# A GLOSSARY OF UK GOVERNMENT AND POLITICS

# Politics Glossaries

Series Editor: Keith Faulks

This series introduces key terms within the core subject areas of politics. The aim is to provide a brief, clear and convenient A–Z guide to the central concepts of the various branches of politics.

The series provides thorough, authoritative and concise reference works which offer clear and consistent coverage of both traditional and contemporary terminology. Students and teachers of politics at all levels of study will find the books invaluable, though the books are aimed primarily at readers new to a subject area. In addition to appealing to mainstream politics students, the series will also appeal to those studying courses in sociology, journalism, media studies and social policy that include elements of politics.

Volumes in the series provide:

- Dedicated coverage of particular topics within politics
- Coverage of key terms and major figures
- Practical examples of the terms defined
- Cross-references to related terms

Titles in the series include:

John Hoffman, *A Glossary of Political Theory*
Alistair Jones, *A Glossary of the European Union*
Alex Thomson, *A Glossary of US Politics and Government*
Duncan Watts, *A Glossary of UK Government and Politics*

# A Glossary of UK Government and Politics

*Duncan Watts*

Edinburgh University Press

Edinburgh University Press Ltd
22 George Square, Edinburgh

Typeset in 10.5/13 Sabon by
Servis Filmsetting Ltd, Manchester, and
printed and bound in Great Britain by
Antony Rowe Ltd, Chippenham, Wilts

A CIP record for this book is
available from the British Library

ISBN  978 0 7486 2554 3 (hardback)
ISBN  978 0 7486 2555 0 (paperback)

Published with the support of the Edinburgh University
Scholarly Publishing Initiatives Fund.

# Contents

# Preface

This book, as its title implies, is a glossary and not a dictionary. It aims to present not only basic definitions and factual details, but also – where appropriate – outline arguments. This is especially true of the lengthier entries dealing with some issues of current controversy. However, it is not and cannot be, given the confines of space, an encyclopaedic study. The intention here is to help the readership by providing a useful explanation of the key personnel, concepts, institutions, issues and events of postwar UK politics – and in suitable cases to point them in the direction of other interesting lines of enquiry.

The mere listing of the contents of such a companion guide illustrates how difficult the task of selecting items for inclusion has been. The aim is to offer information on British government and politics in the post-1945 era, with the emphasis more on the period from 1979 onwards. This is an exacting task and inevitably there will be omissions which disturb some readers. Their omission may reflect an error on my part, for which I apologise in advance. Or their absence may reflect the need to be selective – highly selective – as to what can be included in a work of this length. It is intended that the book can be a handy guide, easily accessible and manageable. Some glossaries are considerably longer and more detailed. They have their value, but their bulk in terms of size and content can detract from their utility as a quick-reference publication.

The selectivity to which I refer is most evident in regard to personalities. My initial listing of people in public life with a claim to be included has been drastically reduced, for one can soon find that the number of available candidates runs into hundreds. My reduced list significantly narrowed the range of 'possibles', confining it to prime ministers, recent leaders of the Opposition and those at the helm of small parties. On further reflection, I have taken the view that all prime ministers of the past six decades should be represented, for often reference is made elsewhere in the text to issues and occurrences that took place during a particular premiership. Indeed, in the cases of Margaret Thatcher and Tony Blair, such has been the longevity of their service that many references relate to some aspect of their leadership. They are people who – when future history books are written – are likely to be seen as having presided over an era.

Otherwise, I have concentrated on people who have figured prominently in important developments of recent decades and who – by their actions – have influenced, sometimes greatly modified, the course of events. On this basis, Neil Kinnock is included not because he was a Labour leader for several years, but rather because in the 1980s his overhaul of the image, organisation and policy of his party laid the basis for New Labour. Similarly, Peter Mandelson does not qualify by virtue of having been a Cabinet minister and later European Commissioner, but because of his notable involvement in the creation and electoral success of New Labour.

Doubtless, some readers will be surprised or even irritated to find that Gerry Adams – as a Sinn Féin Member of Parliament and leader prominent in all the developments and negotiations leading up to the Good Friday Agreement and beyond – is in, whereas the current leader of the Liberal Democrats is not. The decision is no reflection on the personality or performance of the latter, but instead it reflects my wish to highlight individuals who have in some way significantly altered the course of events. Many other people, some of considerable distinction, have also been left out. Hopefully, after delving into the book and looking up particular references, you will at least appreciate the reasons for my choices, even if your own would have been different.

A guide such as this can be very useful as readers peruse more specialist tomes and in so doing come across references that mean little or nothing to them. My hope is that, although the list of entries is not exhaustive, you will find more about the issue or person on which you are seeking information. In some cases, the accounts are very brief, but the cross-references will enable you to pursue your enquiries in more detail. Where a word appears in **bold**, this indicates that it has its own listing within the glossary.

From a personal point of view, I have much enjoyed contributing this glossary to the series. It has made me think carefully about the issues, events and personnel which might be regarded as significant when people examine and assess the postwar era. It has forced me to curb my natural inclination to write at length and made me concentrate on the aspects that matter most. However, I have tried to indicate how and why the various people, ideas and episodes have assumed importance and trust that enough material is included to make your use of this volume worthwhile.

# A Glossary of UK Government and Politics

# A

**accountability** Being answerable, having a duty to justify one's actions or inaction. A system of control and answerability is seen as an inherent part of democratic and **representative government**. Certain political mechanisms are created whereby elected representatives have to account for their stewardship of office, the most obvious being regular elections. The doctrines of **collective** and **individual ministerial responsibility** are intended to ensure accountability, for they involve **ministers** being answerable to **Parliament**. **Parliamentary questions** provides a further opportunity to challenge them over their policies and performance.

*acquis communautaire* The rights and obligations arising from the entire body of principles, policies, laws, practices and objectives which have been developed within the **European Union** and must be accepted by all would-be entrants. Most notably, the term refers to the treaties, all **legislation** to date and decisions of the **European Court of Justice**. Britain recognised and accepted the *acquis communautaire* in its accession treaty (1972).

**Adams, Gerry** (1948– ) Born into a strongly activist and nationalist Catholic family, Gerry Adams soon became involved in the **republican** movement and joined the **Sinn Féin Party**. He has always denied membership of the **Irish Republican Army**, although British and Irish state papers of the early 1970s named him as a leading figure, a claim often repeated. He was interned three times in that decade. He was elected to the **House of Commons** in 1983–92 and again in 1997. He has not taken his seat at Westminster, for as with other Sinn Féiners, he refuses to take the compulsory Oath of Allegiance to the British

Sovereign. He has been instrumental in persuading party colleagues to base their influence on mainstream electoral politics rather than paramilitarism. The reward has been governmental recognition of him as a key player in the peace process and the signing – and subsequent attempts at implementation – of the **Good Friday Agreement**.

Some republican opponents accused him of 'selling out' to the British and Irish governments, but he saw the Agreement as a means of ultimately delivering a united Ireland by non-violent and constitutional means. He was credited with having been much involved in persuading the IRA to decommission its arms in 2005. In March 2007, he met with DUP leader Ian **Paisley** face-to-face for the first time. The two men came to an agreement which paved the way for the reinstatement of the **power-sharing** executive in Northern Ireland.

**additional member system (AMS)**  A hybrid form of electoral system which combines elements intended to increase proportionality with features of **first past the post** (FPTP) such as **single-member** constituencies. There are considerable variations in the possible schemes available, which is why various titles are used such as the 'mixed member proportional' or 'additional member' systems. Several of the newer Central and Eastern European democracies have opted for these 'mixed' systems, which are used in countries as far apart as Hungary and Taiwan. Most varieties involve the voter in making two choices (one for the party and one for the candidate in the individual constituency), but in other respects there is scope for variety. The degree of proportionality will depend upon the split between the constituency and the 'top up' list element. In Germany, it is a 50:50 split, in Italy 75:25.

AMS has been more favourably received in Britain than some other alternative systems, because it retains familiar features such as the link of the elected member to a constituency. It is currently used in the elections for the **Scottish Parliament** and **Welsh National Assembly**, as well as for the **Greater London Assembly**. Scottish nationalists complain that it fails to deliver a fully proportional outcome, for representation in Scottish Parliamentary elections is weighted towards the FPTP constituency element which elects 73 out of 129 members.

Further reading: D. Farrell, *Electoral Systems: A Comparative Introduction*, Palgrave, 2001

**adjournment debate**  The half-hour debate held at the end of each sitting day in **Parliament,** so-named because it takes place on the motion to adjourn the house. Adjournment debates give backbench **Members of Parliament** the opportunity to initiate a debate on a subject of their choice. An all-day adjournment debate is normally held on the final day before each parliamentary recess begins.

**adversary** or **adversarial politics**  'Adversarial politics' are characterised by ideological antagonism and an ongoing electoral battle between the major parties. The term is also used to refer to a period in which there is fundamental disagreement between the parties on the political issues of the day. The opposite end of the spectrum would be the **consensus** model, by which policies are adopted only if there is widespread agreement as to their desirability.

British politics are essentially adversarial in nature. In a **two-party system,** in which one main party is in office and the other is in opposition, the one defends its policies whilst the other attacks them. The shape of the **House of Commons** encourages such conflict across the floor of the House, pitting as it does one side versus the other. The term 'adversary politics' was coined by an American, Professor Finer, to describe the British situation. He felt that the **first past the post** electoral system produced a regular swing of the pendulum, resulting in little continuity of policy. One party came in and undid what its predecessor had done, so that policies lurched from **left** to **right**. The electoral system was therefore based on polarising opinion.

Defenders of the adversarial approach argue that it serves **democracy** well, because **ministers** are forced to justify their performance and their policies in the face of a concerted onslaught. Adversarial politics provide the public with a clear examination of the government's policies and of the alternatives posed by the opposition parties. However, parliamentary business can sometimes be conducted in a very hostile manner, in which there is much point-scoring and conflict seemingly almost for the sake of it.

Further reading: S. Finer, *Adversary politics and Electoral reform*, Wigram, 1975

**advocacy rule**   The rule which prevents **Members of Parliament** (MPs) and **peers** from raising a subject in **Parliament** in which they have a material interest. It was formulated following the publication of a report in 1995 from Lord Nolan's **Committee on Standards in Public Life**. It builds on resolutions of the **House of Commons** that have been in place since the late nineteenth century. The House – not without some opposition – agreed that all paid advocacy should be banned (that is, MPs cannot advocate a cause in **Parliament** for payment). MPs are, nonetheless, still allowed to act as paid consultants offering advice to outside bodies (for example, as to how to best present their case to **Government**). They have to disclose any income from outside agencies given in return for such assistance.

**agenda-setting theory**   The ability to structure political debate by directing people's attention to particular **issues** for their consideration, thereby determining the topics that are discussed and establishing a priority amongst them. Whereas until the 1970s discussion of the effects of the media was much influenced by **reinforcement theory**, Cohen and others wrote of the media 'manufacturing news' and 'setting the agenda'. According to this view, the media influence people by subtle means. They cannot directly tell people what to think, but they can tell them what to think *about*. They influence the public by determining what is shown or read. Many of the viewers/readers come to accept what is offered as a representation of the main events.

Issues may be discussed in the morning newspapers or on the *Today* **programme** on Radio 4 and later picked up by the television news bulletins. Journalists (or more particularly their programme editors and producers) decide on what they consider to be the key issues which are worthy of investigation and follow-up reporting and commentary. If they choose to highlight the character of a political leader, **sleaze** (in the 1992 election) or the problems of the Conservatives over policy towards the **European Union** (in the 1997 election), then these may well become influential factors in shaping the image which people have of personalities or events.

The agenda-setting effect refers to the extent to which the level of media coverage of an issue impacts upon the public's interest in and reaction and attention to the issue.

Further reading: S. Cohen and J. Young, *The Manufacture of News*, Constable, 1973

**all-women shortlist** Intended as a temporary expedient, the policy of all-women shortlists was introduced by the **Labour Party** to guarantee the selection of women as parliamentary candidates and thereby boost female representation in the **House of Commons**.

The Labour Conference (1993) voted to introduce all-women shortlists in 50 per cent of safe and winnable seats.

Thirty-five women were selected in this way, before the policy was abandoned following a successful challenge in the courts. The argument against the policy was that the practice breached anti-discrimination **legislation**. Although the policy was dropped, it did lead to a massive increase in the number of Labour women elected in the 1997 election.

Under the terms of the Sex Discrimination (Election Candidates) Act 2002, parties may now use such lists. They can also provide gender-awareness training for party selection committees and women-only training for potential women candidates. However, in 2005 there was strong local resistance to Labour's choice of a woman in the traditionally safe seat of Blaenau Gwent in South Wales. A prominent local party official, Peter Law, objected to the method used, stood as an unofficial independent Labour candidate in the **General election** and defeated the official party candidate by a substantial margin.

**al-Qaeda**  Al-Qaeda is the name given to a network of radical Islamic fundamentalists intensely opposed to the United States, whose supporters wish to reduce outside influence upon Islamic affairs. It comprises independent and collaborative cells in more than 50 countries, to which it dispenses funding and logistical support. Classified by the US State Department, the United Nations and the **United Kingdom** as an international terrorist organisation, al-Qaeda is believed to have been responsible for a large number of high-profile, violent attacks against civilians, military targets and commercial institutions in both the West and the Muslim world, most notably the **September 11th 2001 attacks on the World Trade Center** in New York and the **London bombings** of July 2005.

See also: **Islamophobia, terrorism**

**al-Qaida**  see **al-Qaeda**

**alternative vote (AV)** A voting system in which the elector ranks the candidates in order of preference, 1, 2, 3, and so on. A candidate who receives a majority of first preferences (that is, 50.1 per cent) on the first count is automatically elected. If no candidate reaches this target, then the bottom one is eliminated with his or her votes distributed to the remaining candidates according to the second preferences on the ballot paper. The process continues until one candidate has a majority.

AV has not been widely used. It operates in **single-member** constituencies and is not a scheme of **proportional representation**. Indeed, in the Australian lower house it has on occasion yielded results which are highly distorted. Yet it is likely that if used in Britain it would give a result which is fairer to third parties such as the **Liberal Democrat Party** than that achieved under **first past the post**. In the elections of 1997–2005, it would also have actually increased Labour's already-strong majorities and further weakened the Conservatives.

If Labour were to contemplate change of the electoral system, AV would be a straightforward system, easy to graft on to present arrangements. Liberal Democrats have traditionally tended to dislike the scheme, preferring a more proportional outcome by which they receive seats approximately in accordance with votes.

Further reading: D. Farrell, *Electoral Systems: A Comparative Introduction*, Palgrave, 2001

**AMS** see **additional member system**

**Amsterdam Treaty (1997)** Formally signed in October 1997, the treaty was the conclusion to discussions concerned with the third major revision of the founding treaties of the **European Union** (the **Single European Act** and **Maastricht Treaty** being the forerunners). It was a further stage in the development of an enlarging body whose institutions and policies needed adaptation to allow for increased membership.

At the Amsterdam summit held in June, it was agreed that: the Union should be brought closer to the people of Europe and made more relevant to their lives; unemployment and EU fraud should be tackled; a green light should be given to **enlargement**; and that there should be a modest extension of majority voting and of the **powers** of **Parliament** whose **law**-making role and consultation rights were enhanced. Many treaty details were concerned with implementation of the **single currency**. In addition, the Social Protocol of the Maastricht Treaty (the **Social Chapter**) was incorporated into the **Treaty of Rome**.

Further reading: N. Nugent, *The Government and Politics of the European Union*, Palgrave, 2003

**anti-Americanism** Opposition or hostility toward the **government**, culture, or people of the United States. In practice, a broad range of attitudes and actions critical of or opposed to the United States have been labelled anti-Americanism. Contemporary examples typically focus on international opposition to United States policies. It is debatable whether hostile sentiment reflects reasoned evaluation of specific policies and administrations, or a prejudiced belief system.

The overwhelming global power acquired by the United States in the post-**Cold War** era and the unilateral exercise of that power, especially after the attack on the World Trade Center, fed the anti-American sentiment contributing to its most militant manifestation. Globally, increases in perceived anti-American attitudes appear to correlate with particular policies, such as the Vietnam and Iraq wars. In Europe as a whole, but also in Britain, **public opinion poll**s have indicated that there is increasing disenchantment with America. The number of people in Britain who value the 'special relationship' has declined, as have the numbers seeing the US as a force for good.

anti-globalisation (movement) Anti-globalisation protest is best thought of as an umbrella term covering the concerns of a wide range of groups – environmentalists, campaigners for debt relief, human rights activists, and so on. The 1990s saw the emergence of a widespread movement of opposition to globalisation. It is not an easy movement to characterise. It is diffuse, lacking accredited leaders or formal organisation, and economic rather than technological or cultural. Anti-globalisation to a large extent equates with anti-capitalism, activists having made business centres and conferences of global financial institutions the targets of their demonstrations. It equates to some extent also with anti-Americanism, the USA being seen as the architect of the existing international economic order, the lair of the most powerful multi-nationals and the world's worst polluter. Several demonstrations have ended in violence (for example, London and Seattle, 1999), although it would be wrong to conclude that most anti-globalisation activists support the use of violence.

anti-terrorist legislation The September 11th 2001 attacks on the World Trade Center have had a highly significant impact on discussions of state security, alerting politicians on both sides of the Atlantic to the dangers presented by terrorist activity. Ministerial warnings of possible acts of terrorism in the United Kingdom (UK) had sometimes been portrayed as means of frightening voters into accepting ever more drastic counter-terrorist measures. But the reality of the danger became apparent in the London bombings of July 2005.

Measures to counter terrorism on a UK-wide basis were contained in **legislation** already passed in 2000 and in an emergency measure passed in 2001. Among other things, the legislation created new offences of inciting terrorist activity from within the UK and specific ones relating to the training of terrorist activists, provided police with powers to seize suspected terrorists who crossed British borders, intensified checks at airports and other places of entry into the UK, and extended police powers to question those suspected of terrorism.

A new and more controversial measure was introduced in 2005 and passed the following year, the **Prevention of Terrorism Act**.

**Attlee, Clement** (1883–1967)  Clement Attlee was elected as a Labour MP in 1922, became party leader in 1935, **Deputy Prime Minister** in the war **coalition** in 1942 and (following a landslide Labour victory) **Prime Minister** in 1945. He presided over the 1945–51 **government**s that introduced the **Welfare State** and embarked upon a programme of widespread **nationalisation**.

A quiet, unassuming figure, Attlee was nonetheless an effective premier noted for his brevity and directness (sometimes terseness) in speech, his generally sound judgement, his unflappability and his ability to chair his **Cabinet**. In his own words, in his early career 'few thought he was even a starter', yet he is now widely regarded as one of the best Prime Ministers. In Professor Pimlott's words, he remains 'top deity in the modern **Labour Party**'s pantheon'.

B. Pimlott, *The Independent on Sunday*, 16 March 1997

**authority**  The ability of **government**s and individuals to direct others and achieve their goals because the mass of people accept that it is their right to tell them what to do, rather than because of the **power** or force they have at their disposal. Power is the ability to influence or determine the behaviour of others; authority is power cloaked in rightfulness. Usually, the exercise of authority implies that others will obey without the use of force having to be used. This is because authority is based on the existence of rules of behaviour or other acceptable criteria that mean some have the right to issue orders which others are obliged to obey.

The German scholar Max Weber believed that the three sources of political authority were tradition (the right to rule deriving from the continuous exercise of political power), charisma (the attraction of support because of the ideas, dynamism and strength of personality of the ruler) and legality (the authority that stems from the political office a person holds, authority which is exercised in a legal manner and is recognised by law).

Whereas power can depend on naked force or coercion, authority is evaluated by the criterion of whether it is justifiable or not. It is closely linked to the idea of **legitimacy**. Governments in a **democracy** derive their legitimate authority from the consent of those over whom they govern, as determined in periodic, free and meaningful elections.

Further reading: M. Weber, *The Theory of Economic and Social Organisation*, University of California Press, 1922

**AV** see **alternative vote**

# B

**backbencher** A member of the **House of Commons** (or some other legislative body such as the **Scottish Parliament**) who does not hold office in **government** or serve as a major opposition spokesperson. He or she may be a new **Member of Parliament** (MP) yet to attain high office, a senior figure dropped from government, or someone who has chosen not to undertake responsibility for some particular aspect of policy. At Westminster, these MPs literally sit on the back benches.

**back to basics campaign**  Originally the name of a platform adopted by John **Major** as **Prime Minister** which placed emphasis upon a return to traditional 'core values' – sound money, respect for authority, individual responsibility and public services which work for people and not the other way round. However, rightwing Conservatives, some of whom were in the **Cabinet,** converted the policy into a campaign about personal morality. This worked to the party's disadvantage when it became apparent that a number of Conservative **ministers** were involved in various forms of **sleaze,** some financial and others sexual. Journalists were only too keen to expose ministerial wrongdoing, so 'back to basics' disastrously backfired.

**Barnett formula**  A formula devised by Joel Barnett, the Treasury Secretary in the **Callaghan government,** which was used to allocate public expenditure between the four countries of the **United Kingdom**. The mechanism provides that any change in public expenditure in one of those countries leads to a readjustment of the total public expenditure in the others – in other words, a change in England and Wales has repercussions for Scotland and Northern Ireland.

Originally adopted as a short-term expedient, the formula remains in operation today. It is controversial, because it is based on population rather than on needs or costs in any particular area: it does not apply to differences of expenditure between the English regions and in particular it has allowed Scotland to benefit from greater expenditure than its level of population merits.

**BBC**  see **British Broadcasting Corporation**

**Belfast Agreement**  see **Good Friday Agreement**

**bicameral legislature**  A **legislature** with two houses or 'chambers'. Lower chambers – comprising deputies or **Members of Parliament** – are usually popularly elected by all adults qualified to vote. Upper chambers vary in their membership and **powers**, some being directly or indirectly elected, others appointed. Across the world, bicameralism is now less common than **unicameralism**, but it remains the norm in large states. Those which operate a federal form of government often use the second chamber to provide for regional or **state** representation. In Britain, the **House of Lords** is the second chamber.

**Bill**  A legislative proposal (draft **law**) introduced by a member of the **government** of the day (be he or she a **minister** at Westminster or a member of the **Executive** in the **Scottish Parliament**) or a **backbencher**. At Westminster, Bills proceed through several parliamentary stages in the **House of Commons** and the **House of Lords,** are liable to amendment and – assuming they have been passed – receive **royal assent**. They then become law and are known as acts or statutes.

**Bill of Rights**  (1689) The Bill of Rights established parliamentary supremacy over the **Crown,** by – among other things – placing restrictions on the **royal prerogative,** asserting some rights of Parliament and making provision for the protection of certain individual **freedoms** – for example, from excessive fines – and the right to petition the **monarch**. As a result of this agreement between **Parliament** and William III, the king or queen no longer had the right to make law without parliamentary approval.

**bill of rights** A statement of a kind to be found in many modern states that provides a comprehensive listing of individual and sometimes group rights. Bills of rights outline such liberties of the **citizen** as freedom of expression, freedom from arbitrary arrest and access to legal redress; they may also provide positive rights for groups such as **ethnic minorities** and gays, protecting them from discrimination. Such bills are normally entrenched by special safeguards. Lacking a written **constitution**, the **United Kingdom** had no such a document until 2000, relying instead on other means for the protection of essential **freedoms**. By incorporating the **European Convention on Human Rights** via the **Human Rights Act**, such a statement now exists and is applied in British courts.

**Black Wednesday** The name given to 16 September 1992, the day on which the **Major government** was forced to withdraw the pound from the **Exchange Rate Mechanism** (ERM) as a result of severe currency speculation. In the wake of the rejection of the **Maastricht Treaty** by the Danish voters in the spring of 1992, ERM currencies trading close to the bottom of their ERM bands came under attack in the foreign exchange markets from currency speculators. When the French Maastricht **referendum** yielded only a very narrow 'yes' vote, speculation which had gathered force in early September began to centre almost exclusively on the pound and the Italian lira. On 16 September, British **ministers** announced a rise in base interest rate from 10 per cent to 12 per cent in order to encourage speculators to buy sterling. They promised to raise the figure to 15 per cent the following day, but dealers kept selling pounds. By early evening, Chancellor Norman Lamont announced that Britain would leave the ERM.

Membership of the ERM was the cornerstone of the government's economic policy. The enforced exit was a devastating blow from which it never fully recovered, for it triggered a loss of trust among voters and an immediate collapse in support among many traditionally sympathetic newspapers. The Conservatives surrendered their reputation for sound economic management.

**Blair, Tony** (1953– ) Tony Blair began his leadership of the **Labour Party** in July 1994 and became **Prime Minister** in May 1997. Having entered the **House of Commons** in 1983 as **Member of Parliament** for Sedgefield, he rose to prominence after the 1992 election, serving as an opposition spokesman successively on trade and industry, energy, employment and home affairs. In 1997, he led Labour to a landslide victory and became the youngest person to enter **Ten Downing Street** as premier since Lord Liverpool in 1812. He was Labour's longest-serving Prime Minister, having won a second landslide in 2001 and a third victory with a substantial majority in 2005. He is the only person to have led the party to three consecutive election victories. Prior to the 2005 election, he announced that he would stand down at some point before the next, held on or before 3 June 2010.

Tony Blair is portrayed by admirers and critics as the main architect of **New Labour** and as moving the party towards the centre ground in British politics. Steps along the way included the rewriting of **Clause IV** of the party's **constitution**, support for a **market economy** rather than the traditional Labour policy of **nationalisation,** and pursuit of a **third way.** He claimed to have retained the party's traditional values but to have brought them into line with present-day circumstances and reality. Opponents believe that he placed insufficient emphasis on traditional Labour priorities such as the redistribution of wealth and the pursuit of greater equality of outcome. They feel that he was harsh on its traditional backers, the **trade union**s and many workers in the public services, and too willing to cultivate business leaders and the voters of **Middle England.**

Following the advent of the **war on terror,** Tony Blair was much concerned with external affairs, especially issues concerning Iraq. He supported many aspects of the Bush foreign policy, sending British forces to participate in the invasion of Iraq and the subsequent occupation. Opponents found it hard to forgive him for the stance he adopted, not least because they feel that they were misled about the threat posed by the regime of Saddam Hussein and the existence of **weapons of mass destruction.**

As his time in office drew to a close, opponents found themselves at odds with other policies, be they **anti-terrorism laws, ID cards** and the commitment to modernise the structure and approach of the public services, especially in educational and health provision. Allegations of **sleaze** proved additionally damaging to his reputation, particularly early in the third administration when the **loans for peerages** story unfolded.

Tony Blair stood down as Labour leader on 24 June 2007 and resigned as Premier three days later. He was appointed Steward and Baliff of the **Chiltern Hundreds,** thus disqualified from continuing as an MP. On the same day, he was appointed as the official envoy of the Quartet (the **United Nations, European Union,** United States and Russia) in the Middle East.

See also: **Blairism, Cabinet Office, Ecclestone affair, Iraq war, presidential government, prime ministerial government**

Further reading: P. Hennessy, *The Prime Minister*, Allen Lane, 2000; P. Riddell, *The Unfulfilled Prime Minister*, Politico's, 2005; A. Seldon, *Blair*, Free Press, 2004

**Blairism** Tony Blair's thinking has often been described as eclectic. Commentators note its debt to: the **New Liberalism** of the early twentieth century (the commitment to progressive non-socialist reform); **Thatcherism** (the emphasis on strong leadership, the pursuit of economic realism and the need for Britain to compete in a global economy); ethical and **Christian socialism** (the emphasis on values and improving the tone of society, rather than on traditional **socialism** with its substantial economic content); Clintonisation (modernisation of the party, as Bill Clinton had modernised the American Democrats, rebranding it as 'New', discarding the tax-and-spend approach and adopting tougher attitudes towards some groups who had traditionally looked to Labour to protect them, such as **trade unions** and the poor to whom he wished to give 'a hand-up rather than a hand-out'); **communitarianism** (associated with Etzioni); and to the **stakeholder society** (as elaborated by Will Hutton).

The Blair approach is a long way from traditional socialism. He uses the term the **third way**, to describe his mid-way position between pure **capitalism** and the excesses of **state** control. It rejects the approaches of the old **Left** and the new **Right**, seeking to combine a **market economy** with a decent society, social justice with economic efficiency.

Much of the language of Tony Blair still echoes traditional Labour vocabulary. He talks of community, cooperation, fairness, partnership, society and solidarity. Some of the actions of his **government** – **constitutional reform**, **devolution**, the introduction of a minimum wage, signature of the **Social Chapter**, the New Deal work programme and the injection of funding into education and the **National Health Service** – seem very much in the Labour tradition and are policies that Conservatives, even many moderate ones, opposed. Blair has been non-doctrinaire, borrowing from several traditions, as the circumstances seem to make appropriate. There is no clear Blairite philosophy. Indeed, Blairism represents a retreat from **ideology**.

Further reading: A. Giddens, *The Third Way*, Polity, 1998; A. Seldon and D. Kavanagh, *The Blair Effect 2001–5*, Cambridge University Press, 2005

**block vote** The method of allocating votes at the Labour Annual Conference via which the **trade unions** have traditionally exercised enormous influence in decision-making. In the decades following the introduction of Labour's 1918 **constitution**, the block vote enabled unions to cast the whole of their affiliated vote behind a proposal. As the weighting of votes at conference was overwhelmingly to the unions' advantage, party leaders who courted the backing of the largest unions could often gain acceptance for their proposals. Under the leadership of John Smith (1992–4), it was agreed with the unions that the union weighting should be reduced from 87 per cent to 70 per cent, a figure subsequently reduced to 50 per cent under Tony **Blair**. There are plans for a further and more drastic reduction in the future. Since the 1990s, rather than casting their votes as a whole, union executives have been expected to consult with their membership and split their vote in proportion to the division of views within the organisation.

**BNP**  see **British National Party**

**Boundary Commission** The body that – via the work of four different Commissions for each of the home countries – determines the distribution and character of constituency boundaries in the **United Kingdom**. At between 8- and 12-year intervals, reviews are conducted and revisions suggested. These are then approved by **Parliament**.

The Commissioners work according to certain principles that may prove difficult to reconcile: broadly equal electoral districts (they establish an electoral quota by dividing the total eligible electorate by the number of seats available, with the size of each constituency to be as near to the quota as is practicable); respect for **local government** boundaries (bearing in mind the quota, it is nonetheless desirable that constituency boundaries do not cut across local government boundaries, unless it is impossible to avoid this); and geographical conditions (including in particular the size, shape and accessibility of a constituency, which may render a departure from the previous two points desirable – in mountainous terrain in Scotland and Wales, where population is thinly scattered, the electorate may be significantly smaller in number than the quota would indicate).

Following the review of 2007, the **Electoral Commission** (UK) undertakes the functions of the Boundary Commissions.

**bovine spongiform encephalopathy (BSE)** In March 1996, the British **Government** broke the news that there could be a link between Bovine spongiform encephalopathy and a fatal human disease, Creutzfeldt-Jakob Disease (CJD). BSE is a disease in which the cow's brain turns to a spongy jelly, leading inevitably to death since there is no known cure.

The Ministry of Agriculture, Fisheries and Food (MAFF) ordered a cull of BSE-infected cows and the **European Union** (EU) agreed to a scheme of compensation payments.

It also imposed a worldwide ban on the sale of British beef. Beef sales to the public collapsed. The **Major** government summoned teams of veterinary experts to argue the case with the **European Commission** for an agreement to lift the ban. Europe remained adamant in its refusal to agree.

An inquiry began its work in March 1998 and within a year reported and gave British beef a clean bill of health, a conclusion shortly afterwards endorsed by the scientific committee of the EU which pronounced British beef to be as safe as any in Europe. After a vote by the **Council of Ministers**, the EU lifted its ban on the export of British beef as of 1 August 1999.

**Britain**  see **Great Britain**

**British Broadcasting Corporation (BBC)** The BBC is the national **public-service broadcasting** service in the UK and the largest broadcasting corporation in the world, its motto being 'Nation shall speak peace unto nation'. Its charter lays down its brief, which is 'to inform, to educate and to entertain'. Theoretically free from political and commercial influence, it has long prided itself on its commitment to provide high-quality coverage via its programmes and information services, broadcasting as it does on radio, television and the internet. It is an autonomous body run by a Board of Governors appointed by the **Government** for a term of four years. Day-to day management of the Corporation is placed in the hands of a Director General, appointed by the Governors.

In spite of its commitment to balanced programming, there are regular accusations from politicians of all persuasions that the BBC is biased against them. Many Conservatives have long been uneasy about the continued existence of a **public corporation** funded from a licence fee, finding it conflicts with their free-market principles.

They have portrayed it as pro-**Left,** hence the occasional labels 'Bolshevik Broadcasting Corporation' and 'Buggers Broadcasting Communism'. During the **Thatcher–Major** years, some claimed that its journalists were over keen to expose the less successful and gloomy aspects of life in **Tory** Britain and detected an alleged pro-**Blair** bias in its political coverage. Particularly over the reporting of events concerning Iraq and other controversies, Labour in office has often had rows with programme editors, culminating in the **Gilligan affair**. Governments long in office tend to see BBC interviewers as excessively combative. In times of war, **ministers** sometimes portray the Corporation as too sympathetic to the views of the enemy.

See also: **Hutton Report**

**British National Party (BNP)**  Created out of a schism in the National Front, the far-right BNP emphasises a strong racial line in its propaganda. Though based in the vicinity of South London, it is strong in West Yorkshire, the East Midlands and the West of Scotland. Its mainly male membership is active around some football grounds and draws considerable support from an element among young people. It has links with white racist groups across Europe. In 2005, it won only 0.7 per cent in the **United Kingdom general election**, but it has fared better in local elections, winning several seats in 2006 and putting up more candidates than ever before in 2007.

The far right has long been known for its tendency to splinter over tactics and **ideology**. Many individuals and groups have come and gone, others have suffered from the secession of leading members.

**broadsheet**  The term traditionally applied to a large, quality newspaper that presents news and information in greater depth and with greater analysis than a **tabloid** newspaper.

The tendency of many long-standing broadsheets such as *The Times* to publish now in tabloid size makes the distinction in terminology less clear cut, which is why those who market the paper prefer to employ the word 'compact' to describe the present form. *The Independent* and *The Guardian* have also abandoned their traditional size.

**Brown, Gordon** (1951– ) Gordon Brown was elected as a **Member of Parliament** for the constituency of Dunfermline East and following a reorganisation of parliamentary constituencies in Scotland was elected to Kirkcaldy and Cowdenbeath. He became head of **HM Treasury** in May 1997, making him the longest continuously serving **Chancellor of the Exchequer** since the early nineteenth century. He was widely regarded as the second most powerful member of the **Blair Government**, having been accorded substantial responsibilities over many areas of domestic policy. He assumed the leadership of the **Labour Party** without facing a challenge on 24 June 2007 and became **Prime Minister** three days later.

Before becoming Prime Minister and in his early months in office, Gordon Brown was keen to emphasise that there would be no radical departure from the New Labour approach. However, he emphasised the need for a different style of government, stressing the necessity for high standards of ministerial behaviour. He made clear his support of the British presence in **Iraq**, but admitted that there was a need to learn the lessons of the mistakes made in policy towards that country.

**Bruges Group** A eurosceptic **think-tank** primarily associated with the **Conservative Party**, although it claims to be an all-party group. Members wish to see Europe develop along the lines of a famous speech made by Margaret

**Thatcher** in Bruges, in which she expressed her preference for a **Europe des patries**. The Group stresses the need for independent nations as Europe evolves, and opposes integration or **federalism**. It reached its peak influence in the **Major** years when it served as a focus for rebellious backbench Conservative **Members of Parliament** (MPs) who were alarmed by the prospect of ratification of the **Maastricht Treaty**. It remains active today, although its appeal to some rightwingers has been reduced by the party's adoption of an increasingly **eurosceptic** approach since 1997. Some of its attitudes and ideas have become mainstream among Conservative MPs.

**BSE**  see **bovine spongiform encephalopathy**

**budget**  A statement outlining estimated British **Government** expenditure and revenue and the financial plans for the ensuing fiscal year, presented annually by the **Chancellor of the Exchequer**, currently in March.

**bureaucracy**  Government by non-elected salaried administrative officers. Such officials conduct the detailed business of public administration and advise on and apply ministerial decisions. In Britain, it is more usual to speak of the **Civil Service** when referring to the administrative machinery of the **state**. 'Bureau' derives from the Old French term *burel* (referring to the cloth that covers a desk or writing bureau), *kratos* from the Greek (meaning 'rule by'), hence 'rule by the desk or bureau' (that is, by officials).

Bureaucracy is often used pejoratively, to refer to the tendency of large organisations to grow in an uncontrolled manner. Bureaucrats are often criticised for preoccupation with 'red tape', wastefulness and pursuit of their own interests and inclinations.

**Butler Report** (July 2004) The report of the five-member inquiry established by the **Government** and headed by Lord Butler into the intelligence relating to Iraq's **weapons of mass destruction** which were a key element in the decision to go to war with Iraq. It met in secret, but had access to all intelligence and other relevant government papers and was able to summon witnesses. The Conservatives and the Liberal Democrats were unwilling to take part in its deliberations, because of doubts over the terms of reference.

Butler did not condemn any individuals for the intelligence failures. He was critical of the style of government practised by Tony **Blair**, barely concealing his disdain for 'the informality and circumscribed procedures' which marginalised the **Cabinet**'s role in decision-taking in the run-up to war. His report made recommendations to the **Prime Minister** for the better evaluation and assessment of intelligence prior to any future action.

**Butskellism** A phrase originally coined by *The Economist* to refer to the similar Keynesian policies pursued by Chancellors of the Exchequer Hugh Gaitskell (Labour) and R. A. Butler (Conservative) in the early postwar era. The term became increasingly popular as a means of describing the broad overlap in social and economic policy pursued by either party when in office during the years of political consensus.

See also: **consensus politics, Keynesianism**

**by-election** A special election in a single constituency which takes place when a **Member of Parliament** dies, loses his or her seat through disqualification or resigns for some other reason. Most by-elections arouse little excitement among those eligible to vote and **turnout** is low. Local issues and the personality of the candidate may be more influential than usual in determining the outcome. Voters tend to use by-elections as a chance to vent their frustrations about the performance of the **government** and record a protest vote. If the survival of the government is not at stake, they might be tempted to vote for one of the many fringe candidates.

If the government lacks a clear majority, by-elections may assume a greater importance than usual, for the loss of a seat may imperil its ability to dominate the **House of Commons** and get its programme through **Parliament**.

**bye-law** A piece of **legislation** introduced by a body subordinate to central **government**, such as a local authority or **public corporation**.

# C

**Cabinet** The committee of senior British **ministers** that meets formally and regularly and is chaired by the **Prime Minister**. It is empowered to make decisions on behalf of the whole **government**, its traditional functions including making policy, reacting to events that occur during the lifetime of the administration and ironing out any disputes that arise between ministers and between departments of State.

Over many years, writers have characterised the importance of the Cabinet in different ways, depending on whether they believe that we have **Cabinet government** or **prime ministerial government**. Some (for example, Walker 1970) portray it as the unique source of **authority**, standing at the pinnacle of British government. Others (for example, Crossman 1963) argue that it has lost its influence to the extent that it has become been relegated to one of the dignified elements of the **constitution**. Reacting to the **Butler Report**, Hennessy argued that: 'The Cabinet is no longer a central organ of Government. Cabinet ministers still matter as heads of departments, but Cabinet meetings no longer really count'. Most would agree that Cabinet influence fluctuates, much depending on the personalities involved and the types of issues and problems they face.

See also: **Cabinet committee**, **Cabinet government**, **Cabinet Office**, **presidential government**, **prime ministerial government**

Further reading: R. Crossman, in an introduction to a re-issue of W. Bagehot, *The English Constitution*, Fontana, 1963; P. Gordon Walker, *The Cabinet*, Cape, 1970; P. Hennessy on Butler, as reported in *The Guardian*, 28 February 2005

**Cabinet committee**  Cabinet committees existed in an unsystematic form in the nineteenth century but it was the impact of two world wars and the rapid expansion of governmental activity in the post-1945 era that created the present committee structure. Up until the 1970s, their existence was officially denied, but within a decade academics and journalists had probed to find out more. **Ministers** are now willing to identify them. There are two types. **Standing committees** are named, permanent committees responsible for a particular policy area such as Northern Ireland, the **European Union** and **local government**. Ad hoc committees vary in number according to the preferences and style of the **Prime Minister** and are concerned with particular policy areas. An early Blairite one dealt with the celebration of the millennium. Once the crisis has passed or the event ceases to be relevant, ad hoc committees are disbanded.

Important deliberative work is done in committees which can consider **issues** in detail. Decisions are often made in committees and not referred to the whole Cabinet, which only gets involved if there are major differences of opinion between ministers and departments. Other decisions are 'reported back' to the Cabinet which can revise or veto committee proposals. But as the Prime Minister chairs several important committees, disagreement is not common.

**Cabinet government**  A form of **government** in which a group of senior **ministers** has executive responsibility, each person having – in theory – equal influence and being subject to **collective ministerial responsibility**: the **Cabinet** makes or can expect to be consulted about all political decisions.

The trend towards enhanced prime ministerial power and the greater use of committees and informal procedures such as bilateral talks leads many observers to conclude that Cabinet government has been seriously undermined to the extent that the term is no longer an accurate description of how government in Britain operates.

See also: **presidential government, prime ministerial government**

**Cabinet Office**  The **Cabinet** has a Secretariat of between thirty and forty senior civil servants whose job is to timetable meetings, prepare agendas and documents, and draft and circulate minutes. The Secretariat is so important that its head is the country's top civil servant, the Cabinet Secretary, who is in daily contact with the **Prime Minister** and Cabinet members. It is assisted by a **Cabinet Office** of some 1,500 civil servants who prepare the work for committees and follow up their decisions. The term Cabinet Office is now generally used to cover the whole machinery that services **Ten Downing Street**, the Cabinet and the Departments, and the word 'secretariat' rarely features. The main tasks of the

Cabinet Office are: to support the Prime Minister as leader of the government; to support the Cabinet in its transaction of business; to lead and support the reform and delivery programme; and to coordinate security and intelligence.

From an early stage as Prime Minister, Tony **Blair** and his team were keen to see a 'dynamic centre'. This involved more power for the Prime Minister's Office which works closely with the Cabinet Office and **HM Treasury** to carry through the Governmental agenda.

**Callaghan, James** (1912–2005)  Leonard James Callaghan was first elected to **Parliament** as a Labour member in 1945. As **Chancellor of the Exchequer** in the **Wilson Government** from 1964, he was forced to accept devaluation of the pound (1967) which he had fought hard to resist. He then served as Home Secretary, during which time he ordered British troops into Northern Ireland to deal with rising levels of inter-community tension. As foreign secretary under Wilson (1974–6), he was responsible for renegotiating the terms of Britain's membership of the **European Economic Community** and supporting a 'Yes' vote in the 1975 **referendum** on whether the UK should remain a member. He became **Prime Minister** in 1976, the only person to do so have previously held all three great offices of state.

The Callaghan premiership was dogged by Labour's lack of a parliamentary majority, forcing him to deal with third and minor parties such as the **Liberals** and the **Ulster Unionist Party**. Plagued by inflation and unemployment, **ministers** found it difficult to restrain **trade unions**' wage demands. Their attempts foundered in a series of paralysing strikes in the winter of 1978–9 (the **'Winter of Discontent'**). Industrial strife damaged the administration and the failure to win referendums on **devolution** in January 1979 led to defeat on a motion of no confidence in late March. In the ensuing **general election**, Labour lost to the **Conservative Party**, led by Margaret **Thatcher**. Callaghan resigned as party leader in 1980 and was created a **life peer** in 1987.

Callaghan cultivated the image of a fatherly, reassuring figure, there to steer the nation through perilous waters. By nature a moderate man, 'Big Jim' was less bold than many members of his party, yet possessed a generally instinctive appreciation of the feelings of working people and trade unionists.

See also: **no-confidence vote**

Further reading: K. Morgan, *Callaghan: A Life*, Oxford University Press, 1997

**Cameron, David** (1966– )  Elected as an MP in 2001, David Cameron briefly served on the front bench before being elected as the twenty-sixth leader of the **Conservative Party** in December 2005 and **Leader of the Opposition**. He describes himself as a 'modern, compassionate conservative' and has spoken of a need for a new style of politics, claiming to be 'fed up with the Punch and Judy politics of Westminster'. He has focused on **issues** such as the environment, work–life balance and international development – issues not recently seen as priorities for the post-**Thatcher** Conservative Party – and is widely seen as more **liberal** on social issues than some of his predecessors. As yet, his views on the specifics of policy have not emerged, but he has launched a series of policy reviews. Some critics are unhappy with his attempts to re-brand and re-position the party and with his interest in presentation. They dislike his emphasis on image as much as substance, seeing it as reminiscent of the political style of the early years of the **Blair** leadership.

**Campbell, Alastair** (1957– )  A former political correspondent with the *Daily Mirror* who became a close adviser to Neil

**Kinnock** but eventually more well known for his services to Tony **Blair**. One of the architects of **New Labour**, he played an important role in the run-up to the 1997 election, working with Peter **Mandelson** to coordinate Labour's campaign. Then and thereafter, he intervened personally to complain whenever media outlets ran stories which he felt to be unfavourable to the leader or party.

After the election, Campbell became the Director of Communications and Strategy for **Ten Downing Street**, having responsibility for the **government**'s press machine. He assumed a role of considerable behind-the-scenes influence, often directing civil servants who were used to taking instructions only from government **ministers**. He was viewed with suspicion, even hostility, by elements within the party, though few questioned his skill in the arts of news management. He became embroiled in controversy in the build-up to and aftermath of the **Iraq war**, being a central figure in the '**dodgy dossier**' episode and then later being accused by Andrew **Gilligan** of having 'sexed up' the Government's case for war in its earlier dossier. Lord Hutton cleared Campbell of acting improperly, but the report was widely seen as a 'whitewash'. Campbell resigned shortly afterwards, although he surfaced again as – in effect but not in title – Labour's director of communications during the 2005 election campaign.

See also: **Hutton Report**

**CAP**  see **Common Agricultural Policy**

**capitalism**  An economic system based on the private ownership of the means of production, distribution and exchange. Decisions on issues of investment and employment are made by private companies which compete with each other and operate in their own interest with a view to maximising profitability. Most developed countries are regarded as capitalist, though in others often labelled as mixed economies there is some degree of **government** ownership and intervention in the economy.

**career politicians** People committed to politics, which they regard as their vocation. They know little else beyond the worlds of politics, policy-making and elections, perhaps having begun their career as a research assistant before working in the party organisation as a political staffer.

**cash for honours** see **loans for peerages**

**cash for peerages** see **loans for peerages**

**cause group** A type of **pressure group**, also known as a promotional group, that does not represent organised occupational interests, but rather promotes causes or ideas.

**CFP** see **Common Fisheries Policy**

**CFSP** see **Common Foreign and Security Policy**

**Chancellor of the Exchequer** The Chancellor is the title held by the **Cabinet minister** who controls **HM Treasury** and is responsible for all economic and financial matters. He (all Chancellors to date have been men) also has oversight of public spending across **government** departments. In recent times, the position has come to be widely regarded as being the most powerful office in British politics after the **Prime Minister**. Under the **Blair Governments**, the Chancellor of the Exchequer was Gordon **Brown**.

**Charter 88** A **pressure group** set up to campaign for major constitutional renewal at the time of the 300th anniversary of the Glorious Revolution of 1688. It urged the introduction of a package of constitutional measures ranging from a written **constitution** to a reconstituted and democratic second chamber, from a **Bill of Rights** to an independent, reformed **judiciary**.

**Chief Whip** A political office employed in many **legislatures** that is assigned to an elected member who administers the **whipping** system that ensures other elected representatives attend and vote as the party leadership desires. In Britain the three main **political parties** have a Chief Whip, who assumes responsibility for issues of party discipline, seeking to ensure that **backbenchers** vote with their party in the division lobbies of the **House of Commons**. A similar position exists in the **House of Lords**, the **Government** Chief Whip often being appointed as Captain of the Honourable Corps of Gentlemen-at-Arms.

On the Government side, the Chief Whip has a seat and a voice in **Cabinet**, plus an official residence at 9 Downing Street. He or she fulfils a key two-way function in transmitting the views, concerns and wishes of the leadership to backbenchers and vice versa, thereby acting as the 'eyes and ears' of the leader in the House.

See also: **whip**

**Child Support Agency (CSA)** The CSA is an **executive agency**, part of the Department for Work and Pensions. Created in 1993, it is responsible for implementing the 1991 Child Support Act and subsequent **legislation**, child support being the contribution from a non-resident parent to the person with whom the child lives towards the financial cost of raising his/her child.

The CSA has attracted much criticism, including complaints over delays, errors and lack of action. Critics have also noted the amount spent on administration, currently more than is raised from absent parents. The Department for Work and Pensions announced that the time taken to clear a new case had risen from an average of 18 days in March 2003 to 287 in December 2005. Following a thorough review, the Secretary of State announced in 2006 that the CSA would be axed to be replaced by a 'smaller, more focused' body.

**Chiltern Hundreds** In the thirteenth century, Chiltern Hundreds (a hundred is a traditional division of an English county) referred to a hilly, wooded area in Buckinghamshire notorious as a hiding place for robbers. A **Crown** Steward was appointed to maintain law and order in the area, but the office ceased to exist in the seventeenth century. The title has subsequently been used as a procedural device to allow resignation from the **House of Commons**, another being Bailiffship of the Manor of Northstead in Yorkshire. Once elected to **Parliament**, MPs cannot technically resign, but upon their appointment to this fictional office they cease to be eligible for Commons membership because they are holding 'an office of profit under the Crown' – even if its tangible rewards are negligible.

**Christian socialism** A strand of nineteenth-century socialist thinking whose adherents were keen to relate **socialism** with the ideas propagated in the Sermon on the Mount. They wanted to see greater social justice: conciliation and fairness in the workplace; the spread of popular education; and alternatives to capitalism based on cooperation. Aspects of the ethical socialism of Tony **Blair** have their roots in the attempt to blend Christian and socialist values.

**Churchill, Winston** (1874–1965)   Famous as a soldier and historian, but most well known as a national leader and statesman. Churchill's reputation was made by his performance as **Prime Minister** in World War Two, when he appeared to be the 'man for the hour' in 1940 and afterwards. He inspired people by his courage, restless energy, unshakeable faith in ultimate victory and memorable rhetoric.

Yet for all of his fame today, if his career had stopped in 1939 it might have been seen as a disappointment, hence the title of James's biography: *Winston Churchill: A Study in Failure*. He served as First Lord of the Admiralty at the outbreak of war and then became Prime Minister for the first time in 1940, a post he held for five years of war leadership. In the elections of 1945, the **Conservative Party** was defeated and he spent much time as opposition leader warning of the new danger presented by Soviet Russia and also supporting the idea of a United States of Europe. He was returned to office as Prime Minister in 1951 and lasted for four more years before handing over to Sir Anthony Eden. He stayed in the **House of Commons** until 1964.

In wartime Britain, his premiership illustrated the full scope of the position of Prime Minister. Between 1940 and 1945, his **power** was enormous. After 1951, he placed much greater emphasis upon more collective decision-making in **Cabinet**.

Further reading: R. Rhodes James, *Winston Churchill: A Study in Failure*, Penguin, 1973

**citizen** A person registered or naturalised as a member of a **state** or political community and thereby accorded the legal rights and duties flowing from membership. Unlike subjects, citizens are related to the state as equals and their freedoms are established in **law**. Reflecting the traditions of ancient Greece and Rome, they enjoy the rights – or arguably have the duties – of **participation** in political and social life.

**citizenship** Individual membership of a **state**, thereby creating a relationship between the **government** and the governed based on recognition of mutual rights and responsibilities. Interest in and debate about citizenship increased during the late 1980s, in part because of a widespread concern among **pressure group** campaigners and opposition spokespersons – particularly of the **Left** – about the supposed erosion of rights and **freedom**s under the Conservative governments from 1979 to 1997. On the **right** there had always been more emphasis upon duties and obligations rather than entitlements, but towards the end of the century there was an increasing call from several commentators for people to play a more active part in their community, for instance by serving on school governing bodies and helping the police. There was also a widespread feeling that measures were needed to develop and improve political participation and in particular encourage voters to turn out on election day.

Since the implementation of the **Maastricht Treaty**, citizenship has involved another dimension, for article 8 states that 'every person holding the nationality of a Member State shall be a **citizen** of the [European] Union'. Some opponents of the treaty saw this as a further move in the direction of a European super-state, because citizenship is normally associated with the relationship of individuals to the state. This is not always the case, for it is commonplace to speak of citizens of the **Commonwealth**. In any case, the decision as to who is a member of a state is specifically left to the national **law** of the state concerned and citizenship of the Union only provides for a modest enhancement of personal rights – most notably that which allows for individuals to move and reside anywhere within the Union.

See also: **citizenship education, turnout**

**citizenship education** Citizenship education was portrayed in the 1997 **White Paper** 'Excellence in Schools' as a necessary preparation for adult life. An Advisory Group on **Citizenship** was chaired by Sir Bernard Crick, its brief being 'to provide advice on effective education for citizenship in schools – to include the nature and practices of **participation** in **democracy**; the duties, responsibilities and rights of individuals as citizens; and the value to individuals and society of community activity'. The Group discerned three elements of citizenship education: social and moral responsibility; community involvement; and political literacy.

Following the publication of the Crick Report, 'Curriculum 2000' made provision for the introduction of Citizenship lessons in primary schools from September 2000 and in secondary schools – as a compulsory subject – from September 2002.

Further reading: B. Crick, *Education for Citizenship and the Teaching of Democracy in Schools: Final Report of the Advisory Group on Citizenship*, QCA, 22 September 1998

**civil disobedience** The deliberate act of law-breaking either because of disapproval of a particular statute or to direct attention to the overall injustice suffered by particular individuals or groups. Such law-breaking is designed to promote **justice**. It has a moral content not associated with ordinarily criminal law-breaking.

See also: **direct action**

**civil liberties** see **civil liberty**

**civil liberty** Civil liberty (or liberties) refers to those areas in which governmental power should rarely intrude on the free choice of individuals. It restrains the interference of government, marking out a sphere of governmental inactivity. Examples include free speech, freedom of worship and freedom from arbitrary arrest, which protect the individual against excessive governmental interference. They are sometimes known negative rights.

A concern for civil liberties is often given as the reason why **state power** should not be extended into areas of life traditionally regarded as private – for example, many British people argue that they should not have to prove their identity by carrying an **ID card**. Critics of the **Blair Government**s suggest that the government been insufficiently sensitive to considerations of personal **liberty** because of its concerns over the threat of terrorist activity.

**civil rights** The term refers to those areas where **government** must act, intruding upon what individuals might otherwise choose to do, in order to see that everyone is treated fairly and that opportunities are available to all able and prepared to seize them. Here – as opposed to **civil liberties** – government is acting positively to protect individuals against discrimination or unreasonable treatment by other individuals or groups and to confer rights on disadvantaged groups, by passing anti-discriminatory **legislation**. They are more controversial because they expand the activities of government, impact on the **freedom** of other individuals and are dependent on the availability of resources.

**Civil Service** In the **United Kingdom,** civil servants were defined by the Tomlin Commission (1931) as 'those who are servants of the **Crown,** other than holders of political or judicial offices, who are employed in a civil capacity and whose remuneration is paid wholly and directly out of moneys voted by **Parliament**'. The Service includes all those civilian officials who work in **government depart-ment**s or **executive agencies**. (Employees of the **National Health Service** and of **local government** authorities are not considered civil servants.) Civil servants are appointed to help the government of the day to carry out its policies and administer the public services for which it is responsible. Higher civil servants advise on policy and on the implementation of the decisions taken by ministers. The relationship between the non-elected but permanent civil servants and the elected but transient **ministers** is a key one in British **government**. Civil servants are expected to be politically neutral and are prohibited from taking part in political campaigns or being members of Parliament. However, the extent of this political neutrality in practice – especially within the ranks of the most senior of civil servants – has sometimes been questioned.

Reform of the Civil Service in recent years – initiated in the **Thatcher** years but continuous ever since – has placed greater emphasis on developing professional expertise and the importance of managerial skills, rather than on its traditional amateurism. It has also resulted in a streamlined organisation whose membership has fallen from three-quarters of a million at its peak in 1976 to some 550,000 in late 2006.

**civil society** The arena of social life 'above' the personal realm of the family but 'beneath' the **state**. It comprises mainly voluntary organisations and civil associations that allow individuals to work together in groups, freely and independently of state regulation. A strong civil society is based upon a large and diverse array of associations and organisations and is widely seen as a bastion of a **democracy**.

**class** see **social class**

**class consciousness** A Marxist term denoting an accurate awareness of **social class** interests and a willingness to pursue them. A class-conscious grouping in society is one which is concerned to acknowledge and advance its own distinctive interests, often seeing itself as relatively disadvantaged.

**class dealignment** The process of decline in the **social class**-based strength of attachment and in the sense of belonging to class-based **political parties** that became a feature of the period from the 1970s onwards. Explanations for class dealignment include: increasing affluence enabling many working-class people to purchase their own homes, a car and even shares and live a life more akin to that of the middle classes; the changing middle-class structure, the middle class no longer being the preserve of business-people, bankers, doctors and lawyers, but including also a large number of public sector professionals (including social workers and teachers); and changing occupational structures, such as the shift from manual to non-manual work, from manufacturing to the service sector and within manufacturing itself, where there has been a severe decline in traditional heavy industries.

See also: **voting behaviour**

**classical liberalism** That form of **liberalism** which was concerned with the extension of **liberty** and tolerance and which flourished in the middle of the nineteenth century. Adherents were concerned to develop the capacities and raise the living standards of its **citizens**, but they felt that the best means towards achieving this object was the self-effacement of the state. They believed in retrenchment, **government** economy and self-reliance, generally taking the view that it was not the government's role to undertake what the individual should be doing for him/ herself.

An updated variant of classical liberalism (neo-liberalism) influenced **New Right** thinkers of the mid-1970s. They also argued for **laissez-faire**, the minimal **state** and human freedom, of which economic freedom was seen as an essential part.

**Clause IV (of Labour's constitution)**  Many early socialists in the **Labour Party** saw socialism in terms of the original Clause IV of their Constitution: 'To secure for the workers by hand or by brain the full fruits of their industry and the most equitable distribution thereof that may be possible upon the basis of the common ownership of the means of production, distribution and exchange . . .' For several years, Clause IV was a 'sacred cow' of the Labour Movement and the **left** of the party acted as its guardian. After World War Two, attempts were made to get Clause IV rewritten, for moderate, right-of-centre Labour MPs saw public ownership (**nationalisation**) as lacking in electoral appeal and no longer a statement of what many of them actually believed in.

On becoming leader, Tony **Blair** boldly tackled the party's Constitution, re-writing Clause IV. The 1995 version stresses community values such as **equality** of **power**, tolerance and respect, rights and duties, the emphasis being on society. It proclaims that 'by the strength of our common endeavour we achieve more than we achieve alone so as to create for each of us the means to realise our true potential and for all of us a community in which power, wealth and opportunity are in the hands of the many not the few . . .' Two distinctive features of the new clause reflect the Blairite outlook: the prominence given to enterprise, competition and the free market; and the moral dimension, with references to personal responsibility, the family and our duty to care for each other.

**clientelism**  The term for a style of politics based on the relationships that link individuals of unequal power (patrons and clients). In a system of patronage and behind-the-scenes favours, public sector jobs and contracts may be allocated on the basis of personal contacts in return for political support.

See also: **croneyism**

**coalition (government)** A coalition is an alliance between groups or parties for some temporary or specific reason. A coalition government is one in which **power** is shared between two or more parties, based on the distribution among them of ministerial portfolios and some agreement on the policies to be pursued. They take joint responsibility for the policies they collectively pursue.

Several types of coalition can be distinguished: the grand coalition in which two main parties share political power (as in the case of the National Government formed in 1931 at a time of national emergency and the German administration formed in 2005); the multi-party coalition involving three, four or even five parties (as in the case of many Italian **governments** since 1945), which may be a rainbow coalition involving several colours from the ideological spectrum; the two-party coalition involving one major and one minor party (as in the case of most German governments since 1945); and less formal agreements by which a small party agrees to sustain another in office, without assuming governmental responsibilities (as in the case of the Liberal–Labour pact of 1977–8).

Coalitions are often portrayed as being weak and unstable: they are said to make it difficult for the voter to pinpoint responsibility on one party or the other for particular policies. On the other hand, they help to moderate the partisan tendencies inherent in **single-party government,** keep politics moderate and consensual and have **legitimacy,** in that the parties in office have usually received the backing of the majority of the voters.

**co-decision**  Co-decision is a legislative procedure that was introduced by the **Maastricht Treaty** and much extended at Amsterdam and Nice. It gives the **European Parliament** – as a last resort – the right of veto over **legislation** proposed by the **Council of Ministers** in several key policy areas, including the single market, consumer protection, environmental protection and research, and research and development. Almost three quarters of EU laws are now made via this procedure. For the veto to apply, the rejection must be by an absolute majority of Members of the European Parliament (MEPs).

**codified constitution**  A **constitution** in which all the main provisions are brought together in a single document, whereas uncodified constitutions exist where the constitutional rules and procedures may be written down but have not been gathered together, as in the case of Britain's constitution.

**cohesion**  Introduced after the first **enlargement** of the **European Union,** the policy aims to reduce inequality between regions and compensate for the costs of economic integration. Its main tools have been the structural funds for poor or declining regions and the cohesion fund for the poorest member states.

**Cold War**  A term which refers to the state of constant rivalry, suspicion and sometimes extreme tension in the post-1945 era between the communist countries of Eastern Europe (which were under the controlling influence of the Soviet Union) and the Western nations (led by the United States). The Cold War began in 1947, peaked at the time of the Cuban Missile Crisis in 1962 and was finally ended by the fall of the Berlin Wall in 1989, the subsequent breakdown of the Soviet system and the establishment of new democracies such as those of Hungary and Poland.

At times the conflict was acute, at other times there was a thaw in diplomatic relations. It was a 'cold' war as opposed to a 'hot' all-out one: protracted tension rather than direct military confrontation.

**collective ministerial responsibility**  The convention by which decisions and policies of the **Cabinet** are binding on all **ministers**, who are obliged to give public support to them in order to maintain a united front. **Government** ministers are deemed to be collectively responsible in two ways. They are expected to be answerable and accountable to **Parliament** for all decisions and policies emanating from the Cabinet or any of its committees. Moreover, if a Government is defeated in Parliament on a vote of confidence, it is expected to resign, paving the way for a **general election**. Ministers unable or unwilling to maintain this display of unity are expected to resign, the theory being that they have been given a chance to express their view; if they cannot abide by it, their duty is to surrender office. This avoids the potential damage done to a Government's reputation when opponents and journalists can point to division and schism.

In practice, the doctrine has been significantly weakened over the last few decades. On two occasions, it has been formally suspended, most recently in 1975 when the **Wilson** Government allowed ministers to campaign on either side in the **referendum** campaign over continued British membership of the **European Economic Community**. Ministers frequently 'sail close to the wind' in their public utterances and their differences with colleagues often become apparent, via coded speeches, press leaks and political biographies and diaries.

**collectivism**  The general theory that human beings are capable of collective action, based on cooperation, and that social and economic policy should be organised for the good of the community as a whole rather than for private enterprise or the self-striving of individuals. Collectivism therefore implies a belief that there is such a thing as society.

**collegiality** A style of decision-making conducted on a genuinely collective basis. Usually applied to **Cabinet government,** it means that all **ministers** can have a chance to express their views prior to a decision being taken by which they can all abide. Collegiality enables ministers to act closely and cooperatively; they can resolve inevitable differences over policy issues by thorough discussion of all viewpoints. It is at the opposite end of the spectrum to **prime ministerial government.**

**Commission for Racial Equality (CRE)** The Commission for Racial Equality is a non-departmental public body in the **United Kingdom** which tackles **racial discrimination** and promotes racial **equality**. It was set up under the Race Relations Act 1976 and is the only body with statutory power to help enforce the act. The CRE's work covers all the areas where people are protected against discrimination under the **race relations legislation**. Its main goals are: to encourage greater integration and better relations between people from different ethnic groups; to use its legal powers to help eradicate racial discrimination and harassment; to work with **government** and public authorities to promote racial equality in all public services; to support local and regional organisations, and employers in all sectors, in their efforts to ensure equality of opportunity and good race relations; to raise public awareness of racial discrimination and injustice; and to win support for efforts to create a fairer and more equal society. In October 2007 the CRE is to become part of the new Commission for Equality and Human Rights (CEHR), although it is keen to see some non-governmental body established to guide, advise and mediate on community relations.

**Committee on Standards and Privileges** A parliamentary committee established in 1995 as a result of the recommendations of Lord Nolan's **Committee on Standards in Public Life**. A new position of Parliamentary Commissioner for Standards had already been created to maintain the **register of members' interests**, advise members on appropriate action in cases of possible conflict of interests and investigate possible breaches of the machinery in place. The new committee oversees the work of the Commissioner and investigates complaints about individual MPs. Once a complaint has been investigated, the Committee reaches its conclusions and then is empowered to apply an appropriate punishment, be it a reprimand or suspension.

**Committee on Standards in Public Life** In response to the damaging revelations that were being revealed during the scandals of the **back to basics** era, John **Major** announced the establishment of the Committee in October 1994. Chaired by Lord Nolan (1994–7), its first report proposed extensive new machinery (including the **Committee on Standards and Privileges**) and outlined seven key principles for the conduct of public life. Specific action included substantial restrictions on **Members of Parliament** (MPs) working for outside interests, which were adopted by the Major **Government** in 1995. Since then, via other reports, the Committee has pressed for more openly codified standards of conduct and introduced strict rules and new enforcement mechanisms as part of a drive to achieve high standards of probity among those who assume public office – whether MPs, **peers** or **councillors** – and in the funding of **political parties**.

**Common Agricultural Policy (CAP)**  The CAP is a system of **European Union** (EU) agricultural subsidies. Its origins are to be found in an agreement made between France and West Germany during the drafting of the **Treaty of Rome** which provided for guaranteed markets for French agricultural products as a quid pro quo for wider markets for German manufactured goods. Formalised in 1962, the CAP was devised at a time when there were still memories of wartime food shortages, hence the emphasis upon encouraging agricultural productivity. However, 20 years later, increased efficiency, in part brought about by technical progress, led to the creation of huge, unsaleable surpluses (the much-derided 'wine lakes' and 'butter mountains'), which had to be placed in storage and often sold off cheaply to countries such as the old Soviet Union.

Subsequent reforms of the increasingly costly CAP were concerned to cut production by means of set-aside schemes, reductions in guaranteed prices and a general move away from subsidising production towards instead making direct payments to farmers in need of financial assistance and a greater emphasis on land stewardship. As a result of such moves, EU spending on agriculture has been reduced to around 44 per cent of overall expenditure.

The CAP was never popular in Britain, being seen as costly, wasteful and inefficient. Britain has a much smaller agrarian sector than many European countries, so that it does not benefit from high agricultural spending.

**Common Fisheries Policy (CFP)**  Devised originally in the early 1970s, the CFP is related to the **Common Agricultural Policy**. The policy lays down fishermen's access to **European Union** (EU) waters, quotas, measures for the conservation and management of resources of stocks of fish which swim in waters of member states, programmes to improve production and the conclusion of fishing agreements with non-EU countries, plus long-term security for the fishermen who depend on the EU for protection.

Britain has the largest stocks of fish in the Union. Its trawlermen have long resented the curbs on fishing imposed by the **European Commission** and the way in which Spanish trawlermen have been allowed to fish in British territorial waters. Some advocate national withdrawal from the CFP.

**Common Foreign and Security Policy (CFSP)** Created as a pillar of the **Maastricht Treaty**, the CFSP covers all areas of foreign and security policy in the **European Union**, including provision for majority voting on them. In practice, it is a policy that is still evolving, designed to provide a framework for intergovernmental cooperation and the coordination of national foreign policies under agreed guidelines and on specific issues such as arms control, nuclear non-proliferation and the transfer of military technology. The trend is towards a strengthening of the CFSP, the **Amsterdam Treaty** making reference to the **European Council**'s role in promoting 'common strategies'.

**common law** Common law is the immemorial **law** of the people, based on custom and precedent. Its elements are common or available to everyone, including the rights of free speech and free assembly. In practice, common law has been determined and implemented by **judges** over hundreds of years.

**Commonwealth** A free and loose association of sovereign states, based on voluntary cooperation between countries of equal status to each other and united by a common allegiance to the **Crown**, the **monarch** being the Head of the Commonwealth. Members are bound by certain ties such as a shared language (English) and common historical connections. Both have helped to create a consensus of political values that include **democracy**, **human rights** and sustainable economic and social development.

The Statute of Westminster (1931) defined the relationship of the white countries of the old British Empire that had been granted independence, making them members of a new British Commonwealth of Nations. Since World War Two, most other countries of the old Empire have achieved their independence and have chosen to join what is now simply called The Commonwealth which has become a multi-racial grouping, with 53 members from 6 continents and containing over 1.8 billion people of many colours and creeds.

**communitarianism** The set of beliefs associated with Amitai Etzioni, arguing that both liberal **individualism** and massive **state** interventionism have failed and that the best way forward is through individuals recognising the importance of community. As **citizens**, they have rights but must also be aware of the duties and responsibilities to society. Communitarian ideas influenced Bill Clinton in the White House and some of its ideas were incorporated into **New Labour**'s outlook and values.

**community charge** A deeply unpopular form of **local government** taxation introduced by the **Thatcher** Government in 1990, levied on adults rather than on a property basis. It was replaced by the **council tax** in 1993.

**community law** The body of **law** developed in the **European Community/Union** comprising the treaties, **legislation** (decisions, **directives** and **regulations**) and case-law embodied in the rulings of **the European Court of Justice**.

Together, these form the substantial part of the *acquis communautaire*.

**compact newspaper**   The term for a **broadsheet**, quality newspaper printed in a tabloid format. It came into use in its current form when *The Independent* began producing a smaller-format edition for London's commuters, designed to be easier to read on the bus, train or tube. *The Independent*, *The Times* and *The Scotsman* all now use the format. *The Guardian* has similarly reduced its size, now publishing in a larger format than the others, known as a Berliner.

**Comptroller and Auditor General (C&AG)**   The official who, with staff, helps the **Public Accounts Committee** to ensure that public money has been spent for the purposes which it was voted by **Parliament**. The C&AG has two specific functions: to authorise the issue of public money to **government** from the Bank of England, having been satisfied that this was within the limits Parliament had approved; and to audit the accounts of all **government departments** and report to Parliament accordingly.

**consensus politics**   Consensus implies a wide measure of agreement. In political life, it refers to a circumstance where a large proportion of the population and of the political community broadly accept certain values, even if there is some disagreement on matters of emphasis or detail.

On the continent, where proportional electoral systems are common, politics and policies tend to be more consensual. Many **governments** are **coalitions** in which representatives of the various parties involved do work together and hammer out policies acceptable to all of them. The semi-circular shape of continental parliaments encourages cooperation among them. By contrast, the design of the **House of Commons** forces **Members of Parliament** to choose whether they are on the Government side or on that of the Opposition.

In modern British politics, the period 1951–79 is often described as an 'era of consensus politics' because there seemed to be general agreement about the policies to be pursued. Governments did accept much of what their predecessors had done and found themselves adopting similar solutions to the problems that arose; peace, prosperity, full employment and welfare were widely accepted goals. Some commentators portrayed elections as a contest to decide which set of politicians would administer the policies on which everyone was substantially agreed. Disputes were often more about the degree, the method and the timing of change, rather than representing fundamental conflicts.

Not all observers have seen the era of consensus politics in the same light. It was, after all, in the 1970s that Samuel Finer first put forward the theory of **adversary politics**. Pimlott noted that the word 'consensus' was little used before the 1980s and that it was then used to distinguish **Thatcherism** from the period that preceded it. His point was that it was much easier to detect consensus in retrospect.

Further reading: B. Pimlott, *Contemporary Record*, Summer, 1989; S. Finer, *Adversary Politics and Electoral Reform*, Wigram, 1975

**Conservative 1922 Committee**  The collective name applied to all Conservative **backbenchers**, although **frontbenchers** – other than the leader – can also attend when the party is in opposition, the name deriving from the year in which the **Members of Parliament** (MPs) who originally formed it were elected. The Committee meets weekly to discuss forthcoming parliamentary business. Its meetings help to keep the leadership aware of the mood on the back-benches, providing MPs with a chance to make their views known. Any leader who loses its broad consent is liable to struggle to retain his or her position.

The Executive Committee, chaired by an influential backbencher, oversees any vote of confidence in the leader (most recently in the case of Iain Duncan Smith) and the process of electing a new one (most recently David Cameron). The chairman announces the result of such leadership contests.

**Conservative Party** British Conservatism has a long history. It embraces a broad spectrum of ideas about the nature of man, society and political change. It is a rightwing creed that emphasises preserving the best of the past (including the traditions and institutions of the country) and allowing society to develop gradually, adapting only where change is proved to be necessary. At different times the party has placed more or less emphasis on conserving the past and on reform. It has always been concerned about electoral success and was – until the setbacks of the last decade or so – astonishingly successful in attaining **power** in general elections. It dominated **government** in the twentieth century.

There has always been a strong element of pragmatism in Conservative policy, although in the **Thatcher** years and subsequently the party has carried more ideological baggage. Key enduring themes for Conservatives are: a cautious approach to change; distrust of the role of 'big government'; an emphasis upon **law** and order; an emphasis upon 'Britishness' (patriotism and the defence of traditional institutions); and a preference for **freedom** over **equality**, and private over **state** enterprise.

The Conservatives used to appear the natural party of government. Their leaders managed to convey the idea that the party was uniquely capable of governing, whereas their opponents were derided as divided, ineffective, extreme or even un-British. By the end of the twentieth century, they had shed much of their reputation and advantages and were no longer seen as competent, united or well-led. They were besmirched by scandals and **sleaze** during the **Major** years.

See also: **Cameron, Churchill, Douglas-Home, Eden, Heath, Macmillan, Major, New Right, One Nation Conservatism, Thatcherism**

**constitution** The constitution is at the heart of most political systems, describing the fundamental rules by which a nation state or body politic is constituted and governed. Usually these rules are contained in a single written document, although in rare examples they may be located in major pronouncements, writings, statutes, precedents and legal decisions. Such constitutions may be an imperfect and incomplete guide to what actually happens in any country, but they help to shape the way in which systems of **government** function and give **legitimacy** to those who rule.

Constitutions declare the existence of the **state** and express the most important principles, rules and procedures of the political system. They establish the formal structure of the state, specifying the **power**s and institutions of central government and its relationship with other tiers of administration. In addition, they usually outline the liberties and rights of **citizen**s and in so doing create restrictions on and obligations of the government.

The British constitution is almost unique, on account of its age, gradual evolution and uncodified status. Its major features are that it is not written down in a single document: it is flexible and therefore easy to amend and its commitment to the ideas of **parliamentary sovereignty**, the **rule of law** and the **unitary state**. Its main sources include major constitutional pronouncements (for example, Magna Carta), authoritative commentaries (for example, **Erskine May**), the **royal prerogative**, **statutes**, **common law**, **conventions of the constitution** and **community law**.

**constitutional reform**  The uncodified, flexible nature of the British **constitution** allows it to adapt naturally to the need for change but there was a reluctance to introduce measures of constitutional reform for most of the twentieth century. Any major changes tended to come about because of a breakdown in the system, rather than from any conscious policy decisions (for example, the introduction of the **Parliament Act** 1911 following the rejection of the **Liberal budget** of two years earlier and the partition of Ireland in 1921 in order to avoid a civil war).

A significant package of reforms had been agreed by **New Labour** and the **Liberal Democrat Party** prior to the 1997 election and following the election a series of changes were introduced. They fell into various categories, themes being democratisation (the attack on the hereditary principle in the **House of Lords** and the introduction of different electoral systems such as the **party-list** system for choosing Members of the European Parliament), decentralisation (the **devolution** of **power** to a **Scottish Parliament** and **Welsh National Assembly**), restoration of rights (the incorporation of the European Convention in the form of the **Human Rights Act**) and modernisation (reforms to the working hours of the **House of Commons**).

The measures represent the most extensive instalment of constitutional change since the 1830s, their number and diversity being remarkable. However, not all of them have received a favourable reception and some critics lament the lack of any guiding theme underlying the package.

See also: **Constitutional Reform Act**

Further reading: K. Harrison and T. Boyd, *The Changing Constitution*, Edinburgh University Press, 2006

**Constitutional Reform Act** (2005)  A statute that signifies the most important shake-up in the relations between the **judiciary** and **Executive** for many years. Passed after a stormy ride in **Parliament**, it provides for: the creation of a new Supreme Court which takes over the judicial work of the **House of Lords**; a new Judicial Appointments Commission to replace the **Lord Chancellor**'s role in appointing **judge**s; and an amended position of Lord Chancellor under which he or she will give up the duties of **Speaker** of the House of Lords and perform a reduced role in relation to the judiciary.

From now on, the Lord Chancellor can be from either the **House of Commons** or the House of Lords. The newly created **Cabinet** position of Secretary of State for Constitutional Affairs (originally created to wholly replace the Lord Chancellor's executive function) will continue, although the holder of that Cabinet post will likely also hold the ancient office of Lord Chancellor.

**constitutional regime**  A regime that operates within the **rule of law** and ensures that there are effective restraints on those who exercise **power**, as laid out in the **constitution**. Constitutional regimes are associated with the provision of a generally democratic and humane political order.

**conventions of the constitution** Unwritten rules of constitutional conduct, customs of political behaviour and practice that are usually observed even if they lack legal force. They are observed partly because they are recognised as useful and practical in the circumstances and also out of a sense of propriety and of what is appropriate or correct. Conventions are useful in any political system, for they provide guidance where formal rules are unclear and/or incomplete and are sufficiently flexible to be capable of adaptation as circumstances change. However, they are sometimes unclear and liable to be ignored.

In Britain, because of the lack of a **codified constitution**, the system of **government** has traditionally made substantial use of conventions. Examples include the widespread acceptance that the choice of **Prime Minister** should be made from the **House of Commons** and the concepts of individual and collective cabinet responsibility, both of which have been modified in recent years.

**core executive** The complex network of institutions and people at the centre that between them are charged with the day-to-day government of the country, the making of policies and the implementation of laws. The core comprises the **first minister**, the **cabinet** and its committees, the offices that serve the first minister and cabinet, and the departments headed as they are by senior **ministers** and including senior civil servants. These groups represent the pinnacle of the decision-making process.

Rather than focusing debate on whether we have **prime ministerial government** or **Cabinet government**, some analysts prefer to think in terms of such a 'core' whose members circle around the Prime Minister and his colleagues. They point out that all of them are involved in a power network with other influential people and organisations in Whitehall and Westminster. Membership of the core is liable to change and it is not always clear who should be included at any given moment. During the invasion and occupation of Iraq, it will include the leaders among the military, but they would probably not normally be involved. Members of most – if not all – **Cabinet committee**s qualify for inclusion. In some listings, so also do the **Chief Whip** and even those who chair backbench parliamentary committees.

Further reading: M. Burch and I. Holiday, *The British Cabinet System*, Prentice Hall, 2004

**COREPER**    The Committee of Permanent Representatives in the **European Union** (EU) made up of the head or deputy head of mission from the EU member states in Brussels. Its defined role is to prepare the agenda for the ministerial Council of the European Union meetings and may also take some procedural decisions. It oversees and coordinates the work of some 250 committees and working parties made up of civil servants from the member states.

**corporatism**    A relationship between the state and major protective (**interest**) **group**s in which decisions on domestic economic and social policy are taken in regular meetings of representatives from the three sides (often known as the social partners) – **government**, business and labour. Via such an approach, governments gain acquiescence of the other social partners in the implementation of policy. Corporatism is a feature of the highly consensual Austrian and Scandinavian democracies. The aim is to make the process of government more consensual and avoid open conflict and to foster harmony among the competitive interests in a **market economy**.

Corporatism was practised in a weaker form in the Britain of the 1960s and 1970s, known as **tripartism**. Since the 1980s, there has been a marked reduction in corporatist activity across Europe, as governments have increasingly moved to free-market competition, with greater use of competition and deregulation.

**councillor** An elected representative who serves on a local council. Some 20,000 councillors currently represent local communities and local residents on the 410 local authorities of England and Wales. Scotland has just over 1,200 councillors. The vast majority of them are part-timers who fit in their council work around full-time employment. Accordingly, they are heavily dependent on the advice they receive from senior officers when making decisions, councillors having a democratic mandate to carry their party's changes through and officers possessing professional expertise. A committee chair will liaise closely with senior officers in his or her area of responsibility, whereas an ordinary ward representative is more likely to be concerned with bringing to the attention of particular officers the cases of individuals or groups of constituents in relation to the particular services.

As the role of party politics in local councils has increased in recent decades, most councillors are party representatives, although particularly in some rural areas and on lower-tier bodies there are members who serve as Independents.

**Council of Europe** A body established in 1949, as the first European political institution of the postwar era. Britain is a member, along with 46 other countries. Its stated purpose was 'to achieve a greater unity between its members for the purpose of safeguarding and realising the ideals and principles which are their common heritage and facilitating their social and economic progress'. A key goal was to work for the 'maintenance and further realisation of **human rights** and fundamental **freedoms'** and the creation of the **European Convention on Human Rights** has been its most significant act. It believes that human freedoms are best upheld by countries which are effective democracies with a 'common heritage of political traditions, ideals, freedoms and the **rule of law'**.

**Council of Ministers** The intergovernmental decision-making body of the **European Union** which makes policy and acts like a **government** of the Union. It is made up of one minister from each member country. Usually, for routine business, the minister concerned is the Foreign Minister, although when farming matters are to be discussed it is the Minister of Agriculture, just as when green issues are on the agenda the Secretary of State for the Environment takes the seat. There are Council meetings throughout the year (around 100 or so); agricultural ministers meet at least monthly. Most sessions take place in Brussels, although in April, June and October they are held in Luxembourg. Preparations for the meetings are handled by **COREPER**.

Each member country in turn acts as President of the European Union for six months (January to June and July to December). During these six months, all Council meetings are chaired by the relevant minister from the country holding the presidency. The UK last held the presidency between July and December 2005.

Further reading: N. Nugent, *The Government and Politics of the European Union*, Palgrave, 2003

**council tax** A local tax on property which was introduced in 1993 by the **Major** Government to replace the unpopular **community charge**. As with the old rating system which was in place before the introduction of the community charge, payment is levied on all householders. All domestic properties are classified in bands. Business rates are applicable to non-domestic property and are determined by central government.

Council tax has also become unpopular, particularly among elderly people living in sizeable properties who find it burdensome. An overdue re-valuation of properties has been postponed until after the next election. **Ministers** are aware that although there will inevitably be winners and losers in the process, it is likely that for many people a substantial increase in payments is likely.

**Court of Justice** see **European Court of Justice**

**CRE** see **Commission for Racial Equality**

**croneyism (cronyism)** A derogatory term referring to partiality shown to long-standing friends and associates, sometimes involving appointing them to key public positions without regard for their qualifications. The term 'Tony's cronies' (coined by **Charter 88** in 2000) implies that Tony **Blair** has shown favouritism towards an elite group of influential friends, often businessmen. In the **loans for peerages** saga, he laid himself open to accusations of croneyism when it was revealed that several businessmen who had loaned money to Labour had received nomination to the **House of Lords**.

See also: **clientelism**

**crossbench peers** The large grouping of **peers** who are not aligned to any **political party** and do not therefore take a party **whip**. They sit on the crossbenches, preferring to maintain their political neutrality. All **House of Lords** committees will have crossbench members, often individuals with a significant depth of knowledge and expertise in the work their committees undertake.

Unlike peers aligned to a party, the nearly 200 cross-benchers do not have a leader. They elect one of their members as a convenor who looks after their interests in the House. Due to their independence, they do not adopt any collective policy positions, speaking in debates and voting in divisions as individuals. There is no system of whipping for the crossbenchers, nor can there be as it would be highly unusual for the bulk of them to vote in one way.

**cross-media ownership** The situation that applies when a person or company has a financial stake in different branches of mass communication – for example, when they own a newspaper and a television channel, or a radio station and a publishing house. For instance, Rupert Murdoch's News International owns several British newspapers, Sky TV and has interests in radio stations, film and publishing. Such cross ownership is allowed, subject to certain rules. For example, regulations allow a newspaper proprietor to have a 20 per cent stake in a television station.

There has been concern in recent years over the extent and growth of cross-media ownership within the media industry. In the discussion there has been broad agreement that there should be: an effective plurality of editorial voices across the media; a diverse supply and range of programmes; proper and effective access to new-media players; and a need to secure adequate investment in the industry and stimulate creative talent. The difficulty is in achieving a balance that allows for genuine competition and diversity, whilst at the same time enabling the media companies to remain strong, viable and able to compete in the rapidly evolving media market place.

**Crown** 'The Crown' is a term used to separate the government **authority** and property of the **government** from the personal influence and private assets held by the current monarch of a kingdom. The Crown is regarded as an impersonal, legal concept representing the total of all powers – including the prerogative – exercised by the **Executive**, that is, by **ministers** and their departments. Crown lands are owned by the **state**. The personal estates of the Queen are at Sandringham and Balmoral.

See also: **royal prerogative**

**CSA**  see **Child Support Agency**

**Cube Law (Rule)** A mathematical formula first noted by David Butler which states that if the popular vote is divided between the two main parties in the proportion of A:B, the seats in **Parliament** will be divided A3:B0. In other words, under **first past the post**, the margin of victory of the leading party was exaggerated, making it easy for a party to win a clear majority in Parliament.

The exaggeration of the performance of the winning party narrowed for several years and the Cube Law seemed to lose its relevance, so that in 1992 there was hardly any exaggerative effect at all, the ratio of votes and seats between the Conservatives and Labour being approximately 55:45. In 1997, the degree of distortion was greater than it had been for many years, leading some commentators to invoke the Cube Law once again. In the 2001 landslide, there was an even greater disparity than the Cube Law would imply.

Further reading: D. Butler, *The Electoral System in Britain since 1918*, Clarendon Press, 1963

# D

**democracy** The word 'democracy' derives from two Greek terms, *demos*, meaning 'people', and *kratia*, signifying 'rule of' or 'by'. Many people therefore see democracy as meaning 'people power', with **government** resting on the consent of the governed. According to Abraham Lincoln, democracy is 'government of the people, by the people and for the people'.

In the classical or **direct democracy** of Ancient Greece, it was possible for all the **citizen**s to come together in one place to make decisions as to how the state should be run. This is no longer viable, other than in very small communities. In modern **indirect** or **representative democracies**, voters choose representatives who will govern on their behalf and according to the wishes of the majority.

Key elements of a modern **representative democracy** include: popular control of policy-makers; the existence of opposition: political **equality**; political **freedom**s; and majority rule. A democratic political system is one in which public policies are made, on a majority basis, by representatives, subject to effective popular control at periodic elections which are conducted on the principle of political equality and under conditions of political freedom.

Over the last three decades, democracy has been widely accepted across the world as the most desirable form of government. Whereas at one time it was seen primarily as a Western creed, strong in Western Europe and former colonies such as Australia, New Zealand and North America, that is no longer true. Democracies are to be found in Southern Europe (Greece and Portugal), most of Eastern Europe (Hungary and Slovenia) and parts of Latin America (Argentina), Africa (South Africa) and Asia (Taiwan). The cause of democracy and its ally the **market economy** appears to have triumphed.

Further reading: M. Cole, *Democracy*, Edinburgh University Press, 2006

**democratic deficit** A situation in which there is a deficiency in the democratic process, usually where a governing body is insufficiently accountable to an elected institution. **Intergovernmental organisation**s have a special problem in achieving the **legitimacy** that direct election confers.

The term often refers to the lack of **democracy** and **accountability** in the decision-making processes of the **European Union** and to the obscurity and inaccessibility of its difficult legal texts. The Union is seeking to overcome these deficiencies via simpler **legislation** and better public information and by allowing organisations representing **citizen**s a greater say in policy-making. But these do not address the demands of those who wish to see a more powerful Parliament and maybe an elected Commission.

**Department for Constitutional Affairs**  A government department created in 2003 with the initial intention of replacing the office of the **Lord Chancellor**. It is primarily responsible for reforms to the **constitution**, the administration of the courts, legal aid and the appointment of members of the **judiciary**. Other responsibilities include issues relating to **human rights**, data protection and freedom of information. It incorporates the **Welsh Office** and the **Scottish Office**.

**Deputy Prime Minister**  Not all **Government**s have a person designated as Deputy Prime Minister. In those that do, the role and significance of the office varies according to the wishes of the **Prime Minister** and the standing of the incumbent. A deputy will stand in for the Prime Minister when the latter is absent, performing at **Prime Minister's Questions** and chairing **Cabinet** or those **Cabinet committee** and sub-committee meetings normally led by him. The incumbent of the office may or may not be given other departmental responsibilities.

William Whitelaw's seniority and popularity within the early **Thatcher** years made him a key element in her administration. Sir Geoffrey Howe had the title during the later Thatcher premiership but found himself unable to make a significant impact on policy issues; nor was his advice sought by the premier. By contrast, Michael Heseltine was allowed more scope under John **Major**, having his own office and being allocated the chairmanship of key **Cabinet committees**. In the **Blair** Government, John Prescott's personal popularity amongst Labour's rank and file made him an obvious candidate for the position. He was allocated his own department with extensive responsibilities in relation to a range of cross-cutting regional and **local government issue**s, although in the 2006 reshuffle many of these duties were removed and he was left to concentrate on resolving difficult, cross-departmental issues in Cabinet committees.

**devolution** Devolution involves the transfer of significant duties and **powers** from a higher authority to a lower one – for example, from a central **government** to subordinate regional forms. The transfer stops short of any cession of **sovereignty**, so that powers devolved can always be taken back by the higher authority. Devolution usually comes about as a result of dissatisfaction with centralised government when **ministers** appear to be unwilling to recognise local needs.

Since coming to power in 1997, Labour has devolved power on a substantial scale and several new institutions have been created, notably the **Scottish Parliament** and the **Welsh National Assembly**. The changes amount to a fundamental restructuring of the **United Kingdom**, leading some to view them as steps along the road to the creation of a federal state. But devolution is distinct from **federalism,** in which sovereignty is shared between a central or federal government and the provincial governments, their respective powers being defined by a written constitution.

Devolution does not require the introduction of any such document and there is no sharing of sovereignty.

Devolution has been the British route to decentralisation, so that power remains theoretically in Westminster's hands although it is politically hard to imagine any administration in London seeking to recover control over areas that have been delegated to Edinburgh or Cardiff.

Further reading: R. Deacon and A. Sandry, *Devolution in the United Kingdo*m, Edinburgh University Press, 2007

**dignified and efficient parts of the constitution** A distinction made by the famous political journalist Walter Bagehot (1826–77) in his classic study (1867). In his view, the **monarchy** and **House of Lords** were examples of the dignified element, in that they continued to exert nominal power. The **Cabinet** and the **House of Commons** were examples of the efficient element, for they were parts of the Constitution that exercised real power and influence.

Further reading: W. Bagehot, *The English Constitution*, re-issued by Fontana, 1963

**direct action** Political action outside the constitutional and legal framework of **representative government**, covering a huge variety of activities, many of which are militant but legal, although some of them are illegal or may be violent. It is essentially an attempt to coerce those in authority into doing something that otherwise they would not do.

Many people might choose to engage in an orderly demonstration against, for example, a motorway development or the export of live animals to the continent. They might find that as passions become inflamed, so disorder creeps in. Protest marches have often turned out to be occasions in which violence erupts and the demonstrators become locked into confrontation with the police who are seeking to maintain law and order.

Direct action is often employed by members of radical **social movements**, among them environmental activists and **anti-globalisation** protesters. In 1999, they demonstrated outside the conference hall and marched through the streets in the 'battle of Seattle', where the World Trade Organization was meeting.

See also: **civil disobedience**

**direct democracy** Popular self-government, characterised by the direct and continuous **participation** of **citizens** in the running of **government** and the taking of decisions.

Direct **democracy** as practised in Ancient Greece involved all the citizens coming together in one place to make decisions as to how the state should be run. This is no longer seen as practicable in today's large and often urbanised states, which is why **representative democracy** is the more usual form. However, the modern way of providing citizens with a direct say in law-making is via devices such as the **referendum**.

Direct democracy caters for the need many people to feel to be involved in decision-taking that affects their lives. Whereas they can only participate in a **general election** infrequently, **initiatives** and referendums provide an opportunity for popular involvement at intervals in between. Direct democracy is popular with pressure-group activists who – in the United States – see initiatives as a means of moving **issues** up the political agenda.

**direct rule** Direct rule was the term given, during the late twentieth and early twenty-first centuries, to the administration of Northern Ireland directly from Westminster. The most recent bout of direct rule came to an end on 8 May 2007, when power was restored to the **Northern Ireland Assembly** following a **power-sharing** agreement among major parties in the province.

Although day-to-day matters under direct rule were handled by government departments within Northern Ireland itself, major policy was determined by the Northern Ireland Office in Belfast, under the direction of the Secretary of State for Northern Ireland.

**directive** A form of **secondary legislation** within the **European Union**. Directives are not as complete and detailed as **regulation**s, consisting more of policy objectives. The results to be achieved are communicated to national **government**s and these objectives are binding on them. But the form and method in or by which these outcomes are achieved is left to the discretion of the national governments. They turn or 'transpose' them into national domestic **law**.

Further reading: N. Nugent, *The Government and Politics of the European Union*, Palgrave, 2003

**dissolution** The formal name given to the process of ending the life of one **Parliament** and calling a **general election**. Theoretically the decision is taken by the **monarch**, but in fact the choice is made by the **Prime Minister** who normally announces the date to the press rather than to the **House of Commons**. Under the terms of the **Parliament Act** 1911, the maximum duration of a Parliament is five years in normal circumstances, although in exceptional circumstances such as wartime, Parliament may continue for longer. In introducing that **legislation**, Prime Minister Asquith observed that this would 'probably amount in practice to an actual working term of four years', which he regarded as just about the right balance to be struck between the competing interests of political accountability and the need for governments to have sufficient time to implement their policy programmes.

**dodgy dossier** A document (*Iraq: Its Infrastructure of Concealment, Deception and Intimidation*) issued to journalists in February 2003 on behalf of the **Blair** Government by Alastair **Campbell**. The ministerial case against the regime of Saddam Hussein had been set out in a dossier released the previous September, the document said by Andrew **Gilligan** to have been 'sexed up' by Campbell. The dodgy dossier, so named by *Channel 4 News*, was written by the Communications team, who had heavily plagiarised the contents from various unattributed sources, most notably an article in a foreign-affairs journal published in September 2002. **Number Ten** conceded that a mistake had been made in not acknowledging sources, but did not see this as detracting from the arguments and facts advanced.

**Douglas-Home, Sir Alec** (1903–95) Born into the Scottish aristocracy, Alec Home became a **Member of Parliament** in 1931 and soon achieved minor office. He lost his Lanark seat in 1945, regained it five years later but within a year had inherited his father's title to become the 14th Earl of Home. He served the Conservatives in the **House of Lords,** before being elevated to the position of Foreign Secretary in the **Macmillan Government** in 1960. On Macmillan's resignation in October 1963, the vacant party leadership and premiership was to be filled via a process of 'soundings' among the party's elder statesmen (later dubbed 'the magic circle'). Senior figures including Macmillan suggested Home, who had emerged as a possible compromise candidate. The Queen invited him to become **Prime Minister** and Home took advantage of the recently passed Peerage Act to renounce his title and become Sir Alec Douglas-Home. He won a by-election and thereby entered the history books as the only Prime Minister to resign as a **peer** to re-enter the Commons. His renunciation of the title illustrated an acceptance that it would be impractical for anyone to serve as Prime Minister whilst sitting in the House of Lords.

He was only briefly Prime Minister, serving at a time when the Conservatives had been damaged by a series of problems and scandals. The party narrowly lost the 1964 **general election**, Home staying on for a few months in order to set a new method of selecting the leader in motion. He returned to office as Foreign Secretary in the **Heath** Government and following its defeat in February 1974 he retired from front-line politics and was later restored to the upper chamber as a **life peer**.

**Downing Street Declaration** (1993) The Downing Street Declaration followed exchanges between London and Dublin concerning the pursuit of peace in Northern Ireland. The joint Declaration was an attempt to reconcile both **loyalist** and **republican** traditions and lure the **Irish Republican Army** to the conference table. It stressed the British role as a neutral facilitator, rather than a country with a strategic interest in the future of the province. London was willing to accept any settlement approved by the people of Ireland, concurrently given, North and South. Dublin accepted that a united Ireland could not be imposed. But nor was it ruled out, if that was what the Irish wanted.

Via this Declaration, both **Government**s demonstrated a readiness to consider negotiations with representatives of **paramilitary organisation**s, in an attempt to bring about a lasting settlement. Although republicans rejected it, the initiative may be viewed as a major step towards their ceasefire of August 1994. The *ouverture* created possibilities for movement, although the road to peace was to prove long and tortuous.

**dries** The nickname applied to those members of the **Conservative Party** in the early **Thatcher** years who shared her admiration for the ideas of two economists, Hayek and Friedman. They supported substantial cuts in public spending, argued that individual freedom and free enterprise were inseparable, shared a strong commitment to market forces, viewed inequality as desirable as well as inevitable, criticised welfarism and believed in **monetarism**, which was perhaps the most widely held tenet of their thinking. The term was applied to distinguish them from the **wets** who were supporters of **One Nation Conservatism**.

# E

**early day motion (EDM)** **Members of Parliament** (MPs) may table motions for debate 'on an early day' which in most cases never comes. The true purpose of the device is to draw attention to an **issue** and canvass for the views of other MPs who can add their names to the motion, so making known to the government the extent of parliamentary feeling on the matter. Sponsors of EDMs sometimes ask the Leader of the House at Thursday business questions if such an opportunity may be made available, the answer usually being 'no'. In 2005–6, nearly 3,000 EDMs were tabled.

**Ecclestone affair** Bernie Ecclestone is a key figure in Formula One motor racing, his influence deriving to a considerable extent from his financial control over the sport. In 1997, it transpired that he had given the **Labour Party** a one-million-pound donation, a move which raised eyebrows when Labour **ministers** changed their policy to allow Formula One to continue to be sponsored by tobacco manufacturers – contrary to its previous decision to ban all sports sponsorship by tobacco companies. Following the resulting controversy, Labour returned the donation. However, the episode dented the claims of the **Blair** administration to be totally untainted by the kind of **sleaze** that had so damaged the **Major Government**. For the first time, there were suggestions that the **Prime Minister** had positioned himself too closely to the interests of wealthy backers and big business. He took the unusual step of going on television to apologise for the ministerial handling of the issue, admitting in the process that mistakes had been made.

**ECJ**  see **European Court of Justice**

**ecology**  The study of the relationships between living organisms and their environment. Ecologists share a sense of environmental awareness with others in the green movement, but they go further and stress the inter-connectedness of all forms of life. They do not see people as being endowed with superior wisdom or with greater rights and wish to see all species treated equally and with respect.

Whereas moderate environmentalists – light greens – see the good life as not being markedly different from the one we lead, radical environmentalist or ecologists – dark greens – have a distinctive vision. They are concerned to change society's present direction, for in their view it currently reinforces values associated with affluence and technology. In Porritt's words, they wish to 'overthrow our whole polluting, plundering and materialistic industrial society and, in its place, to create a new economic and social order which will allow human beings to live in harmony with the planet'.

Further reading: J. Porritt and D. Winner, *The Coming of the Greens*, Fontana, 1988

**economic and monetary union (EMU)**  Economic and monetary union was a bold and ambitious plan for the coordination of economic policy and culminating in the use of a **single currency** in the **European Union**. The adoption of the euro in 1999 involved the unification of monetary and fiscal policy across the member states. The goal of EMU was first mentioned in the **Single European Act**. The provisions governing its introduction were added to the **Treaty of Rome** via the **Maastricht Treaty**, which described the new institutions that would be created and specified the stages by which EMU would be achieved. No other region has come close to this level of economic cooperation.

See also: **euro**


**e-democracy**  The name for those initiatives designed to facilitate electronic interaction between **citizen** and **government** by use of the Internet, web sites, e-mail and on-line voting. It was anticipated by some commentators that they would play an important role in the 2005 election, the third election to be contested using such methods. In the event, it was another campaign tool but did not shift votes or alter the results in any noticeable way. Nor did it do much to engage additional interest, other than that of a small number of existing political junkies.


**Eden, Sir Anthony** (1897–1977)  Having been elected as a **Member of Parliament** in 1923, Eden was soon seen as a rising star in the **Conservative Party**. He served as Foreign Secretary from 1935 to 1938, during the war (1940–5) and during the **Churchill** peacetime administration (1951–5), before taking over as **Prime Minister** on Churchill's resignation. At the time, he was a highly popular figure, in part because of his long record of wartime and public service, but also on account of his charm and good looks. He quickly dissolved **Parliament** and the Conservatives were returned with an increased majority. In his second term, he was responsible for the Anglo-French intervention during the **Suez crisis** in 1956 which greatly damaged his reputation for sound judgement. He resigned for health reasons the following year. He was later made the first Earl of Avon in 1961. In a poll of political science academics conducted by MORI (2004), he was voted the least successful Prime Minister of the twentieth century.

**EDM**  see **early day motion**

**(EEC) European Economic Community**  see **European Union**

**elective dictatorship**  The late Conservative peer Lord Hailsham coined the phrase 'elective dictatorship' to express his anxiety about the growth in **executive power**. Speaking in 1976 in the Dimbleby Lecture, he claimed that a constitutional imbalance had been created, executive power having grown at the expense of parliamentary power. He argued that with a flexible constitution, a majority **Government** in control of a sovereign **Parliament** could bring about fundamental constitutional changes almost at will; it need fear no defeat. Government was portrayed as all-powerful, the checks and balances having been eroded. The only thing said to hold a government in check was its need to retain enough popularity to win the next election.

Hailsham was writing at a time when a Labour administration – elected in October 1974 on the basis of the minority support of only 29 per cent of the whole electorate – was about to lose its majority. Similar concerns have been voiced since the 2005 election, with the election of a Government whose support among the voters was as low as 35.2 per cent (the worst figure for any postwar Government), among the whole electorate only 21.6 per cent.

**electoral college**  An indirect electoral mechanism, by which a body is charged with the task of filling a vacancy for a party or public office. Members of the college are usually chosen to represent the differing sections of a wider constituency; they may themselves be elected. The best-known example is in the USA, where the electoral college, now only a formal body, is popularly elected to choose the president. In effect, all the votes of this college are determined in advance by the original election.

In Britain, the **Labour Party** uses an electoral college comprising three elements (the **Members of Parliament**, the constituency associations and affiliated **trades unions**) to choose its leadership, when the need arises.

**Electoral Commission**  The Electoral Commission was created by the **Political Parties, Elections and Referendums Act** 2000. It is responsible for: advising the **Government** on the reform of electoral law; working with the Boundary Committee in determining the boundary divisions, in accordance with statutory guidelines; deciding the procedures for all **referendums** held in the UK; ensuring that all national and local elections are fully free and fair; regulating **political parties**, including maintaining a register of political parties for the **United Kingdom** and the funding of political campaigns; and promoting public awareness of electoral systems in use in the United Kingdom.

**electoral reform**  A term used in Britain as a shorthand for any attempt to abandon the **first past the post** electoral system in order to introduce some alternative method of voting. In itself this does not necessarily imply a more proportional system of voting and when used in Ireland or Italy has sometimes been associated with a change towards that used for Westminster elections.

**emergency powers**  Reserve powers that are only invoked in times of national emergency, in order to see the country through some urgently challenging situation, such as a terrorist threat or a general strike. Emergency **legislation** may involve derogation from Britain's commitments under the **European Convention on Human Rights**, as set out in the **Human Rights Act**.

**EMU**  see **economic and monetary union**

**English question**  The broad question of whether **devolution** to Scotland, Wales and Northern Ireland should be matched by a similar process of devolution for England, either as a whole (through the creation of an English Parliament) or by region (the creation of some elected regional machinery).

  The issue arises because some people feel that consideration of English interests has been omitted in the process of devolution. They argue that Scotland and Wales are advantageously treated, having their own elected bodies, a Secretary of State with a voice in the **Cabinet,** a higher-than-UK average figure of per capital expenditure and – until the 2005 general election – over-generous representation in the **House of Commons**.

**enlargement**  The process by which new members join the **European Union**. The six original members have now become twenty-seven, as a result of five successive enlargements. The **Treaty of Rome** (1957) makes it clear that the Union is open to applicant countries whose economic and political situation are such as to make accession possible. Subject to that qualification, 'any European **state** may become a member'. (Only Morocco has ever been turned down as an applicant, on the grounds that it does not qualify as a European country.

Turkey – a would-be entrant – has been technically judged a European power).

In 1969, the Hague communiqué laid down the basis on which issues of enlargement were to be approached: 'In so far as the applicant States accept the Treaties and their political aims, the decisions taken since entry into force of the Treaties and the options adopted in the sphere of development'. These principles have remained in force ever since – acceptance of the Treaties, of the *acquis communautaire* (what the Community/Union has achieved, everything that can legally be enforced against a member state) and of the political aspirations of the members.

Further reading: N. Nugent, *The Government and Politics of the European Union*, Palgrave, 2003

**environmentalism**  Environmentalism refers to ideas and theories that share the central belief that human life can only be understood in the context of the natural world. It challenges some accepted ideas about economic growth and human progress, posing a distinctive moral standpoint from which to judge human activities. It does not fit into a neat **Left–Right continuum**.

Environmentalism has been described as green with a small g, as opposed to **ecology** which is Green with a large G. Porritt points out that 'ecologism is not environmentalism . . . it seems quite clear that whereas a concern for the environment is an essential part of being green, it is . . . by no means the same thing as being green'.

Environmentalists are committed to protection of the environment and see the importance of ensuring that human beings meet their obligations to cherish the air, sea and land and all the life forms that inhabit them. However, they do not necessarily claim that all species of life have the same rights and their approach is ultimately human-centred. They want us to protect nature, but ultimately this is for reasons of benefit to men and women.

Further reading: J. Porritt, *Seeing Green: The Politics of Ecology Explained*, Blackwell, 1984

**EOC** see **Equal Opportunities Commission**

**EP** see **European Parliament**

**equality** All men are not equal in any descriptive sense. For instance, they are not equal physically or intellectually. In a prescriptive sense, we might say they should be treated equally, as long as there are not grounds for treating them differently. In other words, men with identical tax returns should be treated equally; men suffering from different ailments should not. The entitlement of all people is therefore to equal consideration. They should be treated equally, unless there are good reasons for not doing so. The principle of equality, understood in this way, does not say that all human beings must be treated alike. We presume that they should be, unless there are grounds for making distinctions.

Equality has traditionally been a political **issue** at the heart of the **Left–Right** divide. Socialists dislike the degree of economic inequality in society and point to the vast discrepancies in wealth and income. They note the extent to which affluence confers social advantage in education, health and other forms of social provision. For many years, the **Labour Party** emphasised the importance of equality of outcome. Most supporters did not favour absolute economic equality, but rather wanted to see their party work towards the creation of a more equal society in which the distinctions of rich and poor were less apparent. **New Labour** has laid less emphasis upon the traditional party belief in working towards greater equality of outcome. It embraces equality of opportunity as a desirable outcome, implying that everyone should start on a level playing-field so that they have the same life chances. Because of individual differences in ability and talent, it is likely to result in economic and social inequality.

Conservatives stress that men are born unequal. They have different abilities, and some will flourish. We therefore need a 'ladder and a safety net', so that in life's competitive race the enterprising can flourish and those who cannot make it can be rescued.

**equality before the law**  All humans have certain fundamental rights and should be treated equally unless there are special circumstances making for an exception. The spirit of the idea is that these fundamentals apply to all people because of their common humanity. Equals in **law** should be treated equally by the law.

Of course, the law is not equally accessible to all. Legal aid is only available to the very badly off, and the rich can hire the services of a prestigious barrister. In beginning court proceedings, education, social standing and wealth can have an influence. The ignorant or poor do not always have the means to establish their rights, whereas the privileged can take action to clear their name and win large damages.

Although the presumption is that the law should treat people equally, some argue for '**positive discrimination**' in favour of the disadvantaged so that those who have for years suffered handicaps – women, members of minority races and the disabled, among them – can have an increased opportunity enabling them to 'catch up' and gain positions hitherto denied to them. 'Equality before the law' is enshrined in the Race Discrimination and Sex Discrimination Acts, but positive discrimination can give the disadvantaged an extra push. The two ideas may seem to be in conflict.

See also: **race discrimination, sex discrimination legislation**

**Equal Opportunities Commission (EOC)** The EOC is an independent non-departmental public body, whose task is to enforce, through court action if necessary, the various gender-equality **legislation** that exists in the UK. Because the **Scottish Parliament** and **Welsh National Assembly** are able to vary the **law** in this area, separate EOC sub-agencies exist for Scotland and Wales. In October 2007 a new Commission for Equality and Human Rights (CEHR) will be formed from the EOC and other categories of equality law bodies.

See also: **sex discrimination legislation**

**Equal Pay Act** (1975) A statute passed by the **Wilson** Labour **Government** which established the principle of 'equal pay for equal work'. The intention was to prohibit discrimination in employment practices, the **law** covering pay, allowances, benefits, holidays and hours of work. The law helped to advance the position of working women, although there were many ways by which employers could redefine jobs in favour of men so that they could be paid more. Since the implementation of the Sex Discrimination Act, the **Legislation** has been monitored by the **Equal Opportunities Commission**.

See also: **sex discrimination legislation**

**ERM** see **Exchange Rate Mechanism**

**Erskine May** A reference to a book, now in its twenty-eighth edition, the *Treatise upon the Law, Privileges and Usage of Parliament*. Written by Erskine May, the clerk of the

House of Commons between 1871 and 1886, the work is much checked and quoted by Speakers of the House of Commons when they have to decide on some obscure issue of procedure. Speakers have been known to tell Members of Parliament that they must go to bed with Erskine May, prior to reaching their verdict.

Establishment  A vague term for the group or class that has authority within a society, usually portrayed as being a conservative influence. According to critics of the Establishment, its members are said to exercise a controlling influence in public life, whichever party is in government. They are sometimes characterised as 'the great and the good', that is, the top people in the realms of the bureaucracy, business, church, law, military and the universities, among other institutions. They share a similar socio-economic background, based on birth into the ranks of the wealthy upper/upper-middle classes, attendance at public school and then an Oxbridge college. This equips them with a set of middle-of-the-road, moderate and consensual attitudes.

ethnicity  Deriving from the Greek word *ethnos*, meaning 'tribe', today the term is used to describe people who, through long association of kinship, culture and often religion – as well as skin colour – share a common sense of identity. It refers to the mixture of different social characteristics that give a social grouping a common consciousness and separates them from other social groups. Ethnicity is widely seen as a more useful concept than race, which has emotive connotations.

ethnic minorities  The labels used to describe Britain's ethnic minority population have changed over recent decades. It was usual back in the 1950s and 1960s to refer to 'immigrants' or 'coloureds' but these terms are little used today. 'Immigrant' seems less relevant now that a large proportion of the ethnic minorities were born here and 'coloured' is often viewed as a condescending and rather meaningless term, the more so as many of those involved have intermarried with the native population. Sometimes ethnic minorities have been known as 'blacks', but this too has disadvantages, not least because many of those involved are dark-skinned and some are considerably fairer. No one is literally black, just as no one is literally white. In the last census (2001), the term Black and Ethnic Minority (BEM) was employed and this remains the language used in governmental statistics. According to that survey, the proportion of minority ethnic groups in the UK rose from 6 per cent to almost 9 per cent over the previous ten years, partly as a result of the addition of a new category, mixed ethnic groups.

'Ethnic minorities' is a convenient, all-embracing term for people of many different origins and skin colours. However, to see those so labelled as in any way homogeneous would be very misleading. We are talking about peoples of very diverse cultural backgrounds, each ethnic group having its own traditions and characteristics.

**ethnic minority** see **ethnic minorities**

**EU** see **European Union**

**euro** The currency now in use in 13 of the countries that make up the eurozone of the **European Union**. The UK is not a member.

**European Coal and Steel Community (ECSC)** The ECSC was established by the Treaty of Paris in 1951, signed by the original six members of the **European Economic Community**

(Belgium, France, Italy, Luxembourg, the Netherlands and West Germany). The treaty provided for the pooling of coal and steel resources, under a supranational High Authority. This was the first major move towards greater economic cooperation in postwar Europe. There were political implications to the treaty, for its ultimate importance was that it marked a step towards European unity, the goal of some leading continental politicians.

See also: **supranationalism**

**European Commission** The Commission is the **executive** of the **European Union,** not only providing the **bureaucracy,** but also able to make policy decisions (like government **ministers**). Among other things, it drafts policy documents for discussion and decision by the **Council of Ministers,** has an executive role after policy decisions have been taken – issuing **regulations**, directions and instructions by which Union rules are executed in member states – and is responsible for preparing the Union's annual budget.

The Commission consists of 27 Commissioners representing all 27 member countries (the political arm of the Commission), and an EU Civil Service of approximately 15,000 full-time officials who work in 26 Directorates-General, each dealing with a different area of responsibility. It is appointed to serve for five years. At its head is the President (now the Portuguese Jose Barroso), appointed by the **European Council** with the consent of the **European Parliament.**

Further reading: N. Nugent, *The Government and Politics of the European Union*, Palgrave, 2003

**European Convention on Human Rights** A document drawn up by the **Council of Europe** which was signed by 15 members in November 1950 and came into force in

1953. Altogether, it has 66 articles and since its original implementation 11 protocols have been added. The language used in the Convention is often vague, deliberately so. All-embracing phrases such as the 'right to **liberty** and security of the person' and the 'right to **freedom** of peaceful assembly and to freedom of association with others' allow for interpretation and enable complainants to include more of their grievances with its provisions. If the terminology were more precise, it would automatically exclude many **issues** from consideration.

Britain played a leading role in devising the Convention and was the first of the original signatories to ratify it. In 1965, the **Labour Party** gave British **citizens** the right of individual access to the machinery in Strasbourg and the **Blair** Government finally incorporated the Convention into British **law** as the **Human Rights Act** in 1998.

**European Council**  At least once every six months there is a 'summit meeting' attended by the Prime Ministers/first ministers of all member countries of the **European Union**. These European Councils are held in the country holding the presidency of the EU at that time. They allow for discussion of broad **issues** and help to move the Union legislation on the basis of a proposal from the **European Commission** in the normal way.

Further reading: N. Nugent, *The Government and Politics of the European Union*, Palgrave, 2003

**European Court of Justice (ECJ)**  The Court is based in Luxembourg and is not to be confused with the European Court (the body which has responsibility for enforcing the **European Convention on Human Rights**), which is located in Strasbourg. It rules on matters of **European Union** law as it is laid down in the various treaties setting up the component communities of the EU; it can arbitrate in disputes between member states and on those between the Commission and member states; it can overrule national **law** where that conflicts with Union law; and it has the power to levy fines on firms found to be in breach of Union law, and on those states which fail to carry out their treaty obligations. The ECJ has 27 **judge**s, appointed by common agreement of the member states for a renewable term of six years.

Further reading: N. Nugent, *The Government and Politics of the European Union*, Palgrave, 2003

**ECSC** see **European Coal and Steel Community**

**European Economic Community** see **European Union**

**European Parliament (EP)**  The European Parliament was first directly elected in 1979, with the number of Members of the European Parliament (MEPs) from each country determined by its size. There are currently 785 members, the UK having 78. The whole Parliament meets in Strasbourg one week in every month, but much of the important work is done in one of the 20 all-party standing committees based in Brussels. MEPs belong to European party groups of which the two largest are the Party of European Socialists (PES) on the **left** and the European People's Party (EPP) on the centre-right.

The main powers of the EP are: to vote on the acceptance of new member states; to reject or amend Council decisions affecting the Single Market; to reject or amend the EU budget; to dismiss the entire Commission, on a two-thirds majority; and to accept or reject a new President of the Commission.

Traditionally derided as a 'talking shop', the EP's bid for a more meaningful role was recognised in the **Single**

**European Act** and in subsequent treaties. But many commentators still feel that it should have a clearer identity and more meaningful functions. Some member states have tried to limit the effectiveness of the Parliament and prevent it from acquiring new powers, fearing that any strengthening of the chamber might endanger the **sovereignty** of national parliaments. However, MEPs have struggled to gain greater influence in the affairs of the EU and in the legislative area, though their powers have increased as a result of treaty changes and in particular **co-decision**.

Further reading: N. Nugent, *The Government and Politics of the European Union*, Palgrave, 2003

**European Union (EU)** The organisation created as the European Economic Community (EEC) by the **Treaty of Rome** (March 1957), whose preamble opens with the words: 'Determined to lay the foundations of an ever closer union among the people of Europe'.

The six countries which had signed up for membership of a **European Coal and Steel Community** (ECSC) were keen to take their limited cooperation into the whole area of economic activity. At the Messina Conference in 1955, they decided to examine the possibility of a general economic union and the development of the peaceful use of atomic energy. In 1957, The Six accordingly established the EEC and Euratom (European Atomic Energy Community), the three Communities eventually merging to become the European Community (EC) in 1967. The EC was transformed into the European Union as the result of the implementation of the **Maastricht Treaty** in November 1993. The founding fathers of the EC recognised that there were political implications in the treaties that they signed. They were inspired by the Churchillian vision of a United States of Europe and wanted to see rapid movement towards their grand design: complete political unification along federal lines.

The Union of 27 members has developed as a result of five **enlargement**s. Under the **Heath** (Conservative) **Government**, Britain joined the EEC in January 1973, membership being confirmed after some re-negotiation of the terms by the **Wilson** (Labour) Government in a **referendum** held in 1975. Membership has at times proved difficult. In particular, as some of its implications have become increasingly apparent, rightwing politicians and members of the public have had doubts about the wisdom of handing over powers to Brussels. Many people have accepted the economic case for being in the Union. They are unhappy about any moves towards closer European integration.

Further reading: N. Nugent, *The Government and Politics of the European Union*, Palgrave, 2003

**Europe des patries**  A Europe made up of independent nation-states that cooperate for purposes of mutual benefit. This was the vision of how Europe should develop advanced by General de Gaulle. He wanted to see the creation of a model of European integration in which the states were to be regarded as the essential building blocks and decision-making was to be conducted via intergovernmental machinery rather than supranational organisations. Margaret **Thatcher** held similar views, as outlined in her Bruges Speech.

See also: **Bruges Group, supranationalism**

**europhile**  A euro-enthusiast, someone who admires the **European Union** and broadly supports its aims, policies and practices; a committed integrationist.

**europhobe**  A person who strongly dislikes and distrusts the **European Union**, its aims, policies and practices, especially as they impact upon Britain. Many europhobes would like to see Britain quit the EU.

**eurosceptic**  The term that became fashionable in the 1990s to describe a person who is opposed to European integration and is sceptical of the **European Union**, its aims, policies and practices. Most eurosceptics wish to try and reverse the tide of integration, often using terms such as 'repatriating' powers to the UK.

**Exchange Rate Mechanism (ERM)**  Introduced as part of the European Monetary System in 1979, the ERM was the first stage of a plan for closer financial integration within the **European Union**. It was designed to minimise currency-exchange fluctuation among the countries which belonged to the system. Each participating country had an exchange rate against the European Currency Unit (the ECU), which was a basket of national currencies. Each currency was supposed to fluctuate within an agreed margin on either side of the central exchange rate. For several years, membership of the ERM was seen as a means of creating monetary stability among member states.

Britain joined in October 1990, the pound being allowed to operate within a broad margin of 6 per cent. But after a period of unprecedented international currency speculation culminating in the events of **Black Wednesday**, it left on the 16 September 1992.

**Executive**  The branch of Government that is responsible for making or carrying out governmental decisions, rather than with passing laws.

In Britain, the political executive is the **Cabinet**, led by the **Prime Minister**. It initiates government action, formulating and implementing public policy, and coordinating the activities of the state. The official Executive comprises the civil servants who implement decisions of the political executive.

**executive agency** 'Next step' agencies were created following the publication of the Ibbs Report (1988), as part of a programme of reform of the **Civil Service** designed to promote managerial efficiency. They carry out some of the administrative functions of **government** previously the responsibility of Civil Service departments. The agencies operate as semi-autonomous agencies at arm's length from the sponsoring department.

Within each government department, there are several agencies which specialise in different areas of public service, with diverse arrangements for recruitment and pay. Within the Department of Social Security, there is the core department in Whitehall which is concerned with advice to **ministers**, relations with **HM Treasury** and public relations. Otherwise, work has been hived off into six agencies such as the Benefits Agency and the **Child Support Agency**.

Agencies remain within their departments, their staff are still departmental civil servants and ministers retain responsibility to **Parliament** for their activities. In theory, ministers decide their policy, targets and financial framework, but the chief executive has responsibility for the day-to-day management of services. Yet in practice the position on responsibility is blurred and ministers are reluctant to admit responsibility when things have gone wrong.

**exit poll** An exit poll is a poll of voters taken immediately after they have exited the polling stations. Rather than asking who the voter plans to vote for or some similar formulation, an exit pollster asks how the voter actually voted. Pollsters – usually private companies working for newspapers or broadcasters – conduct exit polls to gain an early indication as to how an election has turned out, as in many elections the actual result may take hours or even days to count. In 1992, the predictions based upon the exit poll were wide of the mark, but in 2005 they accurately projected the majority of 66.

# F

**Fabian Society** The Society is an association of British socialists which has traditionally advocated the establishment of **socialism** by gradualist means. It derives its name from the activities of Fabius Maximus, a Roman general who avoided fighting pitched battles but instead worked to achieve his objectives by his strategy of harassing his opponents. In the same way, Fabians in their early years worked to permeate the two main parties of the late nineteenth century (the Conservatives and the Liberals) with their ideas, before becoming a key element in the formation and development of the **Labour Party**.

Labour has traditionally followed the Fabian evolutionary route to socialism rather than a more confrontational approach. Several Labour **MPs** belong to the Society, which continues to hold summer schools, produce research papers and debate political issues.

**Fabianism** see **Fabian Society**

**faction** Factions are groupings within **political parties**. They are tightly knit – some would say conspiratorial – and highly organised groupings which seek to press their viewpoint forcefully on the leadership. They advance a programme for **government** and often promote a leader to govern. They take every opportunity to place their supporters in key positions, perhaps putting up a slate of candidates for any vacancies which become available.

Labour was traditionally noted for factionalism, especially in the 1950s. The **Conservative Party** long prided itself on the absence of factional activity within its ranks and spokespersons for **tendencies** disclaimed any suggestion of such activity. But in the 1990s, the term was widely used to discuss the activities of some rightist groupings, often with overlapping membership, who cooperated to press their views. Many of them belonged to the **New Right** and stood for a more ideological, Thatcherite form of conservatism than had been present in the past.

**Factortame case**  A case that came before the **European Court of Justice** in 1991 in which judges upheld the claims of the owners of a Spanish fishing vessel that the British Merchant Shipping Act (1988) was invalid because it conflicted with the **Common Fisheries Policy** of the **European Union**. This was the first time that a British law was effectively set aside by the Court. The ruling indicated that EU law takes precedence over British law.

**Falklands War** (March–June 1982)  An armed conflict between the **United Kingdom** and Argentina over ownership of the Falkland Islands, also known in Spanish as the Islas Malvinas. The Falklands comprise two large and many small islands in the South Atlantic Ocean east of Argentina. Ownership of the Falklands had long been in dispute and periodically Argentine governments had laid claim to them. In 1982, the ruling Argentine military junta of President General Leopoldo Galtieri – in the midst of a devastating economic crisis and large-scale civil unrest – decided to mobilise support by renewing the claim. Tension over the islands increased when 50 Argentines landed on the British dependency of South Georgia (19 March) and raised their flag, an act that is seen as the first offensive action in the ensuing conflict.

On 2 April, Galtieri ordered an invasion of the Falklands, triggering what was expected to be a short, easy war. Though initially taken by surprise by the Argentine attack on the South Atlantic islands, Britain quickly assembled a naval task force to engage the Argentine navy and air force and deployed Royal Marines for fighting on the ground. After heavy combat, the British were eventually victorious. Casualties were relatively low on both sides. The islands remain under British control, although Argentina continues to maintain its claim. In Britain, the war created a wave of patriotic sentiment which bolstered the position of the **Thatcher Government** and helped develop the impression of Prime Ministerial strength.

**federalism** A system of **government** in which responsibilities and powers are shared between the centre and regional or **state** units. The division of **power** is laid down in a written **constitution** and any dispute is arbitrated by a supreme court. There is no possibility of central government abolishing the other tier; the **sub-national government** enjoys constitutionally guaranteed autonomy.

Federalism diffuses political authority to prevent any undue concentration at one point. Federations accommodate sectional diversity, whilst providing the advantages of national unity. Federalism is widely seen as desirable or necessary in situations where the country is geographically vast and/or where there exist diverse ethnic, linguistic or religious elements (India, for example).

Some writers suggest that **devolution** of power to Scotland, Wales and Northern Ireland means that the **United Kingdom** is moving in a federal direction, hence talk of 'creeping federalism'. British opponents of moves towards further integration in the **European Union** are prone to denunciation of a 'federal Europe' which they associate with the creation of some massive, centralised European super-state. By contrast, continental Europeans view federalism as a means of decentralisation.

**feminism** A doctrine or movement that promotes the social role of women and advocates equal rights. Feminist aspirations can be dated back to the publication of Mary Wollstonecraft's *A Vindication of the Rights of Women* (1792), but feminist ideas only really made an impact when women's **suffrage** organisations began to emerge some fifty years later (first-wave feminism). Second-wave feminism developed in the 1960s, in the form of the reformist campaign for equal opportunities and equal pay, and the more radical bid for more gender **equality** and the destruction of male power which characterised the Women's Liberation Movement (WLM).

Three strands within feminism can be distinguished. Liberal feminists are of the reformist type and urge equal rights, including a general improvement in the legal and political status of women and in their educational and career opportunities. Socialist feminists link female subordination to capitalist working methods, arguing that too often women are confined to family life and the rearing of the next generation of capitalist workers whilst their male partners are freed from domestic travail and able to enjoy a richer, more fulfilling life. Radical feminists see gender divisions as representing a fundamental cleavage in society, in which the female half of the population is controlled by the male other half. They want a sexual revolution to restructure personal, family and social life, a tiny element among them wishing to boycott male society altogether.

**fire brigade pressure group** A **pressure group** that is formed to fight a specific **issue**. In a dramatic campaign, members seek to rally support quickly and get **government ministers**, **Members of Parliament** and the general public to take notice. The **Snowdrop Campaign** for the abolition of handguns in 1996–7 used this blitz approach. As with Snowdrop, the Anti-Poll Tax Federation was dissolved once its cause had proved triumphant.

**first Gulf war** (1990–1) A conflict between the Iraq of Saddam Hussein and a coalition force of approximately 20 nations. The Iraqis had claimed that Kuwait was slant-drilling petroleum across its border and used this as a pretext for invasion of the oil-rich kingdom. The Western response was sanctioned by the **United Nations**, so that technically it was a UN-led invasion rather than one led by the Americans. Hostilities began in January 1991. Aerial and ground combat was largely confined to Iraq, Kuwait and bordering areas of Saudi Arabia, although Iraq fired missiles on Israeli cities. The coalition troops scored a speedy and decisive victory.

The **Major Government** was strongly supportive of George Bush senior's efforts to resist Iraqi aggression and sent the largest European contingent of the liberating forces in Kuwait. Both countries agreed that once the freedom of the kingdom was secured, they would not go further and invade Iraq and seek to remove Hussein from power. If this had been done, it is unlikely that the unity of the coalition could have been maintained.

See also: **Iraq war**

**First Minister** The chief executive branch in a parliamentary system is often called the **Prime Minister**, sometimes the Chancellor, in Ireland the Taoiseach and in Scotland and Wales the First Minister. In all cases, their power is based upon their leadership of the largest party and they head either a **single-party** or **coalition government**. They hire, promote and fire colleagues, their position offering them scope for a display of personal leadership. In most democracies, the trend has been towards an increase in power of heads of government, whatever their nomen-clature. This has led to claims that First Ministers have emancipated themselves from **Cabinet** constraints and established a dominant position.

The First Minister in Scotland leads the **Scottish Executive** and is in essence the Prime Minister of Scotland. He heads a ministerial team comprising a Deputy Prime Minister and senior and **junior minister**s.

**first past the post (FPTP)**   see **single-member system**

**fixed-term Parliament** The current practice of holding Westminster elections at a date of the **Prime Minister**'s choosing (within the limits set by the **Parliament Act 1911**) contrasts with that for other types of **United Kingdom** elections, such as the devolved, European and local ones, which are fixed at regular intervals. In 1992, Labour advocated fixed parliamentary terms, as still do the Liberal Democrats. Unsurprisingly, it is opposition parties who seem tempted by the idea. Some commenta-tors and individual **Members of Parliament** have taken up the cause, suggesting that the present arrangement pro-vides an unfair advantage for the **government** of the day. They claim that it is like asking a competitor in a race to fire the starting pistol at a time when most convenient to him. Fixed terms would therefore: be fairer for the oppo-sition and the electorate; remove the lengthy period of uncertainty before an election is called, to the benefit of politics, government and the economy; provide a more stable basis on which businesspeople can plan invest-ment; bring the UK into line with much of the rest of Europe; and be broadly in accordance with public wishes, for voters tend to tire of governments after three or four years. Arguments against fixed terms include the suggestion that they would perpetuate weak and unstable administrations in office, encourage longer election campaigns – as in the case of US presidential contests – and serve no useful point, for in most cases a parliament does not last the full five-year stretch (only three postwar parliaments have done so) . Another difficulty is the need to ensure that elections can be held when necessary, for example after a defeat on a **no-confidence vote**, although in some other states this is perfectly possible.

See also: **dissolution**

**floating voter**    Also known as 'swing voter'. A term much used in early studies of **voting behaviour** to describe the voters who changed their mind about which party to support from one election to another. Today the term has lost much of its former impact. Modern studies point out that the electorate itself is constantly changing, with the death of many voters and the coming of age of others, itself a factor sufficient to impact upon the political balance of the country. But more fundamentally the phrase suggests that the electorate can be divided into two categories, on the one hand the faithful supporters who form a core block of support for their particular **political party** and on the other hand those who – on reflection of the **issues** – are liable to switch their allegiance. In fact, there are many voters who offer far less than fervent support, shading off through those who offer broad sympathy to those whose support is weak and conditional. Moreover, those who do float are often not independently-minded rational thinkers but rather those who are less informed about current affairs and less moved to turn out and vote.

Non-constant electors might be: voters whose involvement with the party of their choice is low and are likely abstainers; those who experiment with alternative parties but generally return to their former allegiances; those who support a minor party but may be deprived of a candidate of their highest preference; and finally those who experience a genuine conversion and transfer their allegiance.

In determining the outcome of elections, much more important than the swing voter is the ability of one party in comparison with another in getting out its core support. As people become disillusioned with their favoured party, they are more likely to abstain than switch.

**focus group**  A group of **citizen**s employed by image specialists to test out party approaches and ideas, in order to allow party strategists to tailor and package ideas appropriately. Deriving from the United States, moderate discussions take place among a small number of respondents who discuss a particular topic. The intention is to find out the thinking and emotions that underlie popular attitudes. Questions are asked in an interactive group setting where participants are free to talk with other group members. In the world of marketing, focus groups are an important tool for acquiring feedback regarding new products. A question may be direct, such as 'How do you rate Tony **Blair**?', or it may be indirect, such as 'if Tony Blair were a colour (or perhaps an animal), which one would he be?' Focus groups were used by Margaret **Thatcher** in preparation for the 1979 election and featured strongly in the **Kinnock**-led reorganisation of the **Labour Party** in the 1980s. In its early years, the Blair administration was much criticised by some purists for its obsession with such groups.

Critics see focus-group campaigning as yet another step which takes politics further away from principles and policies and towards the most cynical kind of market manipulation. The emphasis is on presentation and on finding out what people want and giving it to them. But others see focus groups as valuable in assessing the state of popular feeling about parties, ascertaining popular reactions to policies and personalities.

**freedom** Freedom is a difficult term to define, for it has different meanings to different people. Even when they agree about the definition, they may interpret it in a different manner according to their own attitudes and experiences. In the most general sense, it means the ability to act or think as one wishes without being subject to any external pressure. However, there are several problems with the concept. One is that freedom is a 'good' word, implying something of which almost everyone is likely to approve. Another is that it is one which rests upon personal valuations, for any preference for one system over another as being more 'free' is to some extent dependent upon which freedoms one values most.

Many writers would distinguish between negative and positive freedom. Negative freedom means the absence of restraint and is about preserving the independence of the individual from **state** encroachment. It is *freedom from* something, whereas positive freedom is being *free to do* something. The distinction is not a clear-cut one, however, for almost every freedom from something can be described the other way. Freedom from ignorance can be equated with freedom to be provided with education.

In the postwar era, many people have campaigned for more positive freedoms, wanting to obtain certain economic and social rights. They expect the state to be active in promoting goals such as full employment, educational and health provision, and freedom from discrimination. Under conditions of negative freedom, a **laissez-faire** role is envisaged for the state, so that people can live their own lives unhampered by any shackles. Under positive freedom, the **government** is viewed more as a partner of the individual in the development of rights and freedom.

See also: **civil liberty, civil rights**

**Freedom of Information (FoI) Act** (2000)  Access to information is widely seen as an essential ingredient of **open government**. Some 60 developed countries have FoI laws – known as 'sunshine laws' in the United States – which guarantee **citizens** the right to see a wide variety of public documents, both **state** and personal.

Labour passed the Freedom of Information Act in 2000, although the **legislation** only became fully operative in 2005. Under the legislation, an answer to a request for information has to be met within 20 working days. Authorities that do not disclose information have to show that their refusal is in the public interest. An Information Commissioner and an Information Tribunal are in place to enforce it.

Critics note that it offers a relatively weak access to information when compared to similar legislation in the USA, New Zealand or the Republic of Ireland. There are 23 exemptions, which, among other things, allow **ministers** not to reveal information harmful to national security or law enforcement, the public, the environment or the safety of individuals. Most exemptions are subject to the test of 'public interest', a term left undefined. Refusal can also be made on the grounds of expense, if the costs of gathering it amount to more than three-and-a-half day's work for a **government** department (slightly less for other public bodies). Supporters of the Act portray it as a fundamental step forward, which will make a significant difference in terms of the openness of local authorities. They argue that the exemptions are uncontentious and would only be used in the interest of good government.

**frontbencher** At Westminster and in other similar assemblies, seating is typically arranged in banks or rows, with each **political party** grouped together. The spokespeople for each group will often sit on the benches at the front of their group and are then known as being on the front-bench. Those sitting behind them are known as **back-benchers**. In the Westminster **Parliament**, the **Government** frontbench is traditionally on the right-hand side of the **Speaker**.

**fuel protest** A series of fuel protests were held in the **United Kingdom** in 2000 over the high level of duty payable on diesel and petrol, involving the owners of small businesses (in the road haulage and other industries) and farmers. Their **direct action** began on 7 September with the picketing of an oil refinery in Cheshire and spread rapidly. Within a few days, hardly any fuel was being delivered to fuel stations throughout Britain. As motorists engaged in panic-buying, shortages of fuel quickly developed.

The Government did not immediately back down under pressure, but in November the **Chancellor of the Exchequer** felt able to make a concession, freezing fuel duties until the following **budget** and making other changes that effectively reduced the price of petrol and diesel. At first, there was plenty of popular and media sympathy for the protesters. It began to melt away, as the consequences of the confrontation became apparent.

Further protests took place in September 2005, but on a much smaller scale. The protests have been typical of the new breed of popular movement. They possess a loose and decentralised organisational structure and communication is conducted via the latest means of technology.

# G

**G8 countries**  see **Group of Eight countries**

**general election**  An election that is usually held throughout the country on the same day, to elect representatives to serve in the nation's primary legislative body. In Britain, at least every five years, the voters elect who they want to be their **Member of Parliament** by placing a cross against the name of a candidate on the ballot paper. The candidate with the most votes wins a seat in the **House of Commons** and the **political party** that wins the most seats forms the **Government**.

General elections are held to provide a competition for public office and a means of holding the winners to account. They also promote a dialogue between voters and candidates, between society and the **state**. Free elections are the defining feature of any state claiming to be a **democracy**.

**gerrymandering**  A form of electoral corruption in which electoral boundaries are drawn to the advantage of a particular party or interest. The term derives from a constituency designed by Governor Gerry of Massachusetts in 1812, whose long, narrow shape inspired one observer to say that it reminded him of a salamander, a type of lizard. A journalistic wag retorted: 'Say rather a gerrymander.'

The practice of devising boundaries in favour of one party was a feature of Unionist rule in the days of the **Stormont Parliament**, with boundaries being designed to maximise Protestant and minimise Catholic voting strength.

**Gilligan, Andrew** (1968– )  The journalist best known for his May 2003 report about a British **Government** briefing paper on Iraq and **weapons of mass destruction** (the

September Dossier) while working for **BBC** Radio 4's *Today* programme as its defence and diplomatic correspondent. He claimed that the British Government had deliberately exaggerated the military capabilities of Iraq in order to justify going to war with the country. In particular, he claimed on air that Alastair **Campbell** had deliberately 'sexed up' the governmental document which contained the claim that Iraq could deploy biological weapons within 45 minutes of an order to do so. In the **Hutton Report**, the Government was largely cleared of any wrongdoing and Gilligan's central allegations concerning the role of Campbell were adjudged to have been unfounded.

See also: **Iraq war**

**globalisation** An umbrella term describing the way in which the constraints of geography are receding, so that cultural, economic, environmental and political issues are no longer decided within national boundaries but have become matters of global concern. The growing interdependencies and interconnectedness of the world are said to reduce the autonomy of individual states and the importance of borders.

First coined in the 1980s, the term refers to the way in which the modern world is characterised by diminishing national borders, the fusing of individual national markets, the falling of protectionist barriers, the free movement of capital and the spread of companies around the world. The rise of the internet and recent advances in telecommunications have boosted the process of interconnectedness. For many people, avowed capitalists and consumers in advanced countries, this has brought the benefits of greater consumer choice, rising living standards, a growth in international travel and greater understanding of other cultures, as well as promoting the triumph of **democracy** over autocracy. However, **anti-globalisation** protesters see things differently, arguing that the West's gains are being achieved at the expense of developing countries.

**glorification of terrorism** Clause I of the **Prevention of Terrorism Act** (2006) prohibits the publishing of 'a statement that is likely to be understood by members of the public as indirectly encouraging the commission or preparation of acts of **terrorism**', outlawing 'any statement that glorifies the commission or preparation (whether in the past, in the future or generally) of such acts or offences; and is a statement from which those members of the public could reasonably be expected to infer that what is being glorified is being glorified as conduct that should be emulated by them in existing circumstances'. The maximum penalty is seven years' imprisonment. Critics argue that the clause was both unnecessary and damagingly vague, offering too much latitude to those who would seek to stifle legitimate debate about **government** policy and the causes of terrorism. In their view, it provides the Home Office with too much power to decide who is a terrorist and who is a freedom fighter.

**Good Friday Agreement** (April 1998) Also Belfast Agreement. The formal agreement reached by the **Blair Government** with the unionists, nationalists and government of the Irish Republic to pave the way for the future government of Northern Ireland. Under the terms of the settlement, as ratified by the people on either side of the border, there was to be, among other terms, a devolved assembly with law-making powers in the province, elected on the basis of **proportional representation**, and an **executive** of ten **ministers** who would operate on the basis of **power-sharing** between the leaders of the two communities.

Ever since the conclusion of the agreement, there has been a conflict over the decommissioning of IRA weapons, the reform of the police service, the continued presence of British troops and several other issues. The Assembly and Executive were established, although they have been suspended on four occasions, as they still are today. Meanwhile, government continues via direct rule.

**governance** A wider term than **government**, governance focuses not on formal governmental institutions, but on the whole range of governmental activities in each phase of the policy-making process, including the bargaining process between those representing government and the players involved in the private- and voluntary-sector bodies. Governance is about processes and systems by which we are governed. A government may be established to administer them.

**government** A general term that with a capital G refers narrowly to the group of individuals who in a **democracy** are elected to control the operation of the **state** at any time (for example, the present Labour Government) or with a small g refers more widely to the institutions which are part of the constitutional system (as when we speak of the British system of government) and the actual act of governing. In the second sense, the term includes the institutions of government and those who work in them, which are responsible for making collective decisions on behalf of society – not just elected **minister**s, but also non-elected civil servants, advisers and members of various public and private bodies.

Government is then the mechanism through which order is maintained. A government possesses a monopoly on the legitimate use of physical force within a state, securing the internal and external sovereignty of the state being its major tasks.

**government department**  Ministerial departments are led politically by a **government minister** known as a Secretary of State who in most cases has a seat in the **Cabinet**. He or she is generally supported by a team of **junior ministers**. The administrative management of the department is led by a senior civil servant known as a Permanent Secretary. Examples of the 20 or so ministerial departments are the Home Office and **HM Treasury**. Subordinate to these ministerial departments are **executive agencies**. Non-ministerial departments generally cover matters for which direct political oversight is judged unnecessary or inappropriate. They are headed by senior civil servants. Some fulfil a regulatory or inspection function, and their status is therefore intended to protect them from political interference. Examples include the British Council, the Crown Estate, the Government Actuary's Department, HM Revenue and Customs, and HM Land Registry.

**Great Britain**  The largest island of the British Isles. Lying to the northwest of continental Europe, it makes up the larger part of the territory of the **United Kingdom** (UK). It is the largest island in Europe, the eighth largest in the world. It is surrounded by over 100 smaller islands and islets. The UK **Government** officially distinguishes between Great Britain and the United Kingdom, but the former term (or more often simply Britain) is widely used as a synonym for the latter.

**Great Power**  A country which ranks amongst the most powerful in the world hierarchy, having the capacity to exert significant economic, political and social influence in international affairs. As such, Great Powers are the arbiters of world diplomacy whose opinions must be taken into account by other nations before effecting initiatives. Characteristically, they have the ability to intervene militarily almost anywhere, and they also exert influence in the form of economic investment in less developed portions of the world. After 1945, the United States, the Soviet Union, France, China, and the **United Kingdom** were formalised as the five Powers with permanent seats and veto power in the **United Nations** Security Council. However, since then the industrial and military might of the UK have declined so that many observers would see it as a middle Power, one which cannot dominate other states, but does still retain significant influence in world affairs. Arguably, in the early twenty-first century, the USA is the only Great Power.

**Greater London Assembly** The body based at City Hall that administers Greater London, covering the 32 London boroughs and the City of London. Its 25 members (AMs), elected every four years by the **additional member system**, hold the elected **Mayor of London** to account, scrutinising the incumbent's actions and decisions. The Assembly must accept or amend the Mayor's budget on an annual basis. Its areas of responsibility include economic development, fire and civil protection, planning, policing and transport.

**Green Paper** A tentative statement of governmental thinking on the issues raised by some issue of public policy. Such a paper often sets out alternative means of resolving a problem and invites consultation and discussion of the available options. A Green Paper is usually used at an early stage in the process of making public policy and may be regarded as a first step in changing the **law**. There is no commitment to action, but such a document may be followed by a more specific **White Paper**.

As an example, a Green Paper *A strong BBC, independent of government* was published in March 2005. It marked the launch of a public consultation on the proposals it contained.

**Green Party**    Formed in 1973 as the **Ecology** Party, the Green Party adopted its present title in the 1980s. It enjoyed a brief spell of success towards the end of that decade, winning 15 per cent of the vote (but no seats) in the 1989 European elections. Following a period of internal schism, the party lost its electoral momentum and the mainstream parties moved to thwart any threat it posed by some 'greening' of their own policies.

As yet, the party has not been able to match the success of some continental Green parties. It has never elected an MP, but in European and devolved elections it has won several seats, assisted in both cases by more proportional systems of voting. Since the 2007 devolved elections, it has maintained the SNP in power in the **Scottish Parliament** by offering support on **no confidence votes** and budgetary matters, should this prove necessary.

**Group of Eight (G8) countries**    An informal grouping of the seven most advanced economies in the world, plus Russia. It is essentially a club for the world's most powerful countries in economic terms, members being Britain, Canada, France, Germany, Italy, Japan and the United States. Every year, G8 leaders meet to discuss broad economic and political issues, the stated aims of the organisation being to promote economic growth, reduce global poverty, strengthen good **governance**, promote peace and security and improve global public health. As the agenda of G8 is usually about controversial global issues, critics often refer to the G8 as an unofficial 'world government' which has the **power** to act on areas of worldwide concern. The annual summits are often the focus of **anti-globalisation movement** protests, notably in Genoa in 2001. Pressure has been placed on G8 leaders to take responsibility to combat problems they are blamed for creating. Bob Geldof organised Live 8 global awareness concerts in 2005 to encourage G8 leaders to 'Make Poverty History' at the Edinburgh summit.

# H

**Hansard** The traditional name for the official record of the proceedings of the **House of Commons** and **House of Lords,** named after Luke Hansard who first published reports in the early nineteenth century. **Parliament** took over responsibility for publication in 1909, since when it has been a fully comprehensive – but not verbatim – account of every speech. The term Hansard exists in other countries with a British connection, Australia, Canada, New Zealand and South Africa among them, to describe the printed transcripts of parliamentary debates.

**head of state** The leading representative of the **state**, usually either a president or **monarch.** The incumbent normally has an essentially symbolic role, but like the flag and certain other traditions the office can provide a focus around which people can rally in times of difficulty. It serves as a reminder to people that, beyond the cut and thrust of party strife, there is someone who represents continuity, stability, tradition and who embodies the whole nation.

All European countries have a head of state. In the continent's monarchies, this will be the king or queen. In republics, it will be a president, either directly or indirectly elected. In the United States, two posts are combined in one, head of state and head of government.

**Heath, Edward** (1916–2005) Born the son of a carpenter, Edward Heath attended a state grammar school before gaining entry to Balliol College, University of Oxford. He entered the **House of Commons** as **Member of Parliament** for Bexley in 1950 and from an early stage committed himself to the cause of European unity and an active role for Britain in Europe. He rose swiftly to become **Chief Whip**, the position he held at the time of the **Suez crisis**. Between 1961 and 1963, he conducted the first, abortive negotiations for Britain to join the European Economic Community (see **European Union**). In 1964, **Prime Minister Douglas-Home** rewarded his industry and obvious competence by making him President of the Board of Trade.

In 1965, Heath won the party leadership, making him the first leader to come from a humble background in a party that was accustomed to being led by landowners and businessmen. It was hoped that he would land blows on the Labour Prime Minister, Harold **Wilson**, but as an opposition leader he found it difficult to arouse popular enthusiasm, being noticeably ill-at-ease on television. In 1970, he won a surprise victory, advocating a distinctively rightwing economic programme. He soon found it necessary to reverse some of the ideas he had previously stressed, such as less **government** support for industry and rejection of any form of incomes policy. These and other 'U-turns' upset some rightwingers in the party who did not warm to his new and more consensual approach. The major achievement of Prime Minister Heath was gaining French acceptance for British membership of the European Economic Community from January 1973.

Heath lost the **general election** of February 1974 and another shortly afterwards. He was defeated in a leadership challenge by Margaret **Thatcher** in 1975. After 1979, he was critical of Thatcherite attitudes and policies and was vocal in support of a more pro-European stance

than the Prime Minister favoured. The relationship between them was at best cool, at worst distinctly frosty.
See also: **three-day week**

**hereditary peer** A member of the **House of Lords** who has inherited his or her title. This category constituted the majority of peers until 1999 but was removed in that year under Phase One of the **Blair Government**'s reform of the House of Lords. Ninety-two 'elected hereditaries' remain, chosen from among the ranks of former hereditary peers. This was seen at the time as a temporary measure, prior to the eventual abolition of the voting rights of all hereditaries at some later date.

**HM Opposition Party** The second largest party in the **House of Commons** following a **general election** becomes the official Opposition party. Its importance in British politics is recognised by the payment of an official salary to the **Leader of the Opposition** and Opposition **Chief Whip**. The Opposition also gets a share of the **Short money**, the grant payable to opposition parties to help them carry out their work.

The Opposition plays an essential role in the day-to-day affairs of **Parliament**, at best providing a structured and regular challenge to the measures and actions of **government**. It has three main functions: it opposes the government, at best providing sustained scrutiny, questioning ministerial proposals and testing them through debate; it supports the government, acting in a bipartisan manner when the national interest is at stake, not opposing for the sake of opposition (this is the concept of responsible, constructive opposition); it is also an alternative government which involves regular review of its policies as circumstances change so that it can offer convincing alternative courses of action.

**HM Treasury**  Her Majesty's Treasury, usually known as The Treasury, is the **United Kingdom** government ministry responsible for developing and executing the British **Government**'s public finance policy and economic policy. It is headed by the **Chancellor of the Exchequer** and has one other **minister** of **Cabinet** rank, the Chief Secretary to the Treasury.

**Home, Alec**  see **Douglas-Home, Sir Alec**

**House of Commons**  The lower and dominant chamber of **Parliament**, elected by the people in periodic **general elections**. The House, as it is also known, has its origins in the thirteenth century. In the nineteenth its superiority over the unelected upper house was established. Today its main tasks are representation, deliberation, **legislation**, authorising expenditure and scrutiny. The watchdog function over the actions and policies of the **Executive** has assumed growing importance in recent years, **select committees** playing a key role in making **government** accountable to elected representatives of the people.

The House comprises 646 **Members of Parliament** (MPs), each of whom is elected to represent a **single-member constituency**. Almost without exception, each MP belongs to a **political party**. The House is organised on a party basis, with Labour and the Conservatives dominating parliamentary proceedings. There are MPs belonging to a number of minor parties who may affect the calculations of parliamentary arithmetic in a vote and the organisation of the House. The House is presided over by the **Speaker**.

As an elected chamber, the House is not and is unlikely to ever be a microcosm of the wider British society. MPs are overwhelmingly white, male, middle class and middle-aged. Members are paid and for most of them membership is a full-time occupation, although some combine it with some other professional activity. Recent years have seen the growing importance of the so-called **career politician**. Along with this greater emphasis upon professionalism, there has been a demand for better pay and conditions. The Commons may compare adversely with many other legislatures in these respects, but the working environment has significantly improved in recent decades.

Further reading: P. Norton, *Parliament in British Politics*, Palgrave, 2005

**House of Lords**  The upper chamber of **Parliament** that is subordinate to the elected **House of Commons**. The House of Lords dates back to Anglo-Saxon times. As the Commons came to be elected by a mass franchise in the nineteenth century, its importance in the constitution diminished, as did respect for its hereditary basis. It was widely portrayed as an anachronism in an increasingly democratic age. Its pro-Conservative leanings proved an obstacle for more radical administrations, Liberal and later Labour. Its composition and **power**s were reformed in the twentieth century, primarily by the **Life Peerages Act** (1958), the House of Lords Act (1999) and the two **Parliament Act**s (1911, 1949). As a result of the 1999 changes which removed the right of most **hereditary peer**s to sit and vote in the House of Lords, its membership was virtually halved from 1,295 to 695 and currently fluctuates around 700, with the two main parties broadly equally represented. Labour has yet to produce a viable scheme for Phase Two that can command substantial agreement between the main **political parties**. Many MPs favour an elected or predominantly elected house, although several members of the **Government** have voted for a mainly appointed body.

Upper chambers in **bicameral legislature**s have three important roles: to provide continuity and stability in parliament and law-making; to act as a constitutional longstop, preventing or delaying the passage of radical innovations; and to act as a revising body. The Lords fulfils all of these roles, some 60 per cent of its time being spent on examining **legislation** and 35 per cent on scrutinising the work of government. In addition to scrutinising and revising UK legislation, the House – via its Committee on the European Community – examines proposals advanced by the **European Commission** and draws attention to those that raise important issues of policy or principle. In its judicial capacity, the Lords is also the highest court of appeal in Britain, but this role is due to be transferred to a new supreme court under the terms of the **Constitutional Reform Act**.

Further reading: P. Norton, *Parliament in British Politics*, Palgrave, 2005

**human rights**  Those entitlements which allow us the minimum necessary conditions for a proper existence. In other words, they enable us to develop as individuals and achieve our potential, irrespective of the **class**, ethnic background, nationality, religion or sex to which we belong. They are innate and cannot be bestowed, granted, limited or bartered away.

The concept of human rights is an elusive one which is interpreted differently by different politicians and by different governments. Some place the emphasis on one set of rights, others stress the importance of different ones. Many writers would distinguish between legal rights – the liberties which the **law** allows us and which in democracies are recognised by the judicial machinery of the **state** (for example, freedom of assembly) – and moral or natural rights, sometimes described as inalienable or inviolable rights, entitlements which cannot or should not be removed for they derive from people's common humanity.

In the latter case, a person ought to be granted them because he or she has a morally compelling claim.

As we have seen, legal rights derive from our membership of a particular society rather than from our status as human beings. They can be amended or removed by a change in the law. They can be subdivided into civil and political rights, and economic and social rights.

Listings of basic rights are contentious, but two well known and widely accepted ones are the **Universal Declaration of Human Rights** and the **European Convention on Human Rights**.

See also: **Human Rights Act**

**Human Rights Act** (1998) The Human Rights Act became operative from October 2000. It provides the first written statement of people's rights and obligations by enshrining most – but not all – of the **European Convention on Human Rights** into British **law**. It allows them to use the Convention as a means of securing **justice** in the British courts. **Judges** are now able to apply **human rights** law in their rulings.

The effect of incorporation of the Convention is to introduce a new human rights culture into British politics. In general, decisions by **Parliament**, a local authority or other public body must not infringe the rights guaranteed under the Act. Where rights conflict, such as privacy versus freedom of information, the courts will decide where the balance should lie. Judges have to ask of deciding cases as they come before them, in effect creating new law. If courts decide that a statute breaches the Act, they can declare it 'incompatible' but they cannot strike it down. They cannot overrule Parliament. It will be for Parliament to amend the law, thus preserving the idea of **parliamentary sovereignty**. The ultimate decision in any conflict lies with Parliament, not the courts. Some writers suggest that the measure changes the traditional balance between Parliament and the **judiciary** and gives much greater power to judges. Others suggest that important social change will continue to be brought about by elected politicians rather than judges, this having been the case in other countries that incorporated the Convention many years ago.

There were some initial concerns that the Act would clog up the courts and that the chief beneficiaries would be lawyers. It was expected that the courts would be deluged with all kinds of cases, some of them extreme. This has not happened and the Human Rights Act has changed the outcome of relatively few cases.

**hung council**  A local authority in which no one party has sufficient support to run the council on its own, a situation that prevails in many parts of the country.

**hung Parliament**  A hung **Parliament** is one where – in the aftermath of a **general election** – no party has won a majority of the seats. The outcome is uncertain, the differences between the party performances being not very substantial. In February 1974, when the Conservatives actually outvoted Labour, Labour had four more seats but was well short of having a majority over all other parties combined. In the circumstances, outgoing **Prime Minister** Edward **Heath** tried to stay on as premier, hoping he would obtain **Liberal** backing. But his attempt failed and a **minority government** was formed.

In the event of a hung Parliament, there is some dispute as to the role of the **monarch**. He or she might allow the leader of the previously largest party to carry on in office, invite the leader of the largest party to attempt to form a **government,** or invite an individual from the **House of Commons** to try to form a government which could command a Commons majority, by forming a **coalition**.

**Hutton Report** A judicial inquiry chaired by Lord Hutton, appointed by the British **Government** to investigate the death of a Government weapons expert, Dr David Kelly. Its terms of reference were to 'urgently . . . conduct an investigation into the circumstances surrounding the death of Dr Kelly'. The inquiry opened in August 2003 and reported on 28 January 2004. The inquiry heard evidence from 74 witnesses over 22 days, including Tony **Blair**. In his report, Hutton began by saying that he was 'satisfied that Dr Kelly took his own life'. He then concluded that the **British Broadcasting Corporation**'s (BBC) allegations (made originally by journalist Andrew **Gilligan**) that the Government had knowingly 'sexed up' a report into Iraq's **weapons of mass destruction** – the so-called 'September Dossier' – were unfounded. The inquiry's findings prompted the immediate resignation of the BBC's Chairman and Director General and the journalist at the centre of the allegations. Lord Hutton retired as a **law lord** following the report's publication. The Government was largely cleared of any wrongdoing, much to the surprise of many observers. Having previously been praised for his handling of the witnesses, the chairman found himself criticised for presiding over a whitewash.

See also: **Campbell**

**hybrid Bill** A type of **Bill** which is part private and part public. Such Bills embody a public policy that affects the particular interests of some individuals or organisations in a manner that does not apply to all individuals and groups within the category.

# I

**ID card** Compulsory identity (ID) cards were issued in both world wars but the scheme was abandoned in 1952.

Their use was considered by the **Major Government** but Labour did not pursue the idea after 1997. However, Home Secretary David Blunkett resurrected the idea after the attacks on the World Trade Center in 2001. He portrayed identity cards as invaluable in the fight against **terrorism**, crime, identity fraud and false entitlement to social security benefits. Enabling **legislation** was eventually passed in 2006, providing for the phased introduction of a scheme under which everyone will eventually be compelled to possess an ID card. From 2008, renewal of passports will require the collection of biometric data and become more expensive, to cover the costs of the card. There will be a national data register.

Some people have few fears about being forced to prove their identity, seeing the card as a useful means of so doing. They note that most **European Union** countries have some such scheme and can see its potential benefits. Opponents worry about the implications for the **civil liberties** of individuals being forced to own such a card whether they want one or not, feeling that the storage of biometric features and personal data on a national register places too much knowledge in the hands of the authorities. Others worry about the costs associated with ID cards, the reliability of biometric technology and the way in which the police might harass members of **ethnic minorities**, requiring them to prove their identity.

**identity card**  see **ID card**

**ideology**  A more or less systematic, well developed and comprehensive set of assumptions, beliefs, ideas and values about politics which help us to explain the political world, what it is and why, and what it should be. An ideology consists of both empirical statements about what is and prescriptive statements about what ought to be, examples being anarchism, conservatism, **liberalism** and **socialism**.

**IGO**  see **intergovernmental organisation**

**IMF**  see **International Monetary Fund**

**impeachment** A formal means of removing an individual from public office that could not be enforced through the conventional law courts. Impeachment refers to the charging of a public official, usually an elected politician, with improper conduct in office (usually financial or sexual rather than political) before a duly constituted tribunal, usually the main elected legislative body, prior to removing the official from office if they are found guilty.

Impeachment is little known beyond the United States (and little used there), yet the issue of impeachment was raised in August 2004 by a **Plaid Cymru** MP who announced that he would be attempting to impeach Tony **Blair** over his handling of issues related to the war against Iraq. His initiative won minimal support in the **House of Commons**, the mainstream **Members of Parliament** of both main parties wanting nothing to do with it.

**indirect democracy**  see **representative democracy**

**individualism** A belief in the primacy of the individual. **Classical liberalism** and **New Right** thinking in the 1980s and after have both stressed the supreme importance of the individual over any social group or collective body. Margaret **Thatcher**'s observation that 'there is no such thing as society' is an indication of individualist thinking. Individualism stresses the virtues of independence, perseverance and self-reliance. It is therefore at the opposite end of the spectrum to **collectivism** but it can exist in any community which allows individuals to respect other individuals and their right to personal **liberty**.

**individual ministerial responsibility** Individual responsibility refers to the responsibility of each **Government minister** for the work of his department. He or she is answerable to the **House of Commons** for all that happens within it. The positive aspect of this is that **Members of Parliament** (MPs) know that there is someone to whom they can direct their questions and anxieties about policy, at **parliamentary questions**, in committees, in debates and privately to MPs. The negative aspect is that thereby civil servants are kept out of the political arena and shielded from controversy, making it possible for any future administration to have confidence in **Civil Service** neutrality.

'Responsible' means on the one hand that ministers are required to inform **Parliament** about the work and conduct of their departments, explaining and if necessary making amends for their own and their officials' actions. They take the praise for what is well done and the blame for what goes wrong. In this sense, answerability and **accountability** still apply. But 'responsibility' goes further and implies liability to lose office, if the fault is sufficiently serious. In this second sense, resignations for political or administrative misjudgements and mistakes have in recent decades become extremely unusual. In the nineteenth century, such resignations were not uncommon; few have occurred since World War Two. Many political blunders, misjudgements and departmental administrative failings are committed but they go unpunished by the ultimate sanction. Today, whether or not a minister resigns under the convention will depend on his support from the party, **Prime Minister** and **Cabinet** colleagues. If there is prolonged adverse publicity that may be damaging to the Government, a resignation is more likely to occur. Most resignations today relate to personal indiscretions of a sexual or financial kind.

**initiative** A vote of the electorate on an **issue** of public policy. An initiative is a **referendum** that has been called on the initiative of a section of a community, rather than by the government itself. Common in several American states, this form of **direct democracy** has not been used in national politics in Britain.

**inner Cabinet** All **Prime Minister**s rely on some **ministers** more than others, some being personal friends as well as colleagues. The **Chancellor of the Exchequer**, Foreign and Home Secretaries are likely to be among the 'inner Cabinet' but it is up to the leader to consult whom he or she sees fit. At various times, Tony **Blair** has relied on John Prescott, Gordon **Brown**, David Blunkett and Peter **Mandelson**, among others. On any major issue such as the **Iraq war** (2003), he would want to be sure that his most senior ministers were in support.

**insider group** A **pressure group** which has the opportunity to work closely with elected and appointed officials in national, devolved and **local government**. Insider groups have access to the key personnel who inhabit the place where decisions are made, are often recognised as the only legitimate representatives of particular interests and are often formally incorporated into the official consultative bodies.

**institutional racism** Sometimes known as systemic **racism**, institutional racism is a form of racism that occurs in institutions such as corporations and public bodies. The term was originally coined by black American activist Stokely Carmichael in the late 1960s: he defined it as 'the collective failure of an organisation to provide an appropriate and professional service to people because of their colour, culture or ethnic origin'. In the aftermath of the murder of black teenager Stephen Lawrence in 1993, the resulting MacPherson inquiry detected the existence of institutional racism in the Metropolitan Police. He concurred with the above definition and felt that it can be seen 'in processes, attitudes and behaviour which amount to discrimination through unwitting prejudice, ignorance, thoughtlessness and racist stereotyping which disadvantages minority ethnic people . . . if the result or outcome of established laws, customs or practices is racially discriminatory, then institutional racism can be said to have occurred'.

The suggestion underlying the phrase is that in the organisations affected, there exists a culture in which employees at all levels understand that racist language and practices will be acceptable because they are known to have the tacit approval of those at the helm.

**interest group**  see **pressure group**

**intergovernmental organisation (IGO)**  An organisation that allows national states to cooperate on matters of specific concern to them, in a way that does not compromise their national **sovereignty**. They are usually established by treaty and operate by consent, their day-to-day running being conducted by a secretariat. Most of them lack any means of enforcing compliance with their agreed decisions and on occasion their wishes can be ignored or overridden, as with George Bush's decision to press ahead with an invasion of Iraq without a second **United Nations** resolution. Powerful states tend to comply with IGO recommendations when they endorse what they are already doing or intend to do. Examples include the United

Nations, the International Telecommunications Union and regional bodies such as the **Council of Europe**.

Most established states belong to one or more of the many intergovernmental organisations which inhabit the international environment.

See also: **supranationalism**

**international law** The system of principles and rules which constrains states and other political actors in their mutual relations. There being no international **legislature**, international **law** derives from generally accepted principles (for example, respect for territorial integrity), custom, treaties and the views of legal authorities as set out in international courts. It applies primarily to **states** and their rulers but can also apply to individuals who act under state direction, as in the case of the Nuremberg War Crimes Tribunal (1946).

Coined by the English philosopher Jeremy Bentham (1748–1832), the concept is much admired by idealists who see it as a way of peacefully resolving conflicts via some reference to moral code. Pragmatists are more sceptical, noting that it cannot be enforced and therefore is not so much law but rather a guiding set of moral principles.

See also: **just war**

**International Monetary Fund (IMF)** Established at the Bretton Woods conference (1944) in New Hampshire, the IMF describes itself as 'an organisation of 185 members, working to foster global monetary cooperation, secure financial stability, facilitate international trade, promote high employment and sustain economic growth, and reduce poverty'. Almost all **United Nations** members participate in the Fund, recognising that in an increasingly interdependent world, the economic performance of any country is much related to the performance of others and to the stability of the global economic environment. In particular, the policies pursued by some states tend to impact on how well poorer countries perform. **Globalisation** requires international cooperation and this has increased the need for such international machinery.

In 1976, in the face of a dramatic slide in the pound in the foreign-exchange markets, the **Callaghan Government** in Britain had to seek a $3,900 million loan from the IMF. To obtain this assistance, it had to both increase taxes and make substantial cuts in public expenditure.

**investigative journalism** In-depth and often critical journalism which involves careful, detailed and often time-consuming research which may result in unfolding some scandal or information that those in authority would prefer to remain unknown. For example, *The Guardian* conducted an in-depth probe into the cash for questions affair during the lifetime of the **Major Government**.

**IRA** see **Irish Republican Army**

**Iraq war** (2003)  Since the ending of the **first Gulf war** (1991), relations between the West and Iraq had remained in a state of low-level conflict marked by American and British air-strikes, and sanctions and threats against Saddam Hussein. In the wake of the **September 11th attacks** and the relative success of the United States (US) invasion of Afghanistan in 2001, the Bush administration felt that it had sufficient military justification and public support in the US for further operations against perceived threats in the Middle East. Throughout 2002, while invasion was being contemplated, it was increasingly apparent that removing Hussein from power was a major goal, although the US offered to accept major changes in Iraqi military and foreign policy in lieu of this.

The stated justification for invasion included Iraqi production and use of **weapons of mass destruction** (WMD) which the US claimed were being stored in violation of **United Nations** Security Council Resolution 1441. George Bush, supported by the **Blair Government**, claimed that these weapons posed a grave and imminent threat to the United States and its allies. Critics of the Hussein regime also pointed to the alleged Iraqi links with terrorist organisations and the mass killings and general denial of **human rights** under the Hussein government.

Prior to the invasion, UN inspection teams searched Iraq for WMD and were willing to continue, but were forced out by the onset of war in spite of their requests for more time. The US abandoned its failing efforts to get international endorsement for war against Iraq on 17 March 2003 and began the invasion on 20 March 2003.

Ninety-eight per cent of the invading force comprised United States and **United Kingdom** troops, although numerous other nations also participated. The Iraqi military was defeated and Baghdad fell on 9 April 2003. On 1 May 2003, Bush declared the end of major combat operations, terminating the Ba'ath Party's rule and removing Hussein from office. Coalition forces ultimately captured Hussein on 13 December 2003. Careful inspections after Iraq's capitulation failed to locate any WMD, which has given rise to continued debate about the **legitimacy** under **international law** of the invasion.

Post-invasion Iraq has been plagued by violence caused by a mostly Sunni Muslim insurgency, the involvement of outside powers and the **terrorism** of the **al-Qaeda** militant network. The strife and regular killings between rival religious groups lead some commentators to detect signs of an impending civil war. More positive indications have been the tentative growth of **democracy**, as signified by the country's holding of free elections and the creation – after considerable delay – of a broadly supported government based upon them. However, it has as yet failed to take command of the situation and establish law and order.

The war has proved highly divisive in British politics, some Conservative, several Labour and most Liberal Democrat MPs being opposed to it at the time of the prewar debate. Subsequently, discontent over the basis for and waging of the war has increased, among both politicians and the general public. The controversies surrounding WMD and the enquiries into the evidence on which the case for invasion was made, as well as the handling of the war and its aftermath, have seriously damaged the reputation and credibility of Tony Blair who as **Prime Minister** was widely portrayed as being too unwilling to criticise George Bush and his presidency. The war caused major upset to many traditional Labour supporters, seriously damaging the morale of party activists.

See also: **Butler Report, Hutton Report, just war**

**Irish Republican Army (IRA)** The main **republican** organisation in Northern Ireland. In the late 1960s, the Provisional IRA (PIRA) broke from the original organisation and has subsequently surpassed it in influence. Until the 1990s, PIRA operated beyond the mainstream political process. Members portrayed themselves as true representatives of the nationalist community, but for many years saw no requirement for this to be sanctified by the nationalist population. Some leading figures sought to emphasise the need to participate in the formal political arena and since the beginning of the peace process have been willing to allow the **Sinn Féin Party** to enter into negotiations.

Allegations of republican violence continue to be made, although on occasions such as the Omagh atrocity, it was a splinter group the Real IRA that was responsible for violence. In 2005, the IRA officially renounced the use of violence as the means of achieving Irish unification and has decommissioned a vast stockpile of weaponry under the supervision of the independent decommissioning inspectorate.

**Islamophobia** Prejudice against or demonisation of Muslims which manifests itself in general negative attitudes and stereotyping, discrimination, harassment and, at worst, violence. Fear or hatred of Muslims has been on the increase in recent years. The **September 11th attacks on the World Trade Center** and the **London bombings** provoked anti-Muslim feeling among a section of the white population, some of whom associated the activities of any disaffected young Muslims with **al-Qaeda terrorism**. There have been examples of Muslim communities suffering from mindless and irrational attacks, involving verbal and physical abuse.

Western **government**s have identified al-Qaeda and its network of terrorists as being the instigators of the mass killing in New York, London and elsewhere, but have been careful to point out that in Afghanistan and Iraq they are fighting terrorism, not Islam. The reaction of most British Muslims of whatever background to such events was one of shock, horror and near disbelief that any of their number could have committed or been associated with such actions. Some victims of the explosions were Muslims and so were many of those involved in the rescue exercises and the medical teams. The **Muslim community** is much troubled by the suggestion that they are complicit in or supportive of political extremism. They fear that in the media the image portrayed of Islam is a negative one.

**issue**  A matter recognised as part of the policy agenda over which there is public debate or disagreement. Issues relate to areas of public policy over which opinion is sharply divided, are matters about which the public feels strongly and are matters for the resolution of which voters turn to **political parties**.

Some writers have distinguished between position issues on which people take up a stance (for example, for or against foxhunting or student tuition fees) and valence issues, topics over which there is broad agreement about the goal to be pursued (for example, decreased crime levels and improved provision of personal health) but disagreement over the competence or performance of the parties in tackling the issue.

See also: **issue voting**

**issue network**  A looser and more flexible arrangement than a **policy community**, an issue network comprises all the players who are collectively involved in shaping **government** policy in any given sector. The term takes account of the variety of sometimes discordant voices – organised groups, national and European civil servants who influence policy, regulators, academics and **think-tank**s among them.

**issue voting**  The idea that voters make their decision about whom to support on the basis of their assessment of the **issue** or policy stances of the **political parties**. In other words, it is a calculated decision based on a rational choice. For issue voting to be a significant influence, voters need to be aware of the issue concerned, have an attitude or opinion about the issue, perceive the parties as having different policies on the issue and, finally, vote for the party whose position on the issue is – or is perceived to be – closest to his or her own viewpoint.

In the early decades after 1945, **voting behaviour** was, in Punnett's words, 'habitual and ingrained'. Many voters identified with one party – often on the basis of the **social class** to which they belonged – and tended to maintain that allegiance. Issues did not play a key role, although many people had generalised images of the parties that may have had some policy content. With the development of partisan and **class dealignment**, voting behaviour is more volatile and liable to be influenced by short-term factors. Issue voting has accordingly become more evident. Franklin and Hughes (1999) found that in elections from 1987 to 1997, issue opinions had become significantly more important than **class** as determinants of how people vote.

Further reading: M. Franklin and C. Hughes in G. Evans and P. Norris (eds), *Critical Elections: British Parties and Voters in Long-term Perspective*, Sage, 1999; R. Punnett, *British Government and Politics*, Gower, 1971

# J

**joined-up government** Advocates of joined-up or 'holistic' **government** argue that in order to promote efficient policy-making and effective government, it is necessary to ensure that there is greater integration at all levels and that policies in one area should dovetail with what is being done in other areas. Tony **Blair** was a keen exponent of joined-up government when he became **Prime Minister**, seeing it as essential to the delivery of high-quality public services.

**joint committee** A committee comprising an equal number of members from both houses of **Parliament**, established with a view to save time or for other reasons of convenience, to handle certain issues. They exercise similar powers to **select committees**.

**JP** see **Justice of the Peace**

**judge** Judges in England and Wales are appointed by the Judicial Appointments Commission, an independent non-departmental public body set up under the terms of the **Constitutional Reform Act** (2005). All candidates are to be judged on merit alone, measured by five core qualities: intellectual capacity; personal qualities (integrity, independence, judgement, decisiveness, objectivity, ability, willingness to learn); ability to understand and deal fairly; authority and communication skills; and efficiency. It is the **Lord Chancellor** who actually makes the appointments, but for the most senior judges he will receive one name only from the Commission. Many of the current judges have previously served as barristers.

Judges preside over the courts, following the evidence carefully, giving rulings on points of **law**, summing up the factual evidence for the jury and then passing sentence or, in civil cases, delivering a judgement. They are often criticised for their fundamental conservatism, which allegedly makes them out of step with modern social tendencies. In the past, they have been drawn exclusively from a privileged social background, although in recent years there has been a greater attempt to introduce greater diversity. The lack of social representativeness matters all the more today because of the increased prominence of judges in the political system and is seen as jeopardising their neutrality in the adjudication of cases.

Of course, background is not necessarily a guide to judicial attitude and once on the bench, judges can show a surprising degree of independent judgement and the majority dispense justice of high quality.

**judicial activism**  Judicial activism involves the courts taking a broad and active view of their role as interpreters of the **constitution** and reviewers of **executive** and legislative action. **Judges** are willing to venture beyond making narrow legal decisions and become involved in influencing public policy. Like **judicial restraint**, the term is particularly used in connection with the American Supreme Court, although the development of a more political role for judges in most countries over recent decades has led to its increasing application in countries such as Britain.

**judicial restraint**  The conservative philosophy which maintains that **judges** should simply apply the **law**, irrespective of policy implications and the judge's own values.

**judicial review**  A key function of the courts. It refers to the power of the courts to interpret the **constitution** and to declare void actions of branches of **government** if they are deemed to be in conflict with its requirements. Some countries have a very strong system of judicial review, which is particularly important in federal systems. In the United States, it is the job of the Supreme Court to ensure that each layer of government keeps to its respective sphere and to settle any dispute that arises between them. It has often struck down **legislation** as 'unconstitutional'.

    In Britain, there is a much narrower and more limited version of judicial review, enabling the courts to declare the actions of **ministers** unlawful but not allowing them to question the validity of the **law** itself. No court has declared unconstitutional any act lawfully passed by the British **Parliament**, the sovereign law-making body. But since the 1980s, there has been an increasing resort to the process of judicial review, many of the cases dealing with actions taken by **government departments** and local authorities. The Home Office is the department that has been most challenged in the British courts, attracting as it does some three-quarters of all challenges to government decisions. The doctrine has caused embarrassment to a succession of ministers and on occasion resulted in public confrontations between the courts and the politicians.

**judiciary** The branch of **government** (mainly comprising the **judges** and the courts) responsible for the authoritative interpretation of **law** and the administration of it in particular cases. These include the resolution of civil disputes, disputes between **citizens** and the **state**, trial of suspected criminals and interpretation of the meaning and application of the laws.

**junior minister** A **minister** of state or parliamentary under-secretary who assists the departmental minister (often known as secretary of state) who heads a **government department**. A junior minister usually assumes responsibility for a particular area of departmental policy.

**jury trial** Juries have long been portrayed as bastions of British **liberty**. Trial by jury dates back to the period after the Norman Conquest and became customary during the reign of Henry II in the late twelfth century. It is seen as a cardinal feature of **justice** that the guilt of those charged with a criminal offence should be determined by their peers, bringing the **law** closer to the people. This is seen as a bulwark against oppression, particularly valuable when the decision (as in cases of defamation of character) involves a consideration of the construction which would be placed upon it by the everyday man or woman. Juries provide ordinary people with an opportunity for active participation in the affairs of government. If jurors err, it is more likely to be on the side of the accused. For these reasons, the public have faith in the jury system.

Critics allege that juries are inappropriate to deal with highly technical cases and some civil cases involving the awarding of damages. ('Considerable' damages may mean different things according to the standards of living of those sitting in a particular court.) Sometimes, trials last over several days or weeks, so that jurors, equipped with no special training, have to follow arguments and evidence which can be exceedingly complex.

Recent **legislation**, such as the 2004 Criminal Justice Act, has restricted the right of jury trial.

**justice**  A concept concerned with the morally justifiable treatment of individuals, each person being treated appropriately according to his or her circumstances. It is about fairness or rightness in the application of rule, the settling of disputes and the distribution of benefits and goods between people. It involves 'doing the right thing' which may also mean doing what the **law** demands. But law and justice cannot necessarily be equated, some laws such as those that once supported slavery now being considered 'unjust'. Justice is concerned with ethical considerations, prescribing what the situation should be, whereas law has an objective character rather than a matter of opinion or judgement. Justice is desirable, law is enforceable and binding throughout a political community.

The particular meaning of justice may vary over time, between one society or culture and another. It will be regarded differently, according to the political and religious beliefs and interests of individuals. For instance, one person might consider it wrong and 'unjust' to take human life under any circumstances, whereas many could agree that there are times when it might be necessary, however undesirable.

**Justice of the Peace (JP)**  The 30,000 or so Justices of the Peace are appointed by the **Crown** on the advice of the **Lord Chancellor** who himself is advised by a local advisory committee. Appointees are lay people, normally with a record of public service. Their work is unpaid and as magistrates courts usually sit in the morning, much use has been made of retired persons; men and women are equally liable to be appointed. In the past there were a few stipendiary (paid, full-time) magistrates who handled cases in the larger towns and cities, but since 2000 they have been renamed as district judges (magistrates' courts).

Magistrates' courts form the bottom of the judicial hierarchy, but JPs presiding over them handle many cases from start to finish. For many people who have committed offences, particularly those associated with motoring, they are the only point of contact between **citizen**s and the criminal **justice** system. They have their supporters who see lay participation as a reinforcement of the idea that the prevention of crime and the application of punishment should involve the whole community. JPs are seen as more reflective of the general values of the community than legal professionals. Moreover, the system is much cheaper than the alternative of employing professional **judges**.

On the other hand, critics allege that far from reflecting community values, JPs reinforce concerns about the built-in bias of the judicial system which is in the hands of people whose background and status make them out of touch with the social composition and attitudes of the bulk of British people. They tend to be elderly, white and middle class and to under-represent the young, manual workers and members of **ethnic minorities**. Moreover, JPs lack personal expertise and are often alleged to be too reliant on police evidence and the advice of their trained clerks.

**just war** The tradition dating back to classical and medieval literature that in certain cases it is ethically right to wage war and would be ethically wrong not so to do. Initially a Christian tradition dating back to the conversion of Emperor Constantine to Christianity in the fourth century, the idea has support from the world's other great ethical traditions. Augustine, bishop of Hippo in North Africa, initiated just-war thinking in the Christian West when he wrote that he did not approve of killing in order to defend his own life but that it was right for public functionaries responsible for 'the defence of others' to do so when necessary.

The presumption among supporters of just-war theory is that war is an evil but sometimes it is necessary to fight, although fighting should be limited to the minimum necessary to achieve the desired goal. There is no definitive set of criteria for a just war but it is usual to distinguish between war decision criteria (whether war is justified, *jus ad bellum*) and war conduct criteria (how war should be fought, *jus in bello*), both of which must apply for hostilities to be deemed to be just. War decision criteria include: legitimate **authority**; a just cause; right intention; a reasonable prospect of success; likelihood that the war will lead to a just peace; and last resort. War conduct criteria include proportionality and discrimination (not intentionally harming innocent **citizen**s). **International law** follows the just war *jus in bello* tradition in the limits it places on certain modes of warfare via the Hague and Geneva conventions.

# K

**Keynesianism** A theory named after the writings of British economist John Maynard Keynes (1833–1946) based on

the idea that there needs to be some governmental intervention and management of the economy to achieve economic growth and stability as well as full employment.
Keynesian economics were practised by British **governments** in the postwar years down to 1976, as well as in
much of the Western world.

The idea that governments should 'spend their way out
of a slump' has gone out of fashion and governments
have increasingly over the last two decades or so come to
recognise the importance of tight control over levels of
public spending.

**Kinnock, Neil** (1942– )   Having been brought up in the industrial valleys of South Wales, the young Neil Kinnock
inherited the passionate socialist tradition and oratorical
skills of the Welsh Labour leftwinger Nye Bevan. He was
a **Member of Parliament** from 1970 to 1995, leaving his
'young firebrand' image behind him when he became the
Labour **Leader of the Opposition** following the 1983
election. On becoming leader, he inherited a demoralised
party and was a key figure in its modernisation. He
was responsible for improving its presentational skills,
overhauling its organisation and – following a policy
review – shedding some of the policies that had contributed to its severe defeat in 1983. His finest hour was
perhaps his expulsion of the militants in 1986, an important victory that was an important early step towards
making Labour electable once more. Yet if by the 1992
election he had made the party seem again a credible
alternative party of **government,** he was unable to carry
it to victory, hence his reputation as a 'nearly man' of
British politics. He resigned as leader immediately after
the election defeat.

Kinnock subsequently served as the **United Kingdom**'s
European Commissioner from 1995 until 2004, latterly

serving as vice-president of the **European Commission**. He is now a **life peer** and Chairman of the British Council.

**kitchen Cabinet**  The term refers to the small coterie of advisers and confidantes with which **Prime Minister**s like to surround themselves and talk over issues at the end of the day. It will usually include some politicians (usually members of the Cabinet), public officials and private **citizen**s. Since 1997, more importance has been attached to the views of key personnel such as Alastair **Campbell** and Peter **Mandelson** (both still in close contact, though detached from the day-to-day action), Philip Gould, Jonathan Powell and others.

# L

**Labour Party**  The Labour Party has been the main leftwing British **political party** since the late 1920s. In its **constitution**, it describes itself as a democratic socialist party. Its **socialism** was originally defined in terms of support for the old **Clause IV** but was later interpreted by many members as a commitment to greater economic and social **equality**. It remains a member of the Socialist International but the policies pursued by Labour **government**s in office have been more social democratic than distinctively socialist. The British road to socialism, as pursued by the Labour Party, was always based on a gradualist, evolutionary approach, not a revolutionary one. **Marxism** never made a great impact on many of its supporters.

The first minority Labour administrations were formed in the 1920s under the leadership of Ramsay MacDonald. The first majority Labour government was that led by Clement **Attlee** and formed in 1945. Under the leadership of Tony **Blair**, Labour won a landslide victory in the 1997 **general election** and formed its first government since the 1979 general election. It retained its position with a further large victory in the 2001 general election and a smaller victory (based on only 35.2 per cent of the popular vote) in the 2005 general election. Since June 2007, it has been led by Gordon **Brown**, the current **Prime Minister**.

Now that New Labour has been tested in office, it is easier to see how far the party has travelled over recent years. It was and remains a coalition whose members possess differing shades of opinion, but there are discernible differences between old and new Labour. Old Labour was a working-class party with limited appeal to the middle classes, close to **trades union**s, willing to raise taxes to finance high levels of public expenditure and committed to generous universal welfare benefits, full employment and equality of outcome. It used the language of caring, compassion, social justice and equality. By comparison, New Labour is more detached from the unions, keen to keep public spending under control and direct taxation down, committed to equality of opportunity, more pro-European and less appealing to its traditional supporters as it maintains its bid for support from **Middle England**. It pursues a 'big tent' approach and is concerned about image, having an interest in presentation and **spin**.

**laissez-faire** Literally translated as 'leave to do', the French term refers to the principle that there should be maximum freedom for the economic forces of the market place and minimum interference from the **state** in economic life.

**law** Law is the body of public rules that is binding throughout the political community and is enforced by the **power** of the **state**. It provides the state with legitimate **authority**

over its members. It is related to politics, in that much law has been passed by Parliament and is the product of argument between the main parties. However, if politics is a part of the process by which laws are made, once established law is superior to it and acquires a majesty and importance far beyond that of any political cause or party.

Law is often seen as synonymous with **justice** and morality, both of which concepts are also concerned with the regulation of human conduct. But whereas laws must be observed (otherwise punishment will follow), moral principles enunciate what should happen: if these guidelines are not observed, no sanction will follow. Moreover, something may be illegal without being immoral, such as over-staying one's time limit at a parking meter.

**law lord**  The most senior **judge**s in the UK, who, under the terms of the Appellate Jurisdiction Act (1876) were appointed as **life peer**s in order to fulfil the judicial function of the **House of Lords**. There are usually 12 current law lords (and several former law lords) who sit in the chamber and who in a special committee act as the highest court of appeal in the UK. They and their functions are due to be transferred to the new Supreme Court proposed under the **Constitutional Reform Act** (2005).

**Leader of the Opposition**  The Ministers of the Crown Act (1937) defined the Leader of the Opposition as 'that member of the House of Commons who is for the time being the leader in that House of the party in opposition to His Majesty's Government having the greatest numerical strength in the House', in other words, the leader of the largest opposition party in the **House of Commons**. It recognised the importance of the post by for the first time providing for payment of the incumbent out of public funds.

On certain matters, such as foreign relations, defence policy and **legislation** of a non-party character, the **Prime Minister** may occasionally consult with the Leader of the Opposition before finally committing, especially if the decision is likely to impose obligations on future **governments**. There would also be consultation over the appointment of **life peers** from the main opposition party. The opposition leader also chooses the topic for debate on 17 of the opposition days in the House and has two opportunities to challenge the **Prime Minister** at **Prime Minister's Questions**, every Wednesday.

**Left** A broad ideological disposition associated with support for the principles of **equality**, fraternity, **liberty** and progress. A leftwing person challenges traditional attitudes and practices and wants to see reform. This involves a more active role for **government** in bringing about desirable change. He or she may also believe in higher levels of taxation to pay for improvements, some redistribution of wealth from the better-off to the least well-off and movement towards a more equal and less class-bound society. Some leftwingers are keen to see more **state** control over basic industries, believing that private ownership is unsuitable as a means of running the railways and other essential services.

**Left–Right continuum** A term having its origins in the position adopted by various groups at the first meeting of the French Estates-General in the early days of the French Revolution (1789). It refers to the spectrum on which it is often convenient to locate parties, stretching from the leftwing of parties which believe in radical or even revolutionary change, through the socialists and centre parties, to parties of the moderate right which oppose change, to the extremist parties of a Fascist or

Nazi **ideology**. Inevitably, such labelling over-simplifies the position of some parties, but it enables us to make comparisons between them.

Today, applied in Britain, these labels can be misleading and confusing. People who seem leftwing on one **issue** may adopt a rightwing approach on another. More seriously, the division of **Left** and **Right** has become somewhat blurred, for supporters of **New Labour** increasingly employ terminology and adopt approaches traditionally associated with the British **Conservative Party**. Nonetheless, the term remains convenient shorthand by which to summarise different attitudes on important political, economic and social questions.

**legislation** A body of **law**s passed by the **legislature**. Legislating is the act of initiating, debating and passing laws. Most **Bills** come from the **government**, but the legislature still approves them and may make amendments, usually in committees.

**legislature** The branch of government in which policy **issues** are discussed and assessed and public policies enacted by legislators.

In an **indirect democracy**, representation is a key function of legislatures. Most are elected bodies, whose members act on behalf of those who live in their area, for instance **Members of Parliament** being representatives of their constituents and of the party under whose label they were elected. Legislatures also act as deliberative bodies, considering public matters of national importance in debates in the chamber. They also have responsibility for discussing and passing **legislation** (the roots of the word 'legislature' are the Latin terms *legis* and *latio* meaning 'law' and 'bringing', 'carrying' or 'proposing'), overseeing and scrutinising the **Executive** and authorising expenditure.

**legitimacy** Closely related to **authority**, legitimacy refers in general to the people's acceptance of a **law**, ruling or regime itself as valid. The term is usually used in relation to an entire system of **government**, whereas authority often refers to a specific position. Legitimacy refers to whether people accept the validity of the system, or sometimes of an act of **Parliament**. If the authority of a government is generally accepted by those who are governed, then we describe the regime as being legitimate. Legitimate rule implies some justification for the exercise of rule and **power**, such as the general consent of the governed, as expressed in popular elections. Those who are governed accept the right of the rulers to make decisions.

**Liberal** A member of the Liberal party. Since the late 1980s, most British Liberals now belong to the **Liberal Democrat Party**, although a small Liberal party remains, continuing to subscribe to traditional Liberal nostrums.

With a small 'l' the term can be used to refer to individuals and policies thought to be broad-minded, enlightened, humane, progressive and tolerant.

**liberal democracy** The form of **government** practised in the West that tries to combine the **power**s of democratic government with the liberal values associated with individual **freedom**.

**Democracy** involves more than people having voting rights. It is essential that there are opportunities for **citizens** and the media to exercise freedom of speech, assembly and political opposition. A liberal democracy balances the principle of limited government against the ideal of popular consent. There are checks on the power of government to protect citizens from arbitrary or unfair action, so that a liberal democratic regime is characterised by pluralism, limited government, open government, and an independent **judiciary**.

In liberal democracies, the power of government is limited by the recognition of free play between autonomous voluntary associations within society. There are several checks and balances. Important focuses of power include **trades union**s, professional associations and private companies. The task of government is to reconcile and coordinate these various interests, only imposing coercion when other methods of harmonisation fail to operate effectively.

Liberal democracies are characterised by a spirit of tolerance towards competing groups and particularly towards the views of minorities. There is due recognition of everybody's interests but it is understood that government should be concerned with the good of the whole community.

Further reading: M. Cole, *Democracy*, Edinburgh University Press, 2006

**Liberal Democrat Party** Formed in 1988 out of a merger between the Liberal Party and the short-lived **Social Democratic Party**, the 'Lib Dems' are currently the third largest political grouping in the UK. The party won 62 seats in the 2005 election (and a subsequent by-election), its 63 **Members of Parliament** being the largest 'third force' since 1923. In the **Scottish Executive**, the party has been in **coalition** with Labour since the formation of the **Scottish Parliament** in 1999.

The Lib Dems do not easily fit into the **Left–Right continuum**. Under the leadership of Paddy Ashdown (1988–99), the party abandoned equidistance and moved closer to Labour. As **New Labour** has taken up a position in the centre ground, the Lib Dems have distanced themselves from **ministers** and are generally been seen as having moved leftward over **issues** such as tuition fees and the **Iraq war** over which the Charles Kennedy leadership was highly critical. More consistently pro-European than the main parties, they have also supported higher levels of government spending and if necessary direct taxation. They are wary of the **power** of the **state** over individuals and have been critical of the government's performance on matters concerning **civil liberty** (for example, **ID cards** and **anti-terrorist legislation**). Current leader Menzies Campbell has stressed traditional liberal concerns, such as **human rights** and a foreign policy based on **international law**.

**liberalism**  A political doctrine that emphasises the importance of consent, **freedom** and toleration. It is associated with the protection of individual **liberty** and rights, and limitation of the role of the **state**. **Classical liberalism** was the creed of the Liberal party in the nineteenth century, before it came to embrace a more active role for the state in social protection during the pre-World War One era of **New Liberalism**. Neo-liberal policies influenced the thinking of the **New Right** of the **Thatcher** and Reagan era of the 1980s.

**liberty**  Liberty, or **freedom**, refers to the ability to think and act as one wishes, unrestrained by external pressures. In a negative sense, it means being free from something, non-interference. It is the absence of restraints on individual action which – in its extreme form – becomes licence. In a positive sense, it implies being free to achieve some desired benefit or goal.

Conservatives tend to view liberty in terms of the protection of property rights, the freedoms of the market economy, and from **state** control. Those on the **Left** have traditionally viewed it in terms of the realisation of a certain amount of economic and social **equality** achieved through governmental action. They argue that in any meaningful sense, to be free to pursue a course of action implies not merely the absence of restraint upon so doing, but also having the means to make that choice available.

**life peer**  A member of the **House of Lords** appointed by the **Prime Minister** of the day for their lifetime only. Today, life peers overwhelmingly form the largest segment of the membership of the House of Lords under Phase One of its reform. Announcements of new creations appear in the New Year Honours List, the Monarch's Birthday Honours List, the Dissolution Honours List and the Resignation Honours List of the outgoing Prime Minister.

Life peers derive from a range of backgrounds. Some are appointed to certain important public functionaries upon retirement – for example, Archbishops of Canterbury and **Speakers** of the **House of Commons**.

See also: **Life Peerages Act**

**Life Peerages Act** (1958)  Life baronies under the Act are theoretically created by the **monarch** but in practice they are granted upon the recommendation of the **Prime Minister** (who usually consults with the **Leader of the Opposition**). The measure permitted men and women to be created as peers for the duration of their lives. The purpose of the measure was to diversify membership of the chamber, bringing in individuals from various walks of life who had something to contribute to the deliberations of the upper house. By being used to boost Labour membership, the Act could be seen as a skilful ploy by Conservative Prime Minister **Macmillan** to deflect criticism of the **House of Lords** as one-sided and unfair.

See also: **life peer**

**Limehouse Declaration** A statement issued on 25 January 1981 by a group of four senior Labour **Members of Parliament**, Roy Jenkins, David Owen, Bill Rodgers and Shirley Williams, who subsequently were often referred to as the 'Gang of Four'. They formed the Council for Social Democracy, a preliminary step towards the founding of the **Social Democratic Party** (SDP) of which they were to become leading members. In the document – released from Dr Owen's Limehouse home – they made clear their view that 'the drift towards extremism in the **Labour Party** [was] not compatible with its democratic traditions' and pledged themselves to work for a **realignment** of British party politics.

**Livingstone, Ken** (1945– )  Ken Livingstone served as leader of the Greater London Council from 1981 until its abolition in 1986, prior to becoming the Labour **Member of Parliament** (MP) for Brent East. He was noted for his leftwing views, which earned him the nickname 'Red Ken'. As an MP he did not make a significant impact on national politics, although his forthright views and reputation for plain-speaking won him few friends and sometimes brought him prominence and notoriety.

He was elected as the first **Mayor of London** in 2000 as an independent Labour candidate, having been denied the chance to stand as the official party representative. He was readmitted to the party in early 2004 and – standing this time as the official Labour candidate – was re-elected to the office.

In 2006, he was suspended from duty for one month following his likening of a Jewish journalist to a concentration camp commandant, an example of his bluntness towards and dismissal of those associated with the **tabloid** press.

**loans for honours**  see **loans for peerages**

**loans for peerages** The names given by media commentators and politicians to a political scandal in the **United Kingdom** in 2006 and 2007 concerning the alleged connection between political donations and the awarding of life peerages. The issue of cash for peerages famously featured during the early-twentieth-century premiership of David Lloyd George. It subsequently resurfaced during the Conservative **Government** of John **Major,** when allegations were made that those who contributed generously to the party were granted political honours.

In March 2006, several men nominated for life peerages by **Prime Minister** Tony **Blair** were rejected by the House of Lords Appointments Commission. It was later revealed they had loaned large amounts of money to the governing **Labour Party,** at the suggestion of Labour fundraiser Lord Levy. Suspicion was aroused that the peerages were a *quid pro quo* for the loans. The incident was referred to the Metropolitan Police by a **Scottish National Party Member of Parliament** as a breach of the law against selling honours. Since then various members of the Labour, the Conservative and the Liberal Democrat parties were questioned. More dramatically, Labour's Lord Levy and Ruth Turner, a key Downing Street aide, were arrested and later released on bail.

The original focus was on whether the Honours (Prevention of Abuses) Act 1925 or the Political Parties, Elections and Referendums Act 2000 had been broken. Latterly the focus was on an alleged conspiracy to frustrate or even pervert the course of justice. At the end of the long police inquiry a dossier was sent to the Crown Prosecution Service, which decided that no charges would be brought.

See also: **life peer, Life Peerages Act**

**lobby**  A term variously used to refer to: the ante-rooms of legislative chambers, that is, the area in **Parliament** outside the chamber; the popular collective name for **pressure group**s, the idea originally relating to a group of people representing a particular political interest (lobby-ists) who met with elected representatives in the lobbies or ante-rooms of legislative chambers; and the name given to those journalists who are allowed into the Members' lobby to receive special briefings, as in the **lobby system**.

**lobbying**  The practice of making representations to **Members of Parliament** and **government** by individuals and organ-isations in order to influence actions and policy.

Lobbyists are employees of associations who try to influence policy decisions, especially in the **executive** and legislative branches.

**lobby system**  The name given to 200 or so specially selected correspondents of the main newspapers, television and radio stations who are given confidential information by the **Government** on a non-attributable basis. The system has been widely criticised for allowing **ministers** too much influence over reporting of the news.

Those who belong to the Parliamentary Lobby can roam the corridors of Westminster and enter restricted areas to which normally only elected members have access. They can attend the daily briefings of the Downing Street Press Office and the special ones given by the Press Secretary. As conversations are off the record, the journalists involved resort to such phrases as 'the **Prime Minister** is understood to be intending . . .'. Opinions vary about the system. Many seasoned jour-nalists are happy to acquiesce in it as a means of extract-ing useful information, the basis for a good story. Others see it as too cosy and criticise the way in which selective and sometimes incomplete information is made available. They feel they are being manipulated by the Government, via the Press Secretary.

**local government** The system which allows elected authorities or councils to provide and administer local affairs in their areas. There are 410 local authorities in England and Wales, with more than 20,000 elected **councillors** who lay down policy for their localities. Scotland has just over 1,200 councillors. They are supported by a range of professional and permanent staff. The structure in which they operate is different in the four countries of the **United Kingdom**, England having the most complex system. Labour inherited a system that had been significantly amended even since the major 1974 reorganisation. It has shown little interest in further structural reform, preferring instead to concentrate on issues such as democratic renewal, community leadership and internal management, as well as the best means of delivering efficient services. Local government spends around £80 million of public money and employs more than 2 million people.

Local **governance** is a more all-embracing term to cover also appointed agencies and other local governing bodies. Governance emphasises the process of governing, rather than the institutions of **government**.

**Lome Convention** A comprehensive trade and aid agreement between the **European Union** and 46 African, Caribbean and Pacific (ACP) countries, first signed in 1975, in Togo. As set out in Article 1, its purpose was 'to promote and expedite the economic, cultural and social development of the ACP states and to consolidate and diversify their relations [with the Community and its member states] in a spirit of solidarity and mutual interest'. As well as providing for a substantial package of aid and investment, the agreement allowed all ACP industrial products and most ACP agricultural products free access to the Community market, but the terms were non-reciprocal.

The Convention was renegotiated and renewed on three occasions and now covers 71 countries. Since 2000, a new successor package to Lome IV has applied, known as the Suva (Fiji) Convention. Destined to last until 2020, it transforms the original convention into a system of trade and cooperation pacts with the individual nations involved.

**London bombings** (July 2005)  A series of coordinated bomb attacks that first struck London's public transport system during the morning rush hour of 7 July, three on the underground trains and one on a bus. The explosions created massive disruption of the capital's transport and telecommunications infrastructure. Fifty-six people were killed, including the four suicide bombers, and some 700 injured. An attempted attack took place two weeks later (21 July) when a second series of bombs failed to detonate. In this case, all of the suspected terrorists were arrested and there were no casualties.

These suicide bombings, believed to be the first in Western Europe, were initially thought to be the work of **al-Qaeda** which soon claimed responsibility for them. They are now believed to have been home-grown terrorist actions committed by radical Muslims operating on a shoestring budget.

See also: **Islamophobia, terrorism**

**Lord Chancellor**  The Lord Chancellor has traditionally held both political and judicial responsibilities, the office being a defiance of the principle of the **separation of powers**. The Lord Chancellor has been a member of the **Cabinet**, presides over the **House of Lords** and is head of the **judiciary**, as such having responsibility for a wide range of judicial appointments and for the operation of the machinery of the courts.

The situation has undergone change, following the passage of the **Constitutional Reform Act** (2005). As **Prime Minister**, **Tony Blair** originally intended to abolish the position and transfer many of the functions to the newly created office of Secretary of State for Constitutional Affairs. But it was retained and the holder of the Cabinet post also held the ancient office of Lord Chancellor. Since May 2007, the Lord Chancellor is also Secretary of State for Justice, a post that has superseded that for Constitutional Affairs. The judicial functions of the Lord Chancellor (as opposed to his role in the administration of the court system) have been removed. The Lord Chancellor can in future be from either the **House of Commons** or the **House of Lords**. He no longer acts as **Speaker** of the House of Lords and performs a much reduced role in relation to the judiciary, having ceded his powers to the Lord Chief Justice.

**loyalist** The term used to describe that element of the Northern Ireland Protestant population (the overwhelming majority of it) which wishes to remain part of the **United Kingdom** and expresses its allegiance and loyalty to the **Crown**.

# M

**Maastricht Treaty** (1993) Many issues within the **European Union** were awaiting resolution in the discussions at

Maastricht in December 1991. A treaty was negotiated and signed which in the words of the Preamble was designed to achieve 'an ever closer union among the peoples of Europe'. The treaty created a European Union which had four objectives: the promotion of economic and social progress, particularly via **economic and monetary union**; the implementation of a foreign and security policy; cooperation in the areas of **justice** and home affairs; and the establishment of joint **citizenship** for the inhabitants of the Union. There were also institutional changes, via which the Parliament gained greater powers and an **ombudsman** was established to investigate maladministration. In addition to the main treaty, there were 17 Protocols and 33 Declarations.

The **United Kingdom** secured a double opt-out, John **Major** declining to commit Britain to involvement in economic and monetary union and refusing to sign up for the Protocol which created the **Social Chapter**. The resulting settlement was presented by Major as a negotiating triumph, a victory 'game, set and match'. However, the process of ratification in Britain proved difficult, for with an ever-dwindling majority the **Prime Minister** found himself much criticised by the **eurosceptics** in his own party. British ratification was eventually completed in August 1993 and the Maastricht Treaty and European Union officially came into existence in November of that year.

Further reading: N Nugent, *The Government and Politics of the European Union*, Palgrave, 2003

**Macmillan, Harold** (1894–1986)  First elected to the **House of Commons** in 1924 for Stockton-on-Tees, Harold Macmillan lost his seat in 1929 only to return in 1931. In the 1930s he was stuck on the backbenches, his progressive ideas and sharp criticism of Stanley Baldwin and Neville Chamberlain serving to isolate him. In World War

Two he was part of the wartime **coalition government**. He was returned to **Parliament** in a November 1945 **by-election** and after the Conservatives regained power in 1951 he was **minister** of housing and then of defence under Winston **Churchill** and Foreign Secretary and **Chancellor of the Exchequer** under Anthony **Eden**, whom he succeeded on Eden's resignation as **Prime Minister** in 1957.

During his premiership, there was a considerable increase in the standard of living, which helped to give the Conservatives an increased majority in the 1959 election. He took an active role in **Commonwealth** and world affairs, working to develop closer relations with the United States, achieving a close rapport with John Kennedy. In 1960, he warned the South African parliament that Britain could no longer condone apartheid (separate development of the **races**) for a 'wind of change' was blowing across the African continent. He also moved the Conservatives towards a more pro-European policy but his **government**'s bid to join the **European Economic Community** was vetoed by General de Gaulle of France. This caused the Government to lose popularity and led to a series of by-election defeats. He was greatly embarrassed by a scandal of sex in high places (the Profumo Affair) in 1963. Following ill health and surgery, he resigned in October 1963. In retirement, Macmillan achieved some prominence through his attacks on monetarists and privatisers in the Thatcherite years. In one of his more memorable contributions, he likened **privatisation** to 'selling the family silver'.

**Major, John** (1943– ) John Major served in the **Cabinet**s of Margaret **Thatcher** as Chief Secretary to the Treasury, Foreign Secretary and **Chancellor of the Exchequer** before succeeding her as **Conservative Party** leader and **Prime Minister** of the **United Kingdom** from 1990 to 1997. His premiership enjoyed early successes, for he was at the helm at the time of victory in the **first Gulf war**, negotiated the British opt-outs of the **Maastricht Treaty** and won the 1992 election. After his victory, he continued with Thatcherite economic policies, extending **privatisation** to the mines and railways. However, his new administration quickly ran into serious difficulties over ratification of Maastricht and **Black Wednesday**. The Thatcherite **Right** attacked him over **back to basics**, European policy and taxation. He was widely portrayed as an honest but dull and grey man, unable to rein in the philandering, bickering and general **sleaze** within his party. Following his party's election defeat in 1997, he retired from the leadership and then left the **House of Commons** four years later. His quiet retirement was spectacularly disrupted by the revelation in September 2002 that, prior to his promotion to the **Cabinet**, he had had a four-year extramarital affair with a fellow **Member of Parliament**, Edwina Currie. Commentators were quick to refer to the back to basics platform and throw charges of hypocrisy.

**maladministration**  Bad administration, a broad term which covers errors in the process of decision-making such as bias, delay, ineptitude, neglect and a general failure to observe the procedural rules, rather than in the substance of policy. Often it is used in connection with the jurisdiction of the **Parliamentary Commissioner for Administration**.

**mandarin**  One of a relatively small number of very senior civil servants who have close and ongoing contact with **minister**s in their capacity as policy advisers.

**mandate**  The authority of the **Government** to govern according to the promises as set out in its **manifesto**, as granted by the voters in the previous election.

Each party enters an election campaign with a statement of its intended programme should it gain office. If it wins the election, the manifesto is expected to form the basis of its actions. It has **legitimacy** and the Government a moral right to govern and carry out its policies and the electorate can expect that the programme will be implemented. In a broad sense, it is sometimes said that **ministers** have a 'doctor's mandate', the right to act as they see fit when a particular problem arises, even if it was unmentioned in the manifesto.

There are problems with the concept of the mandate. It is inaccurate for a winning party to assert that the public has demonstrated support for the entire contents of the manifesto. Voters might favour its broad thrust, preferring it to the others on offer, but they may dislike or be unaware of individual elements of what is often a broad and vague set of proposals. Moreover, in postwar Britain no party has ever won more than 50 per cent of the votes cast. In some cases – the **Thatcher** and **Blair** years – the percentage of support has been much lower and has declined in each election contested. Yet they have carried out contentious policies supported by a low percentage of those who voted, let alone of the whole electorate.

**Mandelson, Peter** (1953– )  After working as an economist for the **Trades Union Congress** and a current affairs television producer, Peter Mandelson was appointed as the **Labour Party**'s Director for Campaigns and Communications in 1985, a role in which he is credited as having deployed his considerable presentational skills to modernise the party's image. He became **Member of Parliament** for Hartlepool in 1990 and Tony **Blair**'s campaign manager in the May 1997 election. As an architect of **New Labour** and a member of the Blairite inner circle, he soon gained **Cabinet**

office in the new administration, serving as Secretary of State for Trade and Industry and later Secretary of State for Northern Ireland, from both of which posts he was forced to resign over his personal conduct.

His career in British politics having seemingly come to a premature end, he was nominated by the **Prime Minister** as the British representative on the **European Commission**, for which he serves as Commissioner for Trade Issues.

A long-standing pro-European, his personality and views have involved him in frequent controversy and made him several political enemies. But as a key figure in the repositioning and rebranding of his party in the opposition years and as an influential spokesperson for and writer on **Blairism**, he has been a figure of importance on the political stage in recent years.

Further reading: D. Macintyre, *Mandelson and the Making of New Labour*, HarperCollins, 2000

**manifesto** A document issued by every party prior to each **general election** outlining its general beliefs and the policy proposals it intends to pursue should it gain office.

See also: **mandate**

**market economy** A type of political economy in which there is near total private control of capital, labour and land. The **state** has a generally passive role in the economy, leaving decisions to be decided in the market place.

**Marxism** A **class**-based variant of **socialism**, influenced by the writings of Karl Marx, concerned to produce a society based on **equality** and social justice. Its implementation rests on certain assumptions, namely that: it might be necessary to use violence to overthrow the old economic and political order; an all-powerful **government** will be necessary to restructure society and the economic system; and a small dictatorial leadership group must manage the government and effect the economic and social transformation. This group will cease to be necessary when **equality** is achieved.

**mass media** Those forms of communication where large numbers of people are exposed to an identical message. This catch-all phrase denotes outlets such as radio, television, newspapers, periodicals, magazines and posters, as well as more recent forms such as the internet and e-mail. Whereas sending an e-mail to a friend is a personal communication, sending that message to all members on a list is a form of mass communication. All forms of mass media are concerned with the dissemination of information, entertainment and persuasion, although in popular usage writers on politics are primarily concerned with radio and television broadcasting and the press. Both provide the ideas and images which help most people understand the world they live in and their place in that world.

See also: **British Broadcasting Corporation**

**Mayor of London** Following approval of the scheme in a **referendum** in May 1998, Labour carried out its **manifesto** proposal to create an elected Mayor of London backed by an elected assembly. The holder of the office and his or her advisory cabinet form the executive of the strategic authority for London. The office has a range of duties and powers, relating to issues such as: cultural development; economic development; environmental policy; police, fire and civil defence; transport; and the appointment of personnel for the London Development Agency and many other bodies relating to the areas within its responsibility.

The effectiveness of the mayor probably depends less upon formal powers and more upon profile and personality.

He or she acts a voice for London and is able to promote the capital as a focus of international attention. Ken **Livingstone** is the present incumbent.

**McGuinness, Martin** (1950–  ) An Irish **republican**, McGuinness had an early association with the **Irish Republican Army** (IRA) and was second-in-command of the Provisional IRA at the time of Bloody Sunday. He was involved in negotiations on its behalf with the British **Government** in 1972. He later became increasingly prominent in the **Sinn Féin Party**, adopting the political route to the achievement of his political aims. He was elected as Sinn Féin **Member of Parliament** for Mid-Ulster in 1997 but like his party colleagues, he has refused to take his seat at Westminster. He became the party's chief negotiator in the period leading to the **Good Friday Agreement** and was elected as a member of the currently suspended **Northern Ireland Assembly** established under its terms. He served as Minister for Education in the Northern Ireland **Executive** between 1999 and 2002. Since the restoration of the Stormont administration in May 2007, he has served as Deputy **First Minister** in the **power-sharing** government.

A controversial figure, he has for many years been portrayed by leading unionists as a key figure in the IRA. His accusers doubt his claims to have forsaken his old allegiance, but his achievement (working alongside Gerry **Adams**) in driving the current political strategy of his party to acceptance of **devolution** and attaining political office is a measure of his influence and importance in the republican movement.

**means testing** The targeting of social security benefits on the basis of a person's income and wealth, as opposed to the provision of **universal benefits**. In Britain, means testing was used by the National Government to assist poor people in the early 1930s at the time of the Great Depression. It was then – and often is today – resented by welfare applicants, some of whom may be deterred from applying for that to which they are entitled. Supporters see targeting as inevitable, to ensure that scarce money is allocated to those who need it most. In its modern form, it lacks the shame associated with prewar means testing and is carried out by less overt processes.

**Member of Parliament (MP)** In the **House of Commons**, 646 MPs each represent a **single-member constituency**, having been elected by the **first past the post** electoral system. Almost all MPs are elected for a **political party**, the vast majority of them Labour or Conservative. The number of members belonging to other parties has grown in recent years.

MPs have responsibilities to the nation, party, constituency and to their own conscience. They divide their work between the House of Commons and their constituency. Typically, they spend the early/middle part of the week in London and return later in the week to see their constituents.

MPs do not represent a microcosm of the electorate. Overwhelmingly, they have long been white, male, middle class and middle-aged, although following the 2005 election the female contingent (127) at Westminster is now higher than ever before as is the number of **ethnic minority** MPs (15).

Today, many MPs are **career politicians**. Increased professionalism has been accompanied by improved pay and resources. Opponents of the trend to careerism point to the narrowing of members' experience and consequent lack of expertise.

See also: **women in political office**

**Middle England**  A vague term popularly used by politicians to refer to the aspirational middle classes whom Tony **Blair** and **New Labour** set out to woo prior to and since the 1997 election. The phrase is linked to the middle ground, a political position broadly between the extremes of the political spectrum. The position may not be precisely in the middle, but it is perceived to be the position occupied by a substantial segment of the upper-working- and middle-class electorate.

**Militant Tendency**  The name of a Trotskyite organisation that achieved prominence in the early 1980s by seeking to control local Labour parties with a view to influencing their conduct and thinking. Such 'entryism' was practised in Liverpool where Derek Hatton was able to gain influence over the predominantly Labour city council. Neil **Kinnock** condemned Militant's behaviour and methods in an outspoken attack at the conference in 1985. Under his leadership, the party's National Executive Committee moved to expel members of Militant on the grounds that they were acting as a party within a party.

**Millennium Dome**  A large dome on the Greenwich peninsula in the Docklands area in Eastern London, the largest single-roofed structure in the world. During the whole of 2000 the Dome was open to the public, offering them a large number of attractions and exhibits. The project was financed by the UK **Government** to celebrate the arrival of the third millennium. It was widely portrayed by the press as a flop: badly thought-out, badly executed and leaving the **Blair** Government with the embarrassing question of what to do with it afterwards. In December 2001 it was announced that Meridian Delta Ltd had been chosen by the Government to develop the Dome as a sports and entertainment centre and to develop housing, shops and offices on 150 acres of surrounding land. Following its conversion into a large indoor arena, the Dome will be the largest multi-purpose arena available for the 2012 Summer Olympics.

**miners' strike** (1984–5)  A major industrial action affecting the then nationalised British coal industry. When the National Coal Board (NCB) announced its intention to close 20 uneconomic mines, Arthur Scargill (the President of the National Union of Mineworkers, NUM) argued that the cuts would be the beginning of the end for the mining industry and would have a devastating impact upon miners, their families and mining communities. He urged a robust response from his membership. By contrast, the **Thatcher Government** backed the NCB programme, for in its view mining could not be indefinitely subsidised. The **Prime Minister** was determined to be resolute in the face of the miners' protests, for she had seen the damage inflicted on the **Heath** Government by NUM action. From the early days of her premiership, she had taken steps to ensure that there were substantial stocks of coal to keep power supplies going and so avoid the likelihood of any repetition of the **three-day week** which had contributed to the defeat of the Conservatives in February 1974.

Industrial action began in Yorkshire and in early March Scargill called a national strike without having previously held a ballot of the membership. This fatally undermined his authority within the industrial and political wings of the labour movement. Miners in Nottinghamshire did not back strike action and eventually broke away to form a more moderate union, although elsewhere support was solid. The official strike was marked by much bitterness, with outbreaks of intimidation and violence on the picket lines. It divided families and mining communities. However, after nearly a year on official strike, the miners were forced to admit defeat and return to work. For the Thatcher Government, victory in the confrontation marked a decisive stage in their determination to weaken union power.

**minister** Ministers are the 90 or 100 most senior members of the Government, comprising the **Prime Minister, Cabinet** ministers, ministers of state and parliamentary under-secretaries.

**ministerial code** The handbook of guidelines for **minister**s which suggests how they should behave. Among other things, it covers the way in which they should bring political issues to the **Cabinet,** handling the media and dealing with the ethical issues that arise when receiving gifts.

First made public by the **Major Government** in 1992 and subsequently revised by Tony **Blair,** the code has no binding status and is dependent on the **Prime Minister** of the day for its implementation. It is reissued after each election by the **Cabinet Office,** its current title being A Code of Conduct and Guidance on Procedure for Ministers.

**ministerial responsibility** The doctrine of ministerial responsibility has two aspects: ministers' **collective responsibility** for the work of the government and their **individual ministerial responsibility** for the departments they head. Both forms of responsibility are embodied in **constitutional conventions** which cannot be legally enforced. They developed in the nineteenth century and have been widely recognised as important elements of the **constitution** ever since. However, in recent decades, they have been much modified in practice, leading some commentators to question whether or not they have the same significance once accorded to them.

**minority government** A **government** with under 50 per cent of the seats in the **House of Commons**. It will usually comprise the largest party which seeks to govern on its own, thereby challenging all the elements of opposition to vote it down. In the devolved **Welsh National Assembly** established in 1999, Labour at first governed as a minority administration, before making a **coalition** deal with the Liberal Democrats.

In the **Scottish Parliament** elected in 2007, Alex **Salmond** leads an SNP minority administration which retains power by virtue of support from MSPs of the **Green Party** on a 'confidence and supply' basis. The Greens will back it in all **no-confidence votes** and on budgetary matters, but everything else is dealt with on an issue-by-issue basis.

**mixed economy** An economy that is neither capitalist and market-based nor state controlled but is designed to combine the strengths of both whilst minimising their shortcomings. In other words, there is a mix of private and public ownership, as in Britain – especially between the 1950s and 1990s.

**monarch** The individual person upon whom the **Crown** is conferred.

See also: **monarchy**

**monarchy** A political system in which there is a hereditary sovereign, usually called a king or queen in Europe where monarchy is constitutional and a sheikh in Saudi Arabia and a few other Middle Eastern states where the form may be absolute.

The monarchy in Britain is the oldest of our national institutions. It is a constitutional monarchy, which means that it has lost its political role. In theory it retains certain powers but these are largely exercised by the **Prime Minister**. In a constitutional monarchy, the monarch fulfils essentially ceremonial duties. Under normal circumstances, the monarch has no influence over the choice of Prime Minister, the elected leader of the majority party assuming the office. Nor does the king or queen have any real political power during the lifetime of a Government and has not had any for well over a century. The role is largely symbolic, that of a figurehead who receives visiting dignitaries. The Queen and other leading members of her family also visit parts of the country to perform social functions (opening schools and civic centres), as well as touring abroad to represent Britain in the **Commonwealth** and elsewhere.

Many people – especially the more elderly – find monarchy attractive, admiring the pomp, colour and splendour associated with royal occasions. For them, it seems to satisfy a popular need and evokes respect. It raises their morale and serves as a focus for their patriotic feeling. Others, members of younger generations often among them, are less enthusiastic. In their view, in our less deferential age, respect and loyalty have to be earned. Heredity is no guarantee of capacity. To them, the monarchy seems outdated, an emblem of privilege, costly to maintain and representing the past, not the future.

See also: **royal prerogative**

**Modernisation Committee** A **select committee** of the **House of Commons** established in June 1997, to consider how the procedures and practices of the lower chamber might be improved. It has produced a number of reports and many of its recommendations have been approved by **Members of Parliament**.

**monetarism** An economic policy associated with Milton Friedman and his Chicago school that suggests that

**government** should minimise its involvement in economic policy, except for controlling the **money supply** as a means of defeating inflation. Inflation is seen as the product of an increase in the money supply, with 'too much money chasing too few goods'. Monetarism is associated with free-market, laissez-faire thinking. It was at its peak of influence in the early **Thatcher** years.

**money Bill** A **government Bill** mainly concerned with raising money by taxation or authorising the spending of public money. The **Speaker** has the power to determine which Bills fall into the category and signs a certificate to indicate their status. Under the **Parliament Act** of 1911, money Bills are not liable to amendment in the **House of Lords**.

**money supply** A measure of the amount of cash and credit in general circulation within the economy available to purchase goods, services and securities. The broadest measure is M4, the aggregate of money held in notes and coins, the total amount lent by banks to individuals, companies and other banks, and the total amount of money borrowed by the **Government**. If there is too much money in the economy, interest rates tend to go down and inflation rises. If there is too little, interest rates tend to rise and prices and production go down.

   The figures are important for monetarists, who believe in managing the economy through interest rates and money supply.

**Morgan, Rhodri** (1939– ) Rhodri Morgan has served as a **Labour** representative in the Westminster Parliament and in the Welsh National Assembly. As the Assembly Member for Cardiff West, he is the second and current **First Minister** for Wales. He now heads a coalition administration with **Plaid Cymru** in the Principality.

**MP** see **Member of Parliament**

**multiculturalism** A multicultural society is one in which all ethnic groups feel accepted and included. Multiculturalism is an **ideology** advocating that society should comprise, or at least allow and include, distinct cultural groups of equal status. It began as an official policy in English-speaking countries in the 1970s and was quickly adopted as official policy by most member states in the **European Union**. However, it is currently an extremely divisive **issue** in the UK and in several other Western democracies. Supporters often portray it as a self-evident entitlement of cultural groups, as a form of **civil rights** grounded in **equality** of cultures. They embrace diversity as a positive force, encouraging and enabling different cultures to learn about each other's art, literature and philosophy, and influence each other's cuisine, fashion and music. Opponents tend to see it as an unwanted vision that has been imposed on them by a **liberal** elite which has not sought their consent. They fear it will lead to cultural ghettos and undermine a sense of national identity and unity. In particular, they dislike the way that in practice it means the creation of more single-faith schools and an undue emphasis upon minority rights.

Labour has been sympathetic to multiculturalism, placing much emphasis on the rights of minorities to preserve and celebrate their culture whilst encouraging their **participation** as **citizen**s – that is, integrating without assimilating. However, the policy has come into question. The existence of poor social conditions and **racism** have – particularly in some highly polarised towns and cities in the north of England where there is an absence of shared values – become barriers to the integration of minorities, so that multiculturalism has not functioned as it is supposed to do. In the light of events such as the

**London bombings,** some Labour politicians have seen a need to stress social **cohesion** and inclusion, rather than diversity.

See also: **Islamophobia, multiracial society, Muslim community**

**multi-member constituency** A constituency with two or more elected representatives in the **legislature**. The existence of such constituencies is usually part of some form of pro-portional-voting system.

**multi-party system** A system in which several parties compete for political power with the expectation that no single party will be able to command a majority in the **legislature** – hence the need for **coalition**s of a type common on the continent.

**multiracial society** Literally, a society comprising people of more than one racial or ethnic group, but more often used to refer to a model of **race** relations in which the diverse groups and ethnicities are all accorded equal **legitimacy** and recognition, enabling them to coexist in reasonable harmony.

See also: **multiculturalism**

**Muslim community** British Muslims derive from several countries. They cannot be lumped together as a homogeneous group. They number nearly 1.8 million, many of whom were born in this country. Like everyone else, they have different personalities, different interests and different opinions. In religious matters, some are strict and devout, others less so. Muslims have been in Britain since the 1950s, specific groups settling in particular British cities. Many belong to groups of Sunni Islam but Britain has also received small Shia groups from countries such as Iraq. Muslims from different places often have religious leanings reflecting different shades of Islamic belief.

The first generation of Muslims to arrive in Britain were often victims of racist attitudes and could do little but accept them. The second generation was more willing to challenge them and sometimes this led to fierce confrontations with the police and other authorities. But many members of Muslim communities still wanted to find and share a common set of values, hopes and aspirations that united whites and non-whites and not to separate themselves from the rest of society. In the last decade, a more radical Islam has found a hearing in Britain, particularly among an element of younger Muslims. Adherents have some sympathy with those who engage in armed struggle against the West whether in Afghanistan, Iraq or anywhere else. They are strongly anti-American and disapprove of British governmental support for American attitudes and policies. A very small number among them has been willing to engage in or support terrorist action. The terrorist suspects tend to be aged between 18 and 30, are more likely to be male and are often members of a small cell that contains perhaps a few dozen active members. They are led or inspired by an older individual with more experience and motivation. They are sometimes bound by friendship or family ties, perhaps having spent time in Afghanistan, Iraq or some other theatre of jihad or armed struggle.

See also: **Islamophobia, London bombings**

# N

**National Health Service (NHS)**  The publicly funded system of health provision which provides the majority of medical assistance in the UK. Established by Labour in 1948, the

NHS was for many years widely regarded as one of the most effective and comprehensive system of health care in the world. It is the largest organisation in Europe.

Structural reform has been undertaken by the **Thatcher** and **Blair Government**s, designed to change the way in which different organisations within the NHS are organised and relate to each other. Under the present arrangements, the overall strategic direction and matters of standards and targets are set by the Department of Health, which takes political responsibility for the service. It controls 28 Strategic Health Authorities (SHAs), which are the key link between the Department and the delivery of the NHS at the local level. They ensure that national priorities are reflected in local health service plans, oversee all NHS operations in their area and are responsible for improving the quality of services. Within each SHA, there are a variety of **NHS trusts** that have responsibility for providing the range of NHS services in the community. In addition, several Special Health Authorities provide a health service to the whole of England. These include NHS Blood and Transplants, NHS Direct and the National Institute for Health and Clinical Excellence (NICE).

Having at first adhered to **Tory** spending levels, Tony Blair promised to take spending levels on health care nearer to European levels in the new millennium. Labour has put extra money in, with spending being at an unprecedented level, up by £20 billion since 2000, a 40 per cent rise of more than 7 per cent per annum. Yet in 2006 there is renewed concern about the state of the NHS. For all the extra money put in, there remain serious problems. The NHS continues to cause difficult headlines for **ministers**, with occasional stories of people left on trolleys awaiting treatment, more common stories about people having their treatment indefinitely postponed because of a lack of nurses or hospital beds, problems with computerisation, and alarming and recurring stories of trusts in debt, leading to serious staffing cutbacks.

**National Health Service (NHS) trust**  Trusts have the responsibility for running the range of local NHS services. There are various types, including acute trusts, ambulance trusts, care trusts, mental health trusts, and primary care trusts (PCTs). The 300-plus PCTs are now at the centre of the NHS and control 80 per cent of its budget. As local organisations, they are thought to be in the best position to understand the needs of their communities. Among other tasks, they assess the health needs of their local area, commission the right services to meet these needs (for example, from general practitioners [GPs], hospitals and dentists), ensure the services can be accessed by everyone who needs them, ensure that the services and social-care organisations all work in tandem, take account of patients' views, and carry out an annual assessment of GP practices in their areas. The PCTs report directly to the strategic health authorities (SHAs).

NHS foundation trusts are a new type of NHS hospital run by local managers, staff and members of the public. Only the highest-performing hospitals can apply to become NHS foundation trusts, a status which gives them more freedom in running their services than other NHS trusts. Their creation indicates the shift which is taking place towards delegating decision-making power to front-line staff and the local communities they serve.

**nationalisation**  The taking-over of an industry, services or the land by the **state**, which then runs them in the public interest. Advocated by Karl Marx, it became one of the main doctrines of **socialism**. It was adopted as a policy by the **Labour Party** in 1918, forming **Clause IV** of the party's **constitution**. Early examples of nationalisation were the creation of the Port of London Authority (1909) and the state control of the mines and railways in the two world wars. However, the main era of nationalisation was during the lifetime of the **Attlee Government** from 1945 to 1951 when several industries and services came under state ownership, among them the Bank of England, coal, electricity and gas supplies, the railways and the iron and steel industry. In most cases, they were to be run by a public corporation such as the National Coal Board. The Conservatives restored private ownership to most road haulage and also partially in the iron and steel industry in the early 1950s, but it was not until the **Thatcher/Major** era that they privatised most remaining nationalised concerns.

Nationalisation did not fulfil all of the hopes of its supporters and although the **left** was keen on the policy, the centre-right of the Labour Party was unenthusiastic about any significant extension of public ownership after 1951. Abortive attempts were made to revise Clause IV but this was not finally achieved until Tony **Blair** attained the party leadership.

**nationalism** Refers to the desire of a nation to become a **state**. It is based on the belief that nations are entitled to self-determination, the right to determine their own destiny. It emerged as a political force in the nineteenth century but flourished in the twentieth century during which it became the key **ideology**. The British political philosopher John Stuart Mill was an early supporter. He argued that 'where the sentiment of nationality exists in any force there is a *prima facie* case for uniting all the members of the nationality under the same **government**, and a government to themselves apart'.

See also: **Scottish nationalism**

**NATO**  see **North Atlantic Treaty Organization**

**Neill Committee** Another name for the **Committee on Standards in Public Life**, which at first was chaired by Lord Neill. Under his leadership, the Committee produced reports on party funding and the use of **special advisers** in British government.

**neo-liberalism** The label employed to describe an economic philosophy that has become increasingly prominent since the late 1970s which rejects **state** control and positive **government** intervention in the economy and focuses instead on free market methods, fewer restrictions on business enterprise and the importance of property rights. Associated with the conservative **Right**, the **ideology** stresses the shrinking of the state by lowering tax levels, privatising assets and encouraging and rewarding personal achievement and responsibility. Its adherents oppose **environmentalism**, fair trade and **socialism** and labour policies such as collective bargaining rights and the minimum wage. It is usually described as **Thatcherism** in the **United Kingdom** and Reaganomics in the United States.

**New Labour** The label increasingly applied to the **Labour Party** as it has evolved in recent years but especially associated with Tony **Blair** and his close supporters who employed it in his successful 1994 leadership campaign and during the 1997 **general election**. As he put it: 'We were elected as New Labour and will govern as New Labour'.

New Labour derived much of its early impetus from the experiences of the American Democrat Bill Clinton who rechristened his party as the New Democrats. In its rhetoric, it emphasises the need to adapt party ideas to the reality of modern Britain, places less emphasis on traditional tax-and-spend policies and attaches importance to matters of presentation and style. Devoid of an excess of ideological baggage, it is eclectic, drawing inspiration from ideas such as **Christian socialism, communitarianism** and **stakeholding**, and arguably having a debt to **New Liberalism** and even **Thatcherism**.

New Labour differs from the traditional party outlook in several ways: being more detached from the **trades unions**; keener to keep public spending under control and direct taxation down; tougher on welfare benefits; committed to **equality** of opportunity rather than equality of outcome; adopting a 'big tent' approach which enables it to appeal to **Middle England**; and being pro-European. Its values and priorities are expressed in the revised **Clause IV** and are in line with the **third-way** approach adopted by some other political leaders of recent times. New Labour leader and **Prime Minister** Gordon **Brown** is commonly cited as one of the creators and architects of New Labour, along with Tony Blair, Peter **Mandelson** and Alastair **Campbell**.

See also: **Blairism**

Further reading: D. Macintyre, *Mandelson and the Making of New Labour*, HarperCollins, 2000; A. Seldon and D. Kavanagh, *The Blair Effect 2001–5*, Cambridge University Press, 2005

**New Left** A radical political movement that originated in the United States (US) in the 1960s, especially among college students. Supporters were implacably opposed to the so-called military–industrial complex and US involvement in Vietnam and wanted to see massive changes in society based on public recognition of the needs of dispossessed groups such as the poor and black Americans. Less theoretical than traditional communists, many enthusiasts leaned towards the more participatory approach of Maoism. Members of the British New Left were often to be found in existing popular front organisations of the 1960s that campaigned for causes such as peace, disarmament and global **justice**. Many were student activists involved in campus protest in the British universities. Some joined the International Socialists, which later became Socialist Workers Party, while others became involved with groups such as the International Marxist Group.

**New Liberalism** The term applied to the set of beliefs of a group of reforming **Liberals** in the early twentieth century. New Liberals were conscious of the gulf that existed within society, arguing that the uneven distribution of wealth was wrong in itself and actually harmed the economy because it deprived the mass of the population of the capacity to buy goods. They reinterpreted traditional liberalism and called for increased legislative action. They were still concerned to maintain individual **liberty**, promote individual enterprise and attack monopoly and privilege, but they were beginning to see a greater role for the **state** in protecting the weak. **Churchill**, Lloyd George and other supporters of New Liberalism did not believe in the removal of the capitalist system, but wanted to transform the system of private ownership to make it work to the advantage of a larger section of the community.

**New Right** The label applied in many countries to conservative groups from the late 1970s onwards who advocated a set of neo-liberal ideas. The ideas inspired the development of **Thatcherism** in Britain and Reaganomics in the United States where the New Right developed a political approach and electoral apparatus that carried Reagan into the White House.

In New Right thinking, the free market is seen as the cornerstone of economic and political freedom. Though most notably articulated in the writings of Friedrich Hayek and the American economist Milton Friedman, New Right theory can be traced back to the days of the late-eighteenth-century political economist Adam Smith and his supporters in the following century. Use of the term New Right distinguished conservative proponents from their post-1945 predecessors in Britain and America who were more concerned with pursuing moderate policies and seeking broad agreement or **consensus** on social and economic goals.

**new social movement (NSM)**  A term which seeks to differentiate current popular movements with those of yesteryear. New social movements began to merge in the 1960s, members offering a radical critique of mainstream society in fields as diverse as animal rights, **globalisation**, international peace, nuclear power and the treatment of women and sexual minorities. Such movements are usually non-hierarchical. They tend to have a core group that provides general direction and a network of widespread supporters who are only loosely organised. Often, their activities arise at grass-roots level, before later evolving into national crusades. Members want fundamental change to the status quo and the dominant values in society. They have wider policy interests than most **pressure group**s and are less cohesive than **political parties**.

NSMs provide people with the opportunity to support a cause and by so doing to express themselves and the ideas they hold dear. Various features of modern society facilitate their activities, notably ease of communication among their sympathisers via the mobile phone. Global communications enable protest organisers to cross borders without difficulty, as in the case of the 6 million-strong protest across some 600 cities against the **Iraq war**, just over one weekend.

**NGO**  see **non-governmental organisation**

**NHS**  see **National Health Service**

**Nice Treaty** (2000) The Treaty of Nice (adopted at the Nice European Council by member states of the **European Union,** EU) came into force in February 2003. It was intended to reform the institutional structure of the EU to enable it to cope more effectively with **enlargement.** In the event, there was agreement on the admission of new members (mainly from Central and Eastern Europe) and a commitment to develop EU activity in the field of **citizens'** rights and the **Common Foreign and Security Policy** (the establishment of a Rapid Reaction Force). There was also some re-weighting of votes in the **Council of Ministers** and movement to **Qualified Majority Voting** (QMV) in some 23 policy areas. At Nice, the major **governments** won the major arguments, for – confounding earlier hopes – the summiteers seemed more concerned with national interests than the cause of integration.

Failure to resolve some of the issues on the reform agenda (and to deal with the question of incorporation of the Charter of Fundamental Rights) led to the decision at Nice to establish a European Convention to prepare for a new intergovernmental conference (IGC) in 2004.

Further reading: N. Nugent, *The Government and Politics of the European Union,* Palgrave, 2003

**no-confidence vote** A motion of confidence is a motion of support proposed by the **government** of the day in a **parliament** or other assembly. A 'no-confidence' vote may be proposed by the opposition, in a bid to defeat ministers in the hope that this will precipitate the resignation of the government and a request for a parliamentary dissolution. A motion of confidence has been defeated or a motion of no confidence passed on four occasions in the **House of Commons,** most recently when the **Callaghan** administration was brought down by a single vote in January 1979.

**Nolan, Lord** (1928–2007)  Lord Nolan was the first chairman of the **Commission on Standards in Public Life,** serving for three years until 1997. The Commission and its first report which imposed restrictions on **Members of Parliament** working for outside interests was for a while known by his name.

**non-governmental organisation (NGO)** A national or transnational body that is not part of the governmental apparatus but which is committed to promoting an issue with national or international policy dimensions. The term (often favoured by voluntary-sector organisations and **pressure group**s in the field of overseas aid) signals that, although they may provide public services and seek to influence **government** policy, they are formally separate from the **state.** In many cases, members are drawn from more than one country, as with Médecins Sans Frontièrs ('doctors without borders') and the Red Cross, both of which provide medical assistance.

**North Atlantic Treaty Organization (NATO)** NATO was created in April 1949 as an alliance of 12 states (the United States and Canada, along with several states of Western Europe). It was established as a defensive alliance against the communist bloc, as a result of the growing threat from the Soviet Union in the postwar years. Member countries agreed to treat an attack on any one of them as an attack against them all, each nation being obliged to assist those attacked by taking 'such action as it deems necessary including the use of armed force, to restore and maintain the security of the North Atlantic area'.

Once the **Cold War** ended, NATO's traditional role disappeared. However, members recognise the desirability of retaining the tradition of cooperation they have developed and – at the European end – are keen to ensure that the US retains its commitment to European defence. Now enlarged to 26, it serves as a forum in which member states can consult on issues of common concern and agree on action to advance their interests. It sees its primary purpose as to 'safeguard the **freedom** and security of its member countries by political and military means'. Its main work is in the areas of crisis management and peacekeeping.

**Northern Ireland Assembly**  The Assembly established under the terms of the **Good Friday Agreement** sits at Parliament Buildings at Stormont, in Belfast. It comprises 108 members and is based on the principle of **power-sharing**. It was accorded power to legislate in a wide range of areas and to elect the Northern Ireland Executive. It is the prime source of **authority** for all devolved responsibilities.

The Assembly was first convened in 1998, but attempts to secure its continuing operations have been frustrated by disagreements and a marked lack of trust between the two largest Unionist parties (the Democratic Unionist Party and Ulster Unionist Party) and the **Sinn Féin Party**. For these reasons, the Assembly was suspended on four occasions. After October 2002 responsibility for the direction of Northern Ireland **government** passed to the Secretary of State and the Northern Ireland Office.

However, the Assembly resumed its meetings in early May 2007, following the agreement between Sinn Féin and the DUP over power-sharing.

See also: **direct rule**

**NSM**  see **new social movement**

**Number Ten**  see **Ten Downing Street**

# O

**ombudsman**  The popular word of Swedish origin meaning 'grievance officer'. In Britain, it refers to the **Parliamentary Commissioner for Administration** who hears and investigates complaints of maladministration against public authorities, as a means of safeguarding the rights of the public.

**One Nation Conservatism**  A strand of Conservatism which has its origins in the Disraelian remark that 'the **Conservative party** is a national party or it is nothing'. Those who uphold the tradition emphasise the need to ensure that the Conservatives appeal widely to all **class**es of the population and in all areas of the country.

From the late 1940s to the rise of the **New Right**, rightwing **government**s in Britain recognised the need to embrace the **welfare state** and introduce progressive social **legislation**, in order to lessen the likelihood of class conflict. In the **Thatcher** years, the one nation tendency lost much of its former impact and by the end of the century it was the **Blair** administration that boldly asserted its claims to be the guardian of one nation politics, emphasising that all people of moderate goodwill could be accommodated within Tony Blair's 'big tent'.

**open government** The relatively unconstrained flow of information about **government** to the general public, the media and representative bodies. Open government is relative, not absolute. All governments must keep some secrets, but critics of official secrecy in Britain claim that government is too secretive.

Proponents of greater **freedom** suggest that some relaxation of the tight controls on the supply of information would benefit good government. Excessive secrecy is said to undermine faith in the **authority** and fairness of government, fuelling suspicions that there is much inefficiency, waste or corruption going on behind the scenes. The more policies and their implications are fully unveiled and debated, the more likelihood there is of good decisions being made. Moreover, greater openness would act as a restraint upon **ministers** and officials, who would learn their decisions have to be capable of convincing justification. Opponents believe that open government makes government more difficult to conduct, slowing down decision-making. Furthermore, to reveal documents or evidence that provided honest and candid advice for ministers would be against the public interest, discouraging officials from speaking freely. In the words of the permanent secretary in the TV series *Yes Minister*: 'Open government is a contradiction in terms. You can be open, or you can have government'.

See also: **Freedom of Information (FoI) Act**

**opinion poll** see **public opinion poll**

**Osmotherly rules** A set of rules named after their author that lays down guidance for civil servants who appear before **select committees** of the **House of Commons**, ensuring among other things that **Civil Service** anonymity, impartiality and secrecy are protected.

**outsider group** A group that either does not want access to the corridors of power in Whitehall where decisions are made or is unable to attain recognition. In most cases promotional groups are outsider groups, kept at arms length from **government**, their activists finding that they are denied the chance to present their views to **ministers** and officials.

# P

**pairing** The practice of agreeing with a member of a different party to be absent from a parliamentary division or vote, the lost votes of the two absentees cancelling each other out. Pairing arrangements have to be registered with the **whip**'s Office, approval being automatic in the case of a one-line whip, rare for three-line whips.

**Paisley, Ian** (1926– ) Ian Paisley is best known as the leader of the **Democratic Unionist Party** (DUP) in Northern Ireland and for years was an opponent of any **power-sharing** agreement that involves working alongside the **Sinn Féin Party**. He was the founder of the Free Presbyterian Church of Ulster and has been noted for his expression of anti-Catholic sentiments. (In 1988 he shouted down Pope John Paul II in the **European Parliament**, denouncing him as the Antichrist.) In 1970 he was elected as a **Member of Parliament** for North Antrim, the constituency he still holds – making him the longest-serving member of the **House of Commons** from the province. In 1971 he formed the DUP. In 1979 he was elected as a member of the **European Parliament**. The DUP has steadily increased its popular support and won seats in the local council, province, national and European elections, gradually increasing its hold over the unionist community to become its largest party.

For many years he has often been portrayed in the media as a loud, aggressive figure who makes inflammatory speeches which have sometimes fomented violence. He tends to see issues in stark Biblical terms and his fiery, provocative speeches and denunciations of opponents make 'Big Ian' or 'Dr No' seem an uncompromising enemy, which is why opponents see him as a demagogic wrecker whose extremism makes it difficult for Protestants and Catholics to share **power**. Supporters claim that he is a worthy defender of the union of Britain and Northern Ireland, praise his sturdy defence of unionism and have faith in him to defend them from Dublin/Rome rule.

Paisley remains a key figure in Northern Ireland politics. His decision to stand down from the European Parliament in 2004 seemed to indicate that he was gradually shedding former commitments. However, following talks with Gerry **Adams** in 2007, he now heads the **power-sharing** executive in the **Northern Ireland Assembly**, serving as **First Minister**. Paisley and his Deputy, Martin **McGuinness**, appear to have established a good working relationship.

**paramilitary organisation** An organisation formed out of a group of civilians who are trained and organised to operate in a military fashion. They represent a kind of auxiliary military, not quite military but carrying out military duties. Sometimes such organisations are created by governments as an aid to internal security; others are anti-government armed units that may use traditional or guerrilla warfare; and yet others are neither – private militias intended to enforce order without the niceties of the **rule of law**. All are prepared to resort to violence to achieve their goals.

In the Northern Irish **Troubles** there have been **republican** paramilitaries such as the **Irish Republican Army** and splinter bodies associated with it and **loyalist** paramilitaries who similarly claim to defend the communities they represent (for example, the Ulster Defence Association and the Ulster Volunteer Force).

**Parliament** The British Parliament is **bicameral**, comprising the elected **House of Commons** and the largely appointed **House of Lords**. It has the ability to pass new **laws**, repeal old ones and even to extend its own life. Other than via the right of the courts to interpret its laws, its **authority** cannot be challenged. It derives its authority from the people and is answerable to them alone. Parliament is then supreme, there being no legal limitation upon its **sovereignty** except in so far as it is in conflict with **legislation** deriving from the **European Union**. Yet there are other constraints upon its sovereignty, among them political reality (it is inconceivable that any **government** would seek to abolish the **Scottish Parliament**) and the need to consult with outside interests.

Parliament's duties are wide-ranging. It is, in Harold **Macmillan**'s words, 'the grand inquest of the nation': it provides a forum where Government can explain its policies and where those policies can be debated, subjected to detailed scrutiny and amended by the elected representatives of the people and peers; it raises and spends public money; and it is a channel via which individual grievances can be aired.

For several decades, it has been argued that Parliament – in common with many **legislature**s – is in decline. Its ability to carry out its functions effectively has been questioned, for it has increasingly been dominated by the **Executive**. As **Prime Minister**, Tony **Blair** has distanced himself from the House of Commons further than any of his predecessors, but as a general trend prime ministerial activity in and **accountability** to Parliament has decreased over several decades. It is not just the present Government which has marginalised Westminster.

See also: **elective dictatorship, House of Commons, House of Lords, Member of Parliament, parliamentary sovereignty, peer**

Further reading: P. Norton, *Parliament in British Politics*, Palgrave, 2005

**Parliament Act** (1911 and 1949) The Parliament Act 1911 was introduced by the pre-World War One **Liberal Government**. Passed after the **House of Lords** had rejected the radical People's budget of 1909, the statute removed the permanent veto, so that the second chamber lost its power of absolute delay over **legislation**. In future, any **Bill** which passed the **House of Commons** in three successive sessions would automatically become law. In addition, it took away the power of delay over money Bills which were to become law one month after leaving the Commons, irrespective of whether they had been approved by the Lords or not. It also reduced the maximum time period between **general election**s from seven to five years. The package effectively confirmed the subordinate position of the second chamber in statute.

The Parliament Act 1949, introduced by the post-1945 Labour Government, further limited the delaying power of the Lords, so that any Bill that passed in two successive sessions now became law. This effectively curtailed the delaying power to between eight and nine months and made it more difficult for the upper house to frustrate the wishes of the elected one. It has been used on four occasions, most recently for the passage of the Bill that abolished fox-hunting.

**Parliamentary Commissioner for Administration (PCA)** The office of the Parliamentary Commissioner was created in

1967 by the **Wilson** Government to investigate cases of maladministration in specified public services. The position of Health Service Commissioner was created in 1993. Today, the two posts are held by the same person, who is usually referred to as the Parliamentary and Health Service Ombudsman. It is the official **ombudsman** institution responsible for investigating complaints regarding whether governmental departments, agencies and some other public bodies in the United Kingdom and the **National Health Service** (NHS) in England have acted properly or fairly or have provided poor service.

**parliamentary government** A system in which **government** governs in and through the assembly or parliament, thereby 'fusing' the **legislature** and **executive** branches. The main features are that government **ministers** are normally drawn from and remain members of the legislature; there is a plural executive, in which the first minister shares power with a cabinet; and both first minister and cabinet are liable to be removed should they surrender the confidence of **parliament**.

In Britain, members of the government are chosen from the largest party in Parliament and answerable to it, whereas in a presidential system such as the United States, the legislature and executive are elected separately.

See also: **presidential government**

**Parliamentary Labour Party (PLP)** The PLP comprises all Labour **Members of Parliament**. It meets regularly to make its general views known to the leadership. It attempts to exert influence over policy, especially when Labour is in power. It has a number of committees which study broad policy areas. It provides (but no longer elects) the leader and deputy leader, having a 33 per cent share in the **electoral college**.

**parliamentary privilege** An exception to the ordinary law of the land that refers to the immunity given to members of **Parliament** in order to enable them to conduct their work effectively. Determination of breach of privilege rests entirely with the House concerned, each chamber enjoying the right to punish offenders. In the **House of Commons,** issues used to be dealt with by the long-standing **Select Committee** on Privileges which has now been subsumed into the Select Committee on Standards.

Parliamentary privilege covers the collective immunity of **Members of Parliament** to control their own proceedings and their long-standing immunity against suit for libel.

**parliamentary questions** Oral and written questions may be asked by **Members of Parliament** and peers to **ministers.** Oral ones are answered at question time in the relevant chamber, whereas written ones are printed in **Hansard.** In either case, they must be confined to matters for which the minister has responsibility. They must be questions rather than statements, their purpose being to raise issues, attack or praise ministers and elicit information.

**parliamentary reform** The trend of recent years has been towards a growth in **executive** power at the expense of **legislatures,** a trend not confined to the **United Kingdom.** Supporters of parliamentary reform in Britain worry about the growing imbalance between the **Government** and **Parliament** and advance two main reasons why it is increasingly difficult for Parliament to be an effective and vigilant watchdog: the development of party government, and the increase in the scale and complexity of government work makes it difficult for hard-pressed **Members of Parliament** (MPs) to find the time to master the broad range of material and offer an informed critique of the actions of **ministers.**

Those who detect a need for reforms to make Parliament more effective fall into two main categories. *External reformers* want to see a broad raft of changes designed to weaken executive dominance and strengthen parliamentary control (for example, **electoral reform** for Westminster, reform of the **House of Lords**, a powerful **bill of rights**, strong freedom of information **legislation** and decentralisation of power from London. *Internal reformers* claim that the degree of executive dominance in Britain is over-stated and wish to achieve internal reforms at Westminster rather than measures which would erode the government's power to act. Some have been enacted in recent years (for example, changes to working hours and modest changes in the committee system). Others that might be accomplished include a reduction in the number of MPs, a strengthening of the system of **select committees** and improvements in the legislative process.

Further reading: P. Norton, *Parliament in British Politics*, Palgrave, 2005

**parliamentary sovereignty**  Parliamentary sovereignty is often said to be a cardinal element of the British **constitution**. Constitutional experts such as A. V. Dicey have proclaimed that **Parliament** has legal **sovereignty** (absolute and unlimited **authority**), in that it is the supreme **law-**making body in **Great Britain**. Only Parliament can make, amend and unmake law, and no other institution can override its decisions. Thus no one Parliament can bind its successor.

Membership of European organisations has imposed some limitations on parliamentary sovereignty. The signing of the **European Convention on Human Rights** and membership of the **European Union** both imply that any British **government** must modify its law to take account of European wishes. European law ultimately prevails over British law, as was most clearly indicated in the **Factortame case**. Yet even before such European cases began to make an impact, parliamentary sovereignty was a questionable notion. It implies that Parliament is supreme and all-powerful, yet in the twentieth century it is widely agreed that power has passed from **Parliament** to the **Executive** both because of the growing scale of government and the consequent difficulties of achieving effective parliamentary control, and because of the extent of party discipline. Any government armed with a large majority has a good chance of pushing its programme through and sceptics argue that if the doctrine implies that Parliament has real power, the truth is that it usually acts as a rubber stamp for governmental action. **Devolution** and **judicial review** have created further challenges to parliamentary supremacy.

**participation** Political participation refers to activity by individuals that is intended to influence who governs and/or the decisions taken by those who do so. **Citizen**s can be classified both by the extent of their political involvement, using the Milbrath and Goel division of Americans into a small number of gladiators (an overwhelming number of spectators and a substantial number of apathetics) and by the nature of their engagement (for example, the use of conventional or unconventional approaches).

Broadly, participation in most democracies is greater among high-status social groups (for example, well-educated, professional middle-class men) than among women, young people and disadvantaged/disaffected members of society. Methods of engagement in political action range from voting, through membership of **political parties** and **pressure groups**, to **direct action**.

In Britain, there is evidence of a decline in popular participation via the more traditional routes, particularly among young people, electoral **turnout** has decreased in all types of election, party membership and party activism have declined and there has been a weakening in the level of partisan attachments among the voters. However, not all types of participation have been in decline. There is a growing interest in alternative forms of political engagement, such as contacting one of the numerous media outlets, involvement in pressure-group activity (particularly those groups concerned with animal rights and environmental **issues**) and participation in personal protests such as the boycotting or buying of goods for ethical and political reasons (fair-trade coffee, for example).

Further reading: L. Gilbrath and M. Goel, *Political Participation: How and Why Do People Get Involved in Politics?*, Rand McNally, 1977; see also the report of the Power Commission, *Power to the People*, for the Rowntree Trust, 2006

**partisan dealignment** Refers to the weakening of traditional bonds between the electors and parties and social groups and parties which have occurred to some degree in many democracies. Sharp declines in party identification have been apparent in countries such as Austria, Canada and the United States, moderate declines of between 1 and 10 per cent have occurred in New Zealand and the **United Kingdom**, while there is little or no evident decline in Belgium and Denmark.

Britain has been undergoing a loosening of its former strong and stable voter loyalty and attachment to either of the two main parties, their share of the vote declining from an average 90 per cent in the 1970s to 67.5 per cent in 2005. As a result, **voting behaviour** has become more volatile, with the growing number of **swing voters** leading to less predictable voting patterns and electoral results.

**party cohesion**  The degree to which members of a party vote together in legislative divisions. The main British parties generally show substantial unity in the voting lobbies, whereas party loyalty has traditionally been much weaker in the United States.

**party election broadcast (PEB)**  see **party political broadcast**

**party family**  A grouping of **political parties** across different countries which have similar beliefs, principles and values. In Europe examples of party families are the Conservatives (including, for example, the British Conservatives and Christian Democrats), Socialists (Labour and the Social Democrats), centre parties (the British Liberals) and regional and ethnic parties (**Plaid Cymru**). Even those within the same family can sharply differ over their vision of end goals and the tactics to be pursued in attaining them.

**party finance**  The means of financing **political parties** have been controversial in recent years. Parties need funding to maintain an operational headquarters, run elections and get their message across. Given the decline in party membership, they seek other sources of finance. The **Labour Party** traditionally relied on **trade union** support, although in the **Blair** years it has sought and received money from wealthy supporters, including many businesspeople. The **Conservative Party** has also traditionally wooed the business community, as well as receiving support from affluent individuals; they also raise money via voluntary activity such as holding garden parties.

All parties find themselves short of money. Reliance on institutional or individual backers is controversial and open to abuse. So too is the alternative of greater state funding, which involves using taxpayers' money to support bodies of which they may not approve. The year-long review of Sir Hayden Phillips that reported in March 2007 recommended spending limits on political campaigns and caps on individual donations. However, it found it impossible to achieve agreement between the main parties, although Phillips believed that a deal was possible. The review backed a £25 million-a-year rise in state funding.

See also: **loans for peerages**

**party list** Party-list **proportional representation** systems belong to a family of voting systems that are much used on the continent. Under these systems, parties create lists of candidates to be submitted to the electorate on election day. Seats are then allocated to each party in proportion to the number of votes it receives on polling day.

There are two major varieties of list systems, 'closed lists' and 'open lists'. In the former, voters have no choice over candidates and simply cast a party vote. In the latter, there is an element of voter choice, for the voter votes for individual candidates rather than for the party. The **United Kingdom** uses closed lists for its five-yearly elections to choose members of the **European Parliament**.

**party political broadcast (PPB)** Or party election broadcasts, PEBs. Three- to five-minute television slots in which the **political parties** present their messages to voters, without any intervention from television interviewers or presenters. At election time, PEBs are available only to those parties that have 50 or more candidates standing for election. They are allocated on the basis of performance in the previous election.

PPBs first appeared – in a very amateurish form – on British television in 1951. By the late 1970s they had become highly professional, as the idea that politicians could be packaged and marketed gained a foothold. Their length was reduced, the idea being that shorter broadcasts would be catchy and more memorable. Towards the end of the century, they were a medium in decline, no longer broadcast simultaneously on the terrestrial channels. Their purpose is still to rally core support and endeavour to persuade uncommitted or wavering voters. However, their impact has diminished and they are generally unloved and derided.

**party system**  A country's party system is the more or less stable configuration of **political parties** that normally compete in national elections. It is based on how many parties exist, what support they have and the extent to which competition between them results in dramatic shifts following the outcome of an election. Three broad types exist in democracies: dominant party systems occur when one party is continuously in office (for example, the Japanese liberal democrats); **two-party systems** occur where one of two main parties normally forms a **single-party government** (in Britain, for example); and **multi-party systems** in which a **legislature** comprises several small to medium parties, a selection of which together form some kind of **coalition** government.

**payroll vote**  The label applied to the 100 or more **Members of Parliament** who form the main part of the administration in office. Salaried or unpaid, they are expected to vote with the **Government**, thus providing the **Cabinet** with substantial backing in any division.

**PC**  see **political correctness**

**PCA**  see **Parliamentary Commissioner for Administration**

**peak association** A type of all-embracing **interest group** that coordinates the activities of different organisations operating within the same field. Members of peak or umbrella organisations are not individuals but other organisations, such as business firms and **trades union**s representing the interests of capital and labour. In Britain, the Retail Consortium is the umbrella group for major shops and stores, just as the **Trades Union Congress** provides the same function for many trades unions.

**peer** see **peerage**

**peerage** The peerage refers to a system of titles of nobility that exists in the **United Kingdom** and is part of the British Honours system. The term can be applied to the entire body of titles in a collective sense or to a specific title held by an individual peer. The main categories of peer are the hereditary and **life peers** who have long dominated membership of the **House of Lords**. Since 1999, only 92 hereditaries are entitled to sit in the Lords, the bulk of whose members are life peers appointed on the advice of the **Prime Minister**. Those **hereditary peers** who are not members of the second chamber retain their peerage but have lost their automatic right to sit in the Upper House.

**Peerage Act** (1963) The statute allowing the disclaiming of hereditary peerages for life and permitting female and Scottish **hereditary peers** to sit in the **House of Lords**.

**performance indicator** Key performance indicators (KPI) are quantifiable criteria against which public bodies are judged. They help an organisation define and measure progress towards desired goals and provide a standard against which outcomes can be assessed. They enable comparisons to be made between the staff in one institution and the staff in a comparable one elsewhere. The **British Broadcasting Corporation**'s Environment Unit has developed 12 headline performance indicators via which action priorities within the Corporation can be established and measured. Local councils are measured against a set of Best Value indicators, the results of which may be published in league tables. Such measurements enable government **ministers** and organisational leaders to determine the strengths and weaknesses within any public body.

**PFI** see **private finance initiative**

**photo opportunity** An occasion that lends itself to (or is deliberately arranged for) taking photographs that provide favourable publicity for those who are photographed. In political life, they are carefully stage-managed events designed to portray public figures in a flattering light. At election time, leaders may be photographed against a particular background or on visits to schools and hospitals, in order to demonstrate their concern for the location and those who work within it. Such occasions have a humanising effect, suggesting that the candidate is a 'regular guy'.

**Plaid Cymru** Plaid, in full Plaid Cymru (The Party of Wales), is the principal nationalist **political party** in the Principality. It advocates the withdrawal of Wales from the **United Kingdom** and the establishment of an independent Welsh **state**, although for many years it placed priority upon support for preservation of the Welsh language and its associated culture. In the past, this has tended to limit its appeal to Welsh-speaking areas of North and West Wales, although there have been signs in the **Welsh National Assembly** elections that the party is now extending its support into the southern valleys. In the **general election** of 2005, the party won 12.6 per cent of the Welsh vote and three seats. Following the devolved elections in 2007 it has become a partner in a **Labour**-led coalition administration.

**PLP**  see **Parliamentary Labour Party**

**pluralism**  Refers to the belief that **power** in modern societies is widely distributed between a multiplicity of interests and organisations that compete with each another in different political arenas. From time to time, new groups emerge, ensuring that there is further competition in the political market place. Pluralist societies are ones in which group activity can flourish, the various organised groups each having the opportunity to articulate their various demands

**PM**  see **Prime Minister**

**PMQs**  see **Prime Minister's Questions**

**policy community**  A small, stable and consensual grouping of **government** officials and **pressure group** representatives that forms around a particular policy area, the interaction being close and continual. Both sides place emphasis on the mutual benefits of largely confidential formal and informal cooperation in the establishment and implementation of policy. They are less evident today, having been replaced by **policy networks** which are indicative of a more open style of decision-making.

**policy network**  Compared with a **policy community**, the range of political actors is larger and looser, and the mode of operation often more open, not least as a result of present-day media scrutiny. The network may extend to include academics and regulators, as well as national and European civil servants and representatives of organised groups.

**political correctness (PC)**   A contentious notion, being politically correct refers to speaking and writing about socially sensitive matters such as culture, gender or **race** in a way which avoids the use of potentially offensive terminology which is seen as inappropriate in a tolerant and multicultural society.

Much condemned on the political **right**, the implication is that such language is not only in itself absurd, but also involves censorship and social engineering. Those concerned to employ language that avoids being hurtful or insulting to marginalised or minority groups see critics of PC as those who would distract attention from substantive debates over discrimination and unfair treatment.

**political culture**   Refers to culture in its political aspect. Political culture is the term given to those widely shared political beliefs, values and norms most **citizen**s consciously or unconsciously share concerning the relationship of citizens to government and to one another. These long-term attitudes, ideas and traditions are passed on from one generation to the next. Usually we think of the political culture of a country such as Britain, France or the United States, but it may be the citizens of an ethnic or religious community who are under consideration – perhaps the people living in a geographic community, such as Londoners or Europeans, or those with a shared identity such as French Canadians or Sikhs in the subcontinent.

**political marketing**   Marketing concerns the way in which business organisations seek to gain a market advantage by carefully tailoring their product to popular requirements and promoting it in such a way as to maximise sales. Political marketing is about the way in which political bodies adapt and employ business-marketing concepts and techniques in order to help them fulfil their objectives. **Parliaments**, councils, **government departments** and in particular **political parties** and **pressure groups** seek to identify public concerns via market research, adjust their behaviour accordingly and communicate their product (their ideas and policies) more effectively, using the latest techniques of popular persuasion.

**political participation**  see **participation**

**political parties**  see **political party**

**Political Parties, Elections and Referendums Act** (2000) A statute that sets out how **political parties,** elections and **referendums** are to be regulated in the **United Kingdom**. It implements recommendations made by the **Neill Committee** to clean up British politics. It created the **Electoral Commission,** an independent body which has responsibility to regulate those areas, and transfers to it the responsibilities already created in the Registration of Political Parties Act 1998. The Commission oversees controls of parties' income and expenditure, will keep under review the **law** and practice in relation to elections and referendums, promotes public awareness of electoral systems, and will in due course take over responsibility for the review of parliamentary and **local government** boundaries.

**political party** Parties are organisations of broadly like-minded people who seek political **power** and public office in order to realise their goals and carry out their policies.

Unlike **pressure group**s, which seek influence only, serious parties wish to operate the levers of **government**. Much of their work involves fighting elections via which they can seek to win popular support. To this end, they represent socially or culturally significant interests and aggregate (lump together) their preferences, recruit and select candidates for public office, structure the choices available to voters at parliamentary and local elections, facilitate the formation of governments that produce relatively coherent policy responses to the problems they face, and act as a channel of communication between the **citizen**s and the **state**.

Parties normally have their distinctive beliefs, principles and values. In Western Europe, they often have a fairly coherent ideological framework, a large – if declining – membership base, and operate on the basis of strong party loyalty in the **legislature**. In North America, they are by contrast less ideologically driven, weaker and more decentralised. They may share their broad approaches and ideological stances with parties from across several different countries.

In recent years, there has been much debate over whether or not parties in Western Europe are in decline and moving in the direction of their North American counterparts. This is because in several cases they no longer offer radically distinctive visions and solutions, suffer from weakening popular loyalty and support, have declining and ageing memberships, and have become less relevant as political leaders often speak more directly with the electorate via television rather than through the traditional modes of party electioneering.

See also: **Left–Right continuum, partisan dealignment, party cohesion, party family**

Further reading: P. Webb, *The Modern British Party System*, Sage, 2000

**poll tax**  see **community charge**

**positive discrimination**  Known as affirmative action in the United States (US), positive discrimination refers to policies or programmes designed to give special attention and compensatory treatment to members of some previously under-represented and disadvantaged groups such as women and members of **ethnic minorities**. Supporters claim that active measures are needed to redress past societal unfairness and to ensure that the phrase 'equal opportunities' is meaningful in practice, in areas such as education and employment. They claim that not only do they go some way to remedy accumulated injustice, but they also promote gender and ethnic diversity. Opponents question whether such measures actually achieve the intended goal and suggest that they may have unintended, even undesirable, consequences. In their view, they amount to reverse discrimination.

In Britain and the US, there is widespread suspicion of any **legislation** which confers a seemingly privileged position on some group. Labour's programme of **all-women shortlist**s in the 1990s was an example of positive discrimination.

**poverty trap**  The poverty trap refers to the position when an increase in earnings results in a loss of income-tested benefit payments which – combined with liability for income tax and other deductions – means that the recipient is no better off. This discourages people from taking responsibility for their own lives and finding higher-paid work, whether that involves working longer hours or acquiring skills.

**power**  The ability to get things done, if necessary involving making others do what they would not do by free choice.

Other means of persuasion may be deployed but under-lying their use is the ability to reward or punish. It is a key ingredient of politics, enabling collective decisions to be made and enforced, the tool that enables rulers to serve or manipulate the people over whom they rule. Indeed, writers such as Hay see politics as being 'con-cerned with the distribution, exercise and consequences of power'.

Power may be found in many different locations, depending on the type of power being considered. Britain has a diffuse political system in which no group or indi-vidual has overwhelming power. Three main concentra-tions of power might be distinguished: *Political power* is in reality exercised by the **Cabinet** (increasingly by the **Prime Minister**), although **Parliament** is the legal reposi-tory of political power, for it is a sovereign body. In recent decades, power has increasingly been exercised by other bodies, the **trades union**s in the 1960s and 70s and **quangos** today. *Economic power* is in the hands of **gov-ernment**, which can regulate economic policy via fiscal and monetary policy, but is also exercised by industrial combines (especially multinational companies), financial institutions and, to a much lesser extent, unions. *Military power* is dependent on political decisions, as in the case of the decision to invade Iraq or send troops to Northern Ireland. Weaponry and personnel are the key ingredients of any country's military capability.

See also: **parliamentary sovereignty**

Further reading: C. Hay, *Political Analysis: A Critical Introduction*, Palgrave, 2002

**power-sharing** A system of **government** by which in deeply divided societies **power** is shared between different com-munities or segments of society. It is a strategy for resolv-ing disputes over who should have the most powerful position in the social and political hierarchy. Instead of fighting over who should have power over whom, it relies upon the joint exercise of power. It can take a variety of forms. It can involve allowing minority groups autonomy over some or all aspects of their own affairs. More usually, it is **governance** handled by leaders from each group who work jointly and cooperatively to make decisions and resolve conflicts. Typically, the electoral system will be structured to encourage multi-community **coalitions** within the political system.

In **power-sharing**, the emphasis is upon achieving decision-making by consensus, within some form of grand coalition in which the principal elements of society are guaranteed a place and influence in government. In Northern Ireland, the **Good Friday Agreement** provided for power-sharing which is guaranteed by two constitutional mechanisms: **ministers** are not appointed to the **Executive** by a simple majority vote, rather all parties with a significant number of seats are entitled to at least one minister and ministerial portfolios are divided among the parties in proportion to their strength in the Assembly; and certain resolutions must receive cross-community support or the support of a minimum number of members of the Assembly from both communities. After early false starts, a power-sharing government in the province was finally up and running in May 2007.

**PPB**  see **party political broadcast**

**PPP**  see **public–private partnership**

**PR**  see **proportional representation**

**presidential government** In presidential systems, the **executive** is elected separately from the **legislature**, is outside of and in theory equal to it. The president is chosen by the people rather than from the legislative branch and acts as head of the **government** as well as ceremonial **head of state**. In the United States and several other countries there is a system of presidential government. This does not refer to the fact that these countries have a president rather than a **monarch** as head of state. Both the Irish Republic and Germany have presidents in this role, yet both have parliamentary systems. As Heywood puts it: 'A presidential system is characterised by a constitutional and political **separation of powers** between the legislative and executive branches of government'.

Further reading: Andrew Heywood, *Politics*, Macmillan, 1997

**press freedom** A free press is widely regarded as one of the essential criteria of a democratic system. Writers from John Locke onwards have interpreted press freedom as basic to the right of an individual to get at the truth and as a prerequisite for better **government**. As Keane writes: 'A free press increases the probability of prudent decisions by making publicly available comprehensive information about the world. And a free press casts a watchful eye over the **bureaucracy**, thus preventing the outbreak of nepotism between legislators and administrators'.

In dictatorships such as South Africa in the days of apartheid, draconian powers were used to close down newspapers or prevent the publication of views unpalatable to the regime in **power**. In liberal democracies such as Britain, the publishing industry is free in the sense that newspapers are not owned or controlled by the government or one of its agencies. In as much as there exist restrictions on what can be published, these are aimed at preventing such things as defamation, racial incitement or other behaviour which could be harmful to the interests of individuals or groups. Any danger comes not from governmental interference, but from the concentration of ownership and the resultant limitations on the diversity of views available.

Further reading: J. Keane, *The Media and Democracy*, Polity, 1961

**pressure group** Pressure groups are private and voluntary organisations that seek to influence particular **government** policies but do not wish to become the government or control all government policies. They operate in the space between government and society, consulting with **ministers** and providing continuous opportunities for **citizens** to become involved in political life. Their nature and degree of influence varies from country to country. Generally speaking, business is close to government, for what government does affects business just as the decisions of businesspeople in areas such as job creation and investment have important repercussions for ministers. However, many other interests in society are also affected by ministerial decisions and wish to make their views known in the appropriate quarters. Employees are organised via the **trade union** movement, and various other groups represent farmers, churches and a host of civic, environmental and social causes. Groups are as diverse as they are numerous, ranging from the high-profile National Farmers' Union to the rather more obscure groups that campaign for the provision of better public lavatories. Some 34,000 organisations are recognised by the *Directory of British Associations*, but there are many more that operate at the local level.

Groups overlap with **political parties** but there are important differences. Notably, they wish to achieve influence, whereas parties wish to run the government.

Groups are interested in one broad policy area, whereas party programmes are more wide-ranging. Also allied to group activity is that of the **new social movements**, more loosely knit organisations that try to influence policy on broad **issue**s such as the environment and nuclear energy.

Different categories of group may emphasise different access points as they go about their work. Obvious direct targets are the **executive** and the **legislature**, but groups also work via the courts, political parties, public and media campaigns, devolved bodies, **local government** and at the international level (for example, via the **European Union**).

Further reading: D. Watts, *Pressure Groups*, Edinburgh University Press, 2006

**Prevention of Terrorism Act** (2006) The Prevention of Terrorism Act contained proposals designed to ensure that the police, intelligence agencies and the courts all have the tools they require to tackle **terrorism** and bring perpetrators to **justice**. Though not a direct response to the **London bombings** of July 2005 (**legislation** on terrorism for introduction in the autumn had already been announced), the Bill took account of the reactions to them. In the words of Tony **Blair**, 'the rules of the game are changing'. When the Bill was introduced in the lower chamber, the **House of Commons** voted to reject the plans to allow police to detain terror suspects for up to 90 days without charge, an issue on which the Prime **Minister** was personally unwilling to budge. (An amendment allowing for a maximum period of 28 days was passed.) Other controversial features of the legislation included the creation of an offence of 'glorifying terrorism' in the UK or abroad, new ground-rules for proscribing certain extreme organisations and powers of closure over places of worship used to foment extremism. Many critics portrayed some of the Bill's clauses as an unwarranted inroad into long-established **civil liberties** and might convince members of Britain's Muslim community to turn to violence. **Minister**s countered that it was a necessary response to an unparalleled terrorist threat. It became law on 30 March 2006. The Act aroused considerable media attention, not least because the defeat on the detention clause was the worst suffered by the Blair **Government** on the floor of the **House of Commons**, and the worst such defeat for any government since 1978.

See also: **glorification of terrorism**

**primary legislation, secondary legislation**  Acts passed by the Westminster and **Scottish Parliament**s are primary legislation. Secondary legislation, sometimes known as delegated **legislation** or **statutory instrument**s, modifies the provisions of the Act in a way allowed by the original legislation. Instruments give **authority** to **minister**s or other public bodies to make orders or **regulations** (for example, to vary the fees levied for a particular service) under the provision of the parent statute. At least a thousand are passed every year. Governments like the use of secondary legislation, for it enables changes to be made without having to pass new Bills through **Parliament** and allows flexibility in policy implementation. The parent act stipulates the level of parliamentary approval required for any Bill, the requirement varying from an affirmative resolution to no consent at all.

**Prime Minister (PM)**  The head of the **executive** branch of **government** and chair of the **Cabinet**. In Britain, the Prime Minister's position derives from their leadership of the majority party in the **legislature**. The PM appoints members of the **Cabinet** and **Government** ('hiring and firing'), directs and coordinates government policy and broad strategy, chairs Cabinet meetings, maintains special interest in key policy areas, answers questions in **Parliament** and leads in major debates such as policy on Iraq, provides leadership to the nation in times of crisis (for example, in response to the **London bombings**) and requests a **dissolution** from the **monarch** effectively determining the timing of the next election.

The **power** of prime ministers – sometimes known as chancellors, first or chief ministers or by some local term such as the Taoiseach in Ireland – varies considerably. Their ability to hire, promote and fire colleagues offers much scope for a display of personal leadership, but much depends on the person at the helm, relationships with Cabinet colleagues and parliamentary party, the distribution of patronage, the ability to use the media to advantage, whether the administration is a single party or **coalition** one and other varying circumstances (the complexity of issues that arise during the lifetime of a government). The tendency of the media to focus on personalities and the growth in international summitry and overseas visits provide prime ministers with opportunities to present an image of statesmanship that makes them more than a national politician.

See also: **presidential government, prime ministerial government**

Further reading: S. Buckley, *The Prime Minister and Cabinet*, Edinburgh University Press, 2006

**prime ministerial government** R. H. S. Crossman, a former Oxford don and then a Labour **Member of Parliament**, was the first main exponent of the idea that Britain had acquired a system in which the **Prime Minister** had supreme **power**: 'The post-war epoch has seen the final transformation of Cabinet Government into Prime Ministerial Government', with the effect that 'the **Cabinet** now joins the dignified elements in the **Constitution**'. His observations were matched by those of another writer and politician, Professor John Mackintosh, who similarly discerned the passing of **Cabinet government**: 'The country is governed by a Prime Minister, his colleagues, **junior ministers** and civil servants, with the Cabinet acting as a clearing house and court of appeal'.

Similar claims have been oft-repeated since the early 1960s, observers suggesting that a Prime Minister presiding over a **single-party government** and equipped with the traditional prerogatives of the **Crown** is immensely powerful. But it was the premiership of Margaret **Thatcher** which provided the debate about whether Britain has 'government by prime minister' with a new impetus. She appeared to stretch the power of the office to its limits. So too Tony **Blair** was accused of operating via a system of personal rule or 'too presidentially'.

Prime ministers are now much more visible than ever before, because of the growing trend towards international summitry and a high degree of television exposure. No occupant of **Ten Downing Street** since the last World War has been anything less than very powerful. Any Prime Minister today has a formidable display of powers at their disposal. Yet the thesis of prime ministerial government can be over-stated and suffers from the tendency to over-generalisation. Power can be seriously circumscribed and dependent on the circumstances of the time. It is not merely that some Prime Ministers are more powerful than others, but that any single incumbent will be more powerful at certain times than at others in the course of the premiership. Even the strongest among them are not always able to sustain the same degree of performance throughout their term.

Prime Ministers do not have unlimited power. Individuals have made a greater or lesser impact upon the office. All have been subject to some constraints, among them: the need to maintain Cabinet support; consent on the backbenches and of Parliament as a whole; hostility in the media; and the activities of **pressure group**s.

There has certainly been a remarkable growth in the power of the **executive** branch of government in the last 100 years, but the distribution of power within the Executive is liable to change at any time. If there has been a gradual trend to prime ministerial dominance, it has been characterised by an ebb and flow of power, rather than a continuous increase. A much-quoted observation by Lord Oxford (formerly Liberal PM Asquith) reflects the varying nature of political power. He judged that: 'The office of Prime Minister is what its holder chooses and is able to make of it'. His emphasis on the ability, character and preferences of the incumbent is generally accepted, as is the role of particular circumstances.

Further reading: R. H. S Crossman, Introduction to W. Bagehot, *The English Constitution*, Fontana, 1963; J. Mackintosh, *The British Cabinet*, Stevens, 1977

**Prime Minister's Questions (PMQs)** A 30-minute slot (Wednesdays, 12.00–12.30 p.m.) in the **House of Commons** in which the **Prime Minister** answers oral questions from **Members of Parliament**. As the questions are not given in advance, the Prime Minister has to be prepared to tackle a wide range of issues and to be particularly well briefed on those subjects that the **Leader of the Opposition** is likely to raise.

PMQs is an example of British **adversarial politics**, the cut and thrust of partisan controversy. Media attention focuses particularly on the confrontation between the Prime Minister and their opposite number, for example judging the performances of **Brown** v. **Cameron**. The duels make for good television spectacle, snippets often being used in news programmes. They tend to generate more heat than light.

**private finance initiative (PFI)** A controversial form of partnership between the public and private sector that involves the contracting-out of large public sector capital projects to the private sector which funds, builds and maintains them. It is often used to build hospitals, prisons, roads and schools, among other ventures. Private companies may lease buildings back to the public sector over a period of 25 years or more in return for an annual payment, after which they belong to the public sector. **Governments** like such partnerships, which make more money available for new building enterprises without affecting the **public sector borrowing requirement**, but opponents are either ideologically opposed to the involvement of the private sector in public projects or else question the long-term costs involved.

**private legislation** **Legislation** which applies to a section of the community rather than to the whole country. It provides specified **powers** to particular individuals or organisations, for example allowing a local authority or a body such as Network Rail to acquire and develop a particular tract of land. Such legislation originates in the form of a petition to **Parliament** by the affected body and goes through a distinctive but analogous parliamentary procedure prior to passing into **law**. At the committee stage, the procedure is a quasi-judicial one, with witnesses giving evidence under oath. Few such Bills are introduced and they consume only a small proportion of parliamentary time.

**private members' Bill** A form of public **Bill** introduced into **Parliament** by backbench **Members** of **Parliament**, usually as a result of winning a high position in the annual ballot of members but occasionally via the **Ten Minute Rule**. Such Bills pass through the same stages as a **government** Bill. Many fail, often for lack of parliamentary time or because of governmental opposition, although a few have been high profile and made it on to the statute book. Notable examples are the controversial socio-moral issues of the 1960s that changed the laws on abortion, capital punishment, divorce and homosexuality, although more usually successful **legislation** tends to be that which is less contentious and therefore arouses less opposition, such as the measures concerning ragwort control and Dealing in Public Objects (Offences) passed in recent sessions. The introduction of such Bills can serve to draw attention to a particular **issue** and it may encourage **ministers** to devise their own alternative legislative proposals.

**privatisation** The process of converting public amenities and services into private ones, thereby returning nationalised industries to the private sector. Privatisation was a feature of Conservative economic policy in the 1980s and 90s, the **Thatcher Government** selling off the electrical, gas and telecommunications industries among many others, and the **Major** administration disposing of the **state**-controlled coal and railway industries. Such measures were said to be advantageous in that they raised large sums of money, gave the new management commercial autonomy, weakened the **power** of **trades** unions, widened share ownership and took government out of decision-making. Critics saw them as more concerned with revenue-raising than with sound policy, 'selling off the family silver' according to Harold **Macmillan**. They suggested that the social case for public ownership of key industries and utilities was being sacrificed for short-term gain.

**Privy Council**  Originating in the thirteenth century as a small body of influential advisers to the **monarch**, today the Council is the formal machinery via which the **monarch** exercises their prerogative powers. Nominally extensive (the Council comprises the 500 or so past and present **Cabinet ministers**, as well as some other leading public figures, who are supervised by the Lord President of the Council), Council work is in reality conducted by a small body of Government ministers who come together to witness the Queen signing formal documents – Orders in Council – which may be used to declare war, commit troops or announce a civil emergency. The Council also operates via a number of small committees, the most famous of which is the Judicial Committee (JCPC) which has long been the final court of appeal for **Commonwealth** countries and now also acts as the arbiter of disputes on matters concerning **devolution**. The JCPC comprises the 12 **law lords** and other senior **judges** who are Privy Councillors, some of whom represent the Commonwealth and Scotland.

**promotional group**  see **cause group**

**proportional representation (PR)**  The name given to a series of electoral systems in which there is a broad proximity in the ratio of votes obtained in the election to seats won in the **legislature**. PR systems make use of **multi-member constituencies** or districts which ensure a greater degree of proportionality than that which applies in **single-member systems** such as **first past the post** (FPTP). Most European countries use electoral systems based on some form of PR, **party lists** being common in Western Europe (for example, Netherlands and Spain) and mixed member proportional systems (see **additional member system**) in a number of the post-communist democracies (for example, Hungary and Poland). **Single transferable vote** is used in Ireland and Malta. PR systems are said by their proponents to be fairer to small parties and favourable to the representation in the legislature of minority groups, thus producing a chamber which broadly reflects the composition and outlook of the population as a whole. They also discourage wasted votes on the part of people who vote for candidates or parties that do not get into the parliament. Critics blame PR for encouraging the development of many small parties whose representation in the legislature makes **coalition government** more likely. They prefer the 'strong government' associated with single-party administrations which are more likely to flourish where FPTP is employed.

**prorogation**  The formal end to the parliamentary year which in the **United Kingdom** usually takes place in November, marking the beginning of the period between two sessions of the legislative body. Prorogation is immediately preceded by the prorogation speech, the mirror of the Speech from the Throne (**Queen's Speech**), delivered by the **Lord Chancellor** to both houses. This speech looks back at the legislative session, noting major Bills passed and other actions of the government.

**PSBR**  see **public sector borrowing requirement**

**Public Accounts Committee**  An influential investigative committee of the **House of Commons** that cuts across departmental boundaries, established by **Chancellor of the Exchequer** Gladstone in 1861 and responsible for overseeing **government** expenditures to ensure they are effective and honest and in line with original intentions. The Committee consists of 16 members, nominated at the beginning of each Parliament. The party proportions of the Committee, like other committees, are the same as in the House. The Committee chooses its own chairperson, traditionally an Opposition member, usually with previous experience as a **HM Treasury** minister. Divisions in the Committee are very rare, generally occurring less than once a year.

**public corporation** Many of the well-known public corporations of the post-1945 era were established to run the amenities and industries nationalised by the **Attlee Government**. Their general features were that the boards were 'corporate' (meaning that they had a legal identity, could own property and be sued), owned and controlled the assets of the industry, were provided with general responsibilities in the act of **nationalisation**, operated under the supervision of a government **minister** who appointed board members and were free from **HM Treasury** control over finance and staffing. The intention behind their creation was to harmonise the dynamic enterprise associated with the private sector, public **accountability** and concern for the general good character of the public sector. However, their alleged benefits were not recognised by the Conservative administrations of the 1980s and 90s which privatised many of the utilities and industries formerly run by corporations. The **British Broadcasting Corporation** is the best-known example of a public corporation today, dependent on government for its income (from the licence fee) but able to determine its own programming and staffing arrangements.

**public legislation** Public legislation is applicable to the whole community rather than to some specific groups. It falls into two categories, **government Bill**s and **private members' Bills**. Most Bills that pass into **law** are introduced by government **ministers**, some high-profile ones having been trailed in the party **manifesto** and some enacted in response to events, such as combating a terrorist outbreak. Other public legislation may derive from **European Union directives**. The bulk of it comprises routine and non-contentious measures that have been in the departmental pipeline, following consultation with outside interests.

**public opinion** Refers to the cluster of attitudes and beliefs held by people about a variety of issues, including those concerning politics and policy **issues**. It is the opinion of the majority of the population at a particular time and place. It will vary on and across the issues of the day. By contrast, **political culture** – in Heywood's term – 'is fashioned out of long-term values rather than simply people's reactions to specific policies and problems'. Of course, there can be no single public opinion. Rather, there are several opinions held by members of the public.

Further reading: A. Heywood, *Politics*, Macmillan, 1997

**public opinion poll** Opinion polling has been conducted in Britain since 1938. Most polls are concerned with the voting intention of the person approached, although others are designed to discover the attitudes of voters to specific questions. For party leaders, the polls are a useful guide to the state of **public opinion** and give a broad indication of their relative standing among the electorate. They have become important to the parties in making their policies and planning their strategies, for polling can highlight **issues** on which there is a need for a clear response to public anxieties. In the 1950s and 60s, the polls had a good record and several were remarkably accurate in predicting the outcome of elections. Since 1970, the performance has been more mixed, 1992 being an example of a campaign in which the polls (57 produced by 8 different polling organisations) got the result conspicuously wrong. Throughout the 2005 campaign, the polls generally agreed that Labour seemed destined to win, but with a reduced majority; they differed on how much the majority might fall. Collectively, the final surveys were the most accurate predictions ever made of the outcome of any British **general election**.

**public–private partnership (PPP)** Formal partnerships between **government** agencies and private firms that are formed to deliver a policy or manage a specific **initiative**, be it small- or large-scale. Usually the money derives from the private sector but the risks involved in achieving the desired goals are shared. They have been a key feature of Labour's **Third Way** approach, **private finance initiatives** being a contentious example of such ventures in action. The current programme of investment in the London underground is an example of public–private co-operation. **Ministers** like such schemes which do not affect the **public sector borrowing requirement**.

**public sector borrowing requirement (PSBR)** The amount borrowed by **government** in order to finance its expenditure. According to Keynesian economics, the PSBR should rise at times of economic recession to boost demand and fall in times of rapid growth to prevent the economy from over-heating. Monetarists reject this view and argue that a large PSBR fuels inflation.

See also: **Keynesianism, monetarism**

**public-service broadcasting** The idea that radio and television should not be commercial, but used in the public interest to educate, inform and entertain. When the **BBC** was established, the idea was that its primary function should be educative. Lord Reith, the first Director General, wanted to expose the audience to programming that was worthy and of the highest standards.

# · Q

QMV  see **qualified majority voting**

**qualified majority voting (QMV)**  QMV is now the most commonly used method of voting in the **Council of Ministers** of the **European Union**. It allows for decisions to be taken on a majority basis. Large member states have more votes than small ones and specified numbers of votes constitute 'qualified majorities' or 'blocking minorities'. The original weightings were laid down in the Treaty of Rome but have been subsequently modified. QMV was much extended via the Single European Act 1986.

British critics of the European Union lament the threat to **parliamentary sovereignty** posed by QMV. Its use means that decisions can be taken by the Council that are binding on all member countries, even though they have not been passed by the national **parliament**.

**quango**  Formerly known in full as quasi-autonomous **nongovernmental organisation**s (a term of American origin to describe a newly created form that had become in vogue), quangos are now often referred to as quasigovernmental or non-departmental public bodies. They are financed by the **government** to perform some public service function but are not under direct governmental control. As such, they operate at arm's length from government, allowing management flexibility and political independence. From a ministerial point of view, they help to shield contentious and sensitive political issues from the heat of partisan strife. Critics lament the growth of a quangocracy, in which there are too many quangos. They dislike the way in which they place key public functions in the hands of unelected and unaccountable officials who are appointed by **ministers**. Labour planned to curb their growth, but ministers of either party find them useful. Their numbers have been diminished by the development of the devolved administrations in Scotland and Wales. The term is much less used today, because such bodies are in fact part of the government in terms of funding, appointment and function, so that the acronym does not work as a description. The use of alternative titles represents an attempt to avoid the pejorative associations of the original nomenclature.

**Queen's Speech** The Queen's Speech is part of the ceremony of the State Opening of **Parliament**. It is prepared by the **Prime Minister** and sets out the ministerial agenda for the coming year. In a neutral voice, the Queen reads 'The Most Gracious Speech from the Throne'. Although she uses the term 'my **Government**', this does not imply endorsement for the stated policies which are those of the Government. The speech ends with 'I pray that the blessing of Almighty God may rest upon your counsels' and marks the formal opening of the new session.

# R

**race** The belief that human beings can be clearly categorised on the basis of their skin colour and physiognomy (the study and judgement of a person's outer appearance, primarily the face). In the nineteenth century, it was widely believed that there were important mental, physical, moral and intellectual differences between black, brown, white and yellow-skinned people. Many attempts were made to dignify the idea scientifically. Today, the preferred term for many commentators is **ethnicity**, which lacks the biological and emotive overtones. But the word 'race' is still popularly used in the sense of common descent, based largely on skin colour and physical characteristics such as hair type.

**race relations legislation** Four Race Relations Acts have been introduced in the **United Kingdom**, those of 1965, 1968, 1976 and 2000. All have been introduced by Labour administrations. The **Commission for Racial Equality** and earlier similar bodies have supported the use of **legislation** in this field, believing that: it is necessary to offer an unequivocal declaration of public policy; a **law** supports those who do not wish to discriminate but who may feel compelled to do so by social pressure; a law gives protection and redress to minority groups; a law provides for peaceful and orderly adjustment of grievances and release of tensions; and a law reduces prejudice by discouraging the behaviour in which the prejudice finds expression.

The early statues between them defined what was meant by discrimination and made it illegal in public places, made it an offence to practise **racial discrimination** in areas such as private clubs (as well as the familiar ones of education, employment, housing and the provision of goods and services), outlawed indirect as well as direct discrimination, and made it an offence if the effect of what was done or said was to discriminate against someone, even if that was not the intention. The Race Relations Act 2000 tightened the law further, extending the scope of previous legislation to the police, those working in the prison service and other formerly exempted groups.

**racial discrimination** Discriminatory or abusive behaviour towards members of another **race**. It refers to differences in treatment of people on the basis of characteristics which may be classified as racial, including skin colour, cultural heritage and religion. In Western societies, the term is usually employed in cases involving discrimination against minority racial groups but it can also refer to the opposite situation, in which case it is often called reverse discrimination.

The 1968 Race Relations Act defined discrimination as 'treating a person less favourably than another person on grounds of colour, race or ethnic or national origin'.

See also: **race relations legislation**

**racism** The belief that there are significant differences between **races** or ethnic groups, whether these relate to culture, intellect, morals or physique, and that they provide grounds for treating the different groups in more and less advantageous ways. It is often accompanied by the theory or assumption that one race or group is superior to others.

**realignment** A concept employed in analysis of long-term shifts in the pattern of support in the **party system** and which usually involves a fundamental change in the political loyalty of important social groups.

**referendum** A form of **direct democracy** in which the electorate is asked to pass judgement in order to resolve a particular policy **issue**. The only **United Kingdom**-wide referendum was that held in 1975 to determine whether Britain should remain in the European Community. Other votes have been held in Scotland, Wales and Northern Ireland on issues such as **devolution**. They have also been increasingly held at the regional and local level.

Referendums differ from elections in that the electorate is being asked to vote on a single issue and not about which party should assume political office. They may be advisory or mandatory. In Britain, the outcome of the vote has usually been accepted by those in authority. Supporters see them as a useful means of democratic consultation: they strengthen **legitimacy** by providing the public with an outlet for their views; they promote political participation; and they are useful in settling major constitutional questions or those issues that cut across party lines which **ministers** find it difficult to handle. Opponents believe that in a **representative democracy**, it is an abdication of responsibility for ministers to hand a decision back to the voters, many of whom may find the issues too difficult to comprehend. They point out that a vote only provides a snapshot of opinion at a particular time, they distort complex issues, by presenting them in a simple yes/no form, and for resolving social issues they are less appropriate, for there is a danger that the public may be susceptible to emotional media campaigns.

Further reading: D. Butler, *Referendums around the World*, Macmillan, 1994

**regionalism**  Regions are geographical areas within a country and regionalism involves providing them with some form of special representation in order that the views of their inhabitants can be articulated. Gestures towards regional **government** have been made over several decades, but as yet in Britain there have been no elected regional councils. The voters of the North East overwhelmingly turned down the opportunity to have such a body in a **referendum** in September 2004. Of course, the peoples of Scotland, Wales and Northern Ireland have received recognition via the devolved machinery established in recent years.

**register of members' interests** In 1974 the **House of Commons** voted to establish a compulsory register of members' interests and a select committee to administer it. **Members of Parliament** (MPs) are required to declare in the register the sources of any extra income or gifts which they receive, so that there can be no suspicion that their behaviour in **Parliament** is unduly influenced by outside interests.

When an MP takes part in a debate that may affect a business with which he or she has a financial connection, the MP concerned must declare this interest to the House before speaking.

**regulations** A form of **law** which emanates from the **European Union** (EU). Regulations are directly applicable in all member states, binding in their entirety over the goal to be pursued and the form of implementation. Much of the day-to-day management of the **Common Agricultural Policy** is conducted via regulations.

Regulations may also refer to the system of rules via which public sector organisations and companies are expected to operate, in order that the public interest may be promoted and preserved. State regulatory activity has increased in recent years with many new regulatory bodies, ranging from the Financial Services Authority (FSA) to the Office of Fair Trading (OFT). The EU has introduced further regulation into British life, especially in areas such as health and safety, the workplace and the environment.

Further reading: N. Nugent, *The Government and Politics of the European Union*, Palgrave, 2003

**reinforcement theory** A theory concerning media influence on the electorate. Supporters of reinforcement theory, which became fashionable in the years after 1945, suggested that voters used the media to reinforce their own outlook. They know what they need from the media and take that, and that alone. In other words, as free agents rather than mindless victims, they filter information which substantiates their own pre-determined beliefs. Hence the name sometimes employed for this theory, the 'uses and gratifications model'.

The reinforcement theory held sway for many years, but as television became more pervasive and played such a key part in people's daily lives, its adequacy was called into question. It gave way in the 1970s to the **agenda-setting theory**, stressing that by deciding on the issues that are granted coverage, television and papers help to determine what the public is thinking about, if not actually what they think.

**representative democracy**  A form of **government** in which **citizens** elect people to rule on their behalf, representative democracy is more attuned to the needs of larger and more complex societies than **direct democracy**, for sheer numbers make the direct and continuous **participation** of citizens in government impossible. Self-government has evolved into elected government. Freely elected representatives of the people make decisions subject to popular control, so that in effect the few govern on behalf of the many. The majority are vote-casters every few years at election time, but in between have little say in what goes on.

Modern democracies are representative in form, even semi-democracies having representative institutions. Many can be described too as a **liberal democracy**.

Further reading: M. Cole, *Democracy*, Edinburgh University Press, 2006

**representative government**  A political system is representative if it is one in which representatives of the people share, to a significant degree, in the making of decisions. For this to apply there must be a good number of representatives meeting in some kind of free assembly. They are chosen to protect and advance the interests of the individuals on whose behalf they are acting and must be freely elected. In Western democracies, it is the manner of choice – free elections – which is seen as the key component of representative government.

But what is a representative of the people? The term is commonly used in different ways: a person whose task it is to protect and advance the interests of the group being represented; a person or assembly who or which has been freely elected; an elected body which mirrors or reflects the characteristics of the community as a whole.

In the West, the main meaning of representation is concerned with election. Representation by election is the most important form of representation, with people choosing an assembly to reflect their wishes. Electoral reformers will, however, point out that the assembly chosen is not truly representative, for **governments** have been chosen by less than half of the voters in every election postwar and might therefore be said to have lacked **legitimacy**. This is particularly true of recent experience: Labour won in 2005 on the basis of a low level of popular support (35.2 per cent of those who voted, little over 20 per cent of the whole electorate), a 'success' achieved on a low **turnout**. Also, Britain an assembly in which minority parties have traditionally been seriously under-represented.

**republican** The term may refer to someone who favours the ending of monarchical rule and instead the election of a president as **head of state**. It also refers to those inhabitants of Northern Ireland who wish to see the province become part of a united Ireland. Here many but not all republicans are Roman Catholics, although by no means are all Catholics republicans.

**responsible government**  As with **representative government**, the term can be used in several ways in political discussion. Three main meanings can be discerned. (1) Responsiveness: those who are chosen to represent us are expected to be sensitive to the needs, opinions and wishes of the constituents. (2) **Accountability**: elected officials are obliged to be answerable to the people for their actions or any lack of action (**collective responsibility** and **individual ministerial responsibility** are **constitutional conventions** which seek to make **ministers** responsible, individually and collectively, in the sense of being answerable for **government** policy). (3) Moral obligation: holders of high office are expected to be 'responsible', in the same way that a nurse cares for a patient, a prison governor for the fate of their prisoners and a teacher for the welfare of their students. In other words, they have to pursue a prudent policy and not behave recklessly or irresponsibly.

Many people would wish to see politicians show regard for all three meanings outlined. They want politicians who listen to **public opinion**, pursue wise and consistent policies and are accountable to the voters. Of course, sometimes the aims may be in conflict. For example, listening to popular demands may not make for a consistent or realistic policy.

**Right**  In European countries, the Right has traditionally acted in defence of the interests of the established propertied classes. It supports the maintenance of the status quo and generally adopts a cautious attitude to political, economic and social change. It dislikes too much **government** intervention and regulation, favours private ownership over

**state** ownership and likes to seek people left in freedom to run their own lives. Rightwingers favour lower levels of taxation, rewards for effort and enterprise and the pursuit of **freedom** rather than **equality**; indeed, they accept an unequal society as inevitable. They tend to emphasise a belief in authority, duties, order and tradition.

In Britain, the Right is primarily represented by the **Conservative Party**.

**Rome Treaty** The treaty signed in March 1957 (and operative from January 1958) by the six member states ('the Six') of the **European Coal and Steel Community**, which decided to extend their cooperation into a **European Economic Community** (the EEC). At the same time, a further treaty established Euratom (European Atomic Energy Community), a body intended to promote the peaceful development of atomic energy. The EEC established major objectives, including: a customs union in which all internal barriers to trade would be removed and a common external tariff applied to the outside world; the development of a **Common Agricultural Policy**; the harmonisation of social security arrangements; the free movement of labour and capital; and the development of regional and social funds to assist poorer regions. With the fulfilment of these objectives, there would be a Common Market. The Six were aiming for 'a harmonious development of economic activities, a continuous and balanced expansion, an increased stability, an accelerated raising of the standard of living, and closer relations between its member states'. The Common Market was a means to this end, not the end in itself. The aim was economic unity. Political unity was not mentioned, but the Founding Fathers knew there was clear political language in the treaty they had signed, the intention being 'to lay the foundations of an ever closer union among the peoples of Europe'.

Further reading: N. Nugent, *The Government and Politics of the European Union*, Palgrave, 2003

**royal assent** The granting of royal assent is the formal method by which a constitutional **monarch** completes the legislative process of law-making by formally assenting to an Act of **Parliament**. While the power to withhold royal assent was once exercised often, it was last deployed in 1707.

**royal prerogative** The royal prerogative comprises a number of powers or privileges performed in the past by the **monarch** but now performed in his or her name by **ministers**. Their **authority** derives from the **Crown**, rather than from **Parliament**, so that parliamentary authority is not required by the **Executive** as it conducts these tasks. Prerogative powers are exercised by ministers individually or collectively. They include the rights to: exercise mercy (a prerogative of the Home Secretary); declare war; make treaties; give orders to the armed forces; appoint ministers; and dispense honours (all duties performed by the **Prime Minister** and his colleagues). Because of the opportunity to act in this way, the **Thatcher Government** was able to deploy troops in the Falklands conflict (1982). So too was Tony **Blair** able to commit British troops to a military invasion of Iraq, in 2003. In neither case was it legally essential to have parliamentary approval, although over Iraq in particular many **Members of Parliament** (MPs) felt entitled to – and were given – an early debate and vote on the controversial decision. This has probably created a precedent, for it is unlikely that in future any British government would send forces into action without allowing MPs a chance to express their opinion.

Former leftwing Labour MP Tony Benn campaigned

for the abolition of the royal prerogative in the **United Kingdom** in the 1990s, arguing that all governmental powers in effect exercised on the advice of the Prime Minister and **Cabinet** should be subject to parliamentary scrutiny and require parliamentary approval. At the time, ministers argued that – given the breadth of topics involved – requiring parliamentary approval in each instance where the prerogative is currently used would overwhelm parliamentary time and slow the enactment of legislation. However, Gordon **Brown** has indicated a willingness to cede some prerogative powers, most notably the Prime Minister's right to take the country into war without parliamentary approval.

See also: **monarch, monarchy**

**rule of law** In a free society, there is a concern to maintain human **liberty** in the face of increasing **state** activity. The problem is how on the one hand to provide **powers** for those in **government** to operate effectively, yet on the other hand to ensure that in exercising those powers they do not encroach arbitrarily upon the rights of individuals. Liberty is protected by the rule of law, the restriction of governmental activities as authorised by **law**. The idea of the rule of law therefore implies the moral and legal acceptance by government of certain restrictions upon its activities. Government recognises that **justice** demands that the rights of individuals must be respected. In essence, the rule of law is the network of legal rules which guide and restrain political behaviour.

A. V. Dicey, the foremost constitutional lawyer of the late nineteenth century, was the person who most clearly articulated the idea of the rule of law. He saw it as the cardinal principle of government in a democratic system, one which seeks to equate law and justice. He discerned three ideas in the concept: **equality before the law** – the belief

that no person should be punished except for a breach of
the law, just as no person should be viewed as 'above the
law'; that laws are clearly published and accessible, so
that everyone is capable of knowing what they are; and
that, as the laws of the **constitution**, especially essential
liberties, derive from judicial decisions based on **common
law**, they cannot be removed.

# S

**Salisbury convention** The convention developed shortly after
the formation of the post-1945 Labour **Government** that
the **House of Lords** would not vote down the second
reading of any legislative proposals which had been
included in the election **manifesto** of the winning party.
Named after the person responsible for originally stating
the doctrine, the convention has been in force ever since,
although in its more assertive mood of recent years, the
House of Lords has shown a greater willingness to challenge ministerial policies. A number of **peers** take the view
that the convention was designed to protect a non-
Conservative Government from being thwarted by a built-
in hereditary and pro-Conservative majority in the
chamber. They suggest that its impact has been diminished, in part because the original House has not existed
since 1999 (because of the near-abolition of hereditary
peerages) and also because the level of popular support for
the Government elected in 2005 is much lower (35.2 per
cent) than that which applied to the **Attlee** Government
elected 60 years earlier.

**Alex Salmond** (1954– )  Alex Salmond was elected as an **MP**
for the **Scottish National Party** in 1987, serving as its
leader between 1990 and 2000, and has been an MSP

since 1999. He left the Scottish Parliament in 2001, but returned in 2007 and as party leader for a second time (2004– ) became the first nationalist to be elected **First Minister** of Scotland. He heads a **minority government**.

Although fully committed to an independent Scotland, Alex Salmond antagonised some hard-line fundamentalists in the SNP by campaigning for **devolution** in 1997. As leader, he has been pragmatic, having moderated his one-time more leftwing views and steered the party towards adopting a gradualist – but still pro-independence – strategy.

**Schengen Agreement**  The agreement, originally signed by five **European Union** (EU) countries (France, Germany and the Benelux countries) in 1985, which refers to the gradual abolition of controls at the common frontiers. Some measures taken under Schengen referred to short-term issues (for example, visa regulations), others were long-term ones (for example, strengthening external frontiers and duty-free allowances). Its more sensitive provisions cover questions such as control of drugs, control of firearms and extradition. So far, a total of 30 countries – including the EU and three non-EU members (Iceland, Norway and Switzerland) – have signed the agreement, having implemented it. Like the Republic of Ireland, the **United Kingdom** has signed up, but both are involved in measures for police cooperation but do not participate in the border and visa provisions. The British position has been that the country will opt in to those parts of Schengen that it finds palatable. **Ministers** have strenuously argued that the country should not surrender the advantage conferred by its island status of being able to check people's identity and bona fides before they enter the UK. Britain remains free to maintain its own controls at national borders.

Further reading: N. Nugent, *The Government and Politics of the European Union*, Palgrave, 2003

**Scotland Act** (1998) Following the successful **referendum** in September 1997, the Scotland Act became **law** a year later. Under the terms of the statute, the first **Scottish Parliament** in 292 years was to assume the responsibilities previously exercised by the **Scottish Office**. This meant that it had primary legislative **power**s over nine broad areas, among them: economic development and transport; education and training; health; and law and home affairs. In all, there are 47 devolved issues grouped under these headings, so that the Scottish Parliament and the **Executive** chosen from it have a wide range of responsibilities. There are, however, a series of 'reserved matters' over which power resides in London, for it is considered that they can be more effectively handled on a **United Kingdom** basis. These include defence and national security, foreign affairs, and major economic policy and fiscal affairs.

By the Act, the Scottish Parliament was also given a tax-varying power, enabling the Executive to collect additional taxation from the people of Scotland of up to three pence in the pound.

Further reading: P. Lynch, *Scottish Government and Politics*, Edinburgh University Press, 2001

**Scott inquiry report** (1996) The inquiry conducted by Lord Justice Scott which followed a controversy over sales of British arms to Iraq in the late 1980s. Critics of the Conservative **Government** claimed that **minister**s had relaxed their own guidelines on the sale of arms to Iraq, in spite of their statements to the contrary in the **House of Commons**. The episode only came to light as a result of the prosecution by Customs and Excise of three businessmen of the Matrix Churchill company for illegally exporting arms to Iraq.

**Prime Minister Major** set up the inquiry which comprehensively examined the inner workings of the British Government and produced a thorough, exhaustive and revealing review of what had happened, one which was highly damaging to the reputation of the Government. He found that **Members of Parliament** had been misled by a process of deliberate deception on the part of ministers and their civil servants, that the criminal prosecution of the businessmen was wrong, and that the Government had used its **powers** to block the release of information that would have assisted in their defence. The Government survived a vote on the report by one vote. No minister resigned as a result of the findings.

**Scottish nationalism** Scotland used to be a distinct nation with its own **parliament** before the Act of Union in 1707. Thereafter, a feeling developed among some Scots that their culture, history and language which gave their country a distinct identity were being neglected. Proud of their history and distinctiveness, they wanted their nation to be recognised as a separate **state**. The campaign for self-government, involving the creation of a **Scottish Parliament** meeting in Edinburgh, was on their political agenda for much of the twentieth century, for they saw it as the most effective means of meeting distinctively Scottish needs.

Scottish **nationalism** became high profile in **United Kingdom** politics in the 1960s, although the **Scottish National Party** had been arguing the nationalist case for many years before that decade. Particular causes of the upsurge in national feeling included: dissatisfaction with the performance of central **government** which was seen as remote and uncaring; economic discontent – the conviction that Scotland suffered from unfair burdens, bearing the worst impact of economic recession and suffering from industrial decline, high unemployment, poor housing and an infrastructure in need of regeneration; and in the 1970s, the discovery of 'Scotland's oil', which fuelled their belief that Scotland could be a viable independent state.

**Scottish National Party (SNP)** Formed in 1934, the SNP originally supported a romantic form of **nationalism** which was strong in rural, Gaelic-speaking areas. For years, the SNP was cursed by internal division and feuding. But since its take-off of the late 1960s when it won a dramatic by-election victory in Hamilton and resurgence in the mid-1970s, it has appealed much more widely. It emphasises culture and language much less than does the Welsh nationalist party, **Plaid Cymru**. Many SNP members want more: they stress the separatist goal more strongly than their Plaid counterparts. Their party is left-of-centre on many issues, such as nuclear power, tuition fees and the Iraq war.

In the last 15 years or so, the SNP has made much of the European dimension, arguing that an independent Scotland should be able to attract **European Union** funding and noting how small countries in the Union have proved their viability. It has campaigned on the slogan 'Scotland in Europe'. It campaigned for **devolution** in 1997 but views it as a halfway house to full independence, its ultimate goal. In recent years, it has regularly won representation in the Westminster, Scottish and European parliaments. Since the 2007 elections, it has acted as a **minority government** in the Scottish Parliament, sustained by limited support from Green MSPs.

See also: **Salmond**

Further reading: P. Lynch, *Scottish Government and Politics*, Edinburgh University Press, 2001

**Scottish Office**  The position of Secretary of State for Scotland and a new Scottish Office were created in 1885. In 1939, the Office was moved from London to St Andrew's House, Edinburgh, although a small office in London was retained. Even prior to **devolution**, a very large part of Scottish government was administered from Edinburgh, through the Scottish Office and its component departments. It was the focus for **pressure group**s that wished to influence the direction of policy within their area of operation.

Post-devolution, the functions of the Office were transferred to the new devolved machinery, although it remained in existence, staffed by a small number of people who serviced the Secretary of State. In June 2003, Tony **Blair** announced that the role of Secretary of State for Scotland, to represent Scottish interests in the **United Kingdom** Cabinet, would be combined with other posts within the **Cabinet**. The Scottish Office, together with the **Welsh Office**, was moved to become part of the new **Department for Constitutional Affairs**.

**Scottish Parliament**  Scotland did not have its own **parliament** between the passage of the Act of Union with England in 1707 and 1999. The present parliament was created by the **Scotland Act** of 1998. It is elected every four years by the **additional member system**, 73 members (Members of the Scottish Parliament, MSPs) being elected in constituencies under **first past the post**, the other 56 being chosen by a **party list** system (based on the European constituencies) which introduces an element of proportionality.

Now located in the costly new Holyrood building, the Scottish Parliament was from the beginning of the debate on the form of **devolution** meant to be a very different body from that in Westminster. It was supposed to be less adversarial, to be based on power-sharing, to emphasise equal opportunities, to be open to consultation and embrace participation, and to operate through a strong committee system, so that much of its work would not take place on the floor of the chamber.

Further reading: P. Lynch, *Scottish Government and Politics*, Edinburgh University Press, 2001

**Scottish Socialist Party (SSP)**  The SSP was founded in 1998 as an anti-capitalist party whose goal is to build a socialist Scotland that will stand up to the forces of global capitalism. It is a pro-independence, pro-internationalist and anti-imperialist party. It is unrepresented in the **Scottish Parliament** but has one member in the **European Parliament,** in both cases its cause being helped by pro-portional-voting systems.

**SEA**  see **Single European Act**

**second-order elections**  Second-order elections are contests other than general elections, for example local and regional ones. Some voters take the view that these are less important than first-order ones, because they do not determine which party is in government. They therefore feel free to take the opportunity to punish the current governing parties. Their protest may be registered by abstention or voting for different (often minor) parties. Elections to the **European Parliament** are also considered to be second-order national elections. Again, voters use their choices for representatives to the Strasbourg body to send signals to their national governments.

**secondary legislation**  see **primary legislation**

**secondary picketing**  The picketing of firms not themselves party to an industrial dispute, banned by the Conservative Government in the Employment Act 1990.

**Section 28 of the Local Government Act**  By the contentious Section 28 (Clause 2A) of its 1988 Local Government Act, the **Thatcher Government** prohibited the 'promotion of homosexuality in schools'. The clause was offensive to many sections of the community and was repealed in the **United Kingdom** in 2000.

**select committee**  A parliamentary committee which possesses a strong scrutiny role, of the type introduced in the **House of Commons** in 1979 and now an established feature of the political landscape. Established on a departmentally related basis, there are currently 18. They exist to 'examine the expenditure, administration and policy' of the relevant department and associated public bodies. Enthusiasts for the system see their creation as perhaps the most important step taken towards improving the scope for the House of Commons to scrutinise the workings and policies of **government** in an effective manner. They conduct enquiries, publish reports and, at best, operate on a bipartisan basis.

**selective benefit**  A state benefit distributed according to individual circumstances such as age, income or disability. The most controversial aspect of benefits targeted by income is that the process of application to receive them involves some kinds of means test.

**separation of powers**  The idea that the legislative **power**, the **executive** power and the judicial power of any **state** should be placed in separate hands, through the creation of three independent branches of **government**.

    The doctrine was advocated by the French Enlightenment thinker Montesquieu in the eighteenth century in his classic book *L'Esprit des lois*. He felt that it was desirable to keep the three branches separate, for this would provide a safeguard against too much concentration of power in one single authority. By fragmenting power, **liberty** could be defended and tyranny kept at bay. He based his assessment on his understanding of the British system, and felt that in Britain good administration derived from the fact that no one person or body could control the three arms. Each could exercise control over the other. Montesquieu's ideas much influenced the writing of the American **Constitution**.

In Britain there is not the clear separation of powers which Montesquieu detected. In reality there is a considerable overlap between the three branches. For instance: the heads of the executive (the **Prime Minister** and members of the **Cabinet**) are drawn from, and sit in, **Parliament**; some judicial functions are exercised by an elected politician, the Home Secretary (for example, the prerogative of mercy) and leading members of the **judiciary** are appointed by the Prime Minister (for example, the **law lords,** who constitute the final court of appeal and yet sit in the **legislature**); and the **Lord Chancellor** has powers in all three branch of Government (he is a member of the Cabinet, the senior figure in the judiciary and sits in the **House of Lords** where he acts as **Speaker**). These judicial aspects have been addressed in the **Constitutional Reform Act** (2005).

**separatism** The quest to secede from a political formation with a view to establishing an independent **state**. The **Scottish National Party** prefers the term 'independence' to separatism as a description of its goal. In its view, the term implies that there will be no cooperation with England, Wales and Northern Ireland should their aspiration be achieved.

**September 11th attacks on the World Trade Center** Often referred to as the events of 9/11. The attacks comprised a series of coordinated suicide terrorist assaults upon the United States (US), carried out on Tuesday, 11 September 2001. That morning, terrorists associated with **al-Qaeda** hijacked four commercial aeroplanes. Operating in teams which each included a trained pilot, the 19 hijackers then launched 4 attacks. Two planes crashed into the Trade Center in New York, one targeting each of its Twin Towers. A third flew into the Pentagon (in Virginia), whilst the fourth crashed into a field in rural Pennsylvania. None of the 246 people on board the hijacked planes survived and in all almost 3,000 were killed or presumed dead.

Within the US, opinion quickly rallied to the President in the face of external aggression, enabling the easy passage of emergency **legislation** and the introduction of a policy of rescue, recovery and compensation. Abroad, there was a wave of sympathy for the American people from governments and media outlets worldwide. Within a month, a '**coalition** of the willing' had been assembled, resulting in troops entering Afghanistan, the first step in the **war on terror**. Their brief was to hunt al-Qaeda terrorists and their leader Osama bin Laden and to topple the Taliban regime that had harboured them.

The axis of Tony **Blair** and George Bush that has so shaped world events in the last few years was cemented by the attacks. The **Prime Minister** was seen as a dependable ally and articulate salesman for US/**United Kingdom** policy. From the start he believed in a forceful response to world **terrorism** and as a 'progressive' of the centre-left he was able to reach out to peoples in parts of the world that the President could not. The repercussions of 9/11 are to be found in the drive for further and stricter **anti-terrorist legislation**, a global view that tends to link terrorism in one country with terrorism elsewhere and in Britain and the United States sporadic signs of **Islamophobia**.

**Sewel convention** The Sewel convention (or motions) refers to a mechanism created by the **Scotland Act** 1998. The convention – named after the **minister** responsible for the idea – applies when the **Executive** hands a decision or debate on a devolved matter over to Westminster. The intention was for the motions to be used only in discussion of non-controversial matters, for the purposes of legislative economy and for clarity. Their critics – often found in the **Scottish National Party** – claim that they have been used for more contentious issues where the Executive does not wish to allow the **Scottish Parliament** to consider an issue in detail, to avoid any adverse political consequences and to confine the legislative bickering to Westminster only. For these reasons, they are said to stifle debate, acting as a means of making unsuitable English policy apply north of the border and thereby preventing the taking of Scottish decisions on Scottish issues.

**sex discrimination legislation** In 1975, the Labour **Government** supplemented its equal pay legislation with the Sex Discrimination Act which among other things sought to outlaw discrimination in recruitment, training and fringe benefits. It also provides for protection against direct and indirect discrimination on the basis of sex or marital status. The Act established an **Equal Opportunities Commission** to monitor the workings of this statute and the equal pay **legislation** and to investigate allegations of discrimination.

See also: **Equal Pay Act**

**SF** see **Sinn Féin Party**

**Shadow Cabinet** The frontbench spokespersons of the official **HM Opposition Party**. They seek to present themselves as an alternative team of **ministers** to the existing **Government**.

**Short money** A subsidy designed to help opposition parties perform their parliamentary duties. Named after the Leader of the **House of Commons** who introduced it in 1975 (for the same reason known as Cranleigh money in the **House of Lords**), the amount payable to any party is calculated according to the number of seats and votes won at the previous election.

**simple plurality system**  see **single-member system**

**single currency** The euro, the currency in operation in 12 countries of the **European Union** but not Denmark, Sweden, the **United Kingdom** or the ten new entrants, some of which are planning for its early use.

A timetable for the introduction of a single currency was laid down in the **Maastricht Treaty**. Britain opted out of the single currency, which was originally to be called the ecu but which has been known as the euro since the Madrid summit of December 1995. It was introduced in 1999 by 11 countries, Greece joining in 2002 at the time when euro notes and coins became the sole currency in use in the 'eurozone', sometimes known as 'euroland'.

**Single European Act (SEA)** (1986) The SEA came into force in July 1987, the first substantial revision of the **Treaty of Rome**. The main changes introduced were: the establishment of December 1992 as the deadline for the establishment of a single market, 'an area without internal frontiers in which the free movement of goods, persons, services and capital is ensured'; the introduction of **cohesion**; a recognition of the importance of environmental policy; the extension of **qualified majority voting** (QMV); and modest new **powers** for the **European Parliament**.

The Act has subsequently proved controversial in Britain, for by providing for the introduction of QMV it meant that in certain areas of policy, **European Union legislation** could be enforced without British representatives in Brussels ever having agreed to it.

Further reading: N. Nugent, *The Government and Politics of the European Union*, Palgrave, 2003

**single-issue politics** The concentration on single **issue**s of popular concern and interest such as abortion, animal welfare and the abolition of foxhunting, rather than on the advancement of broad programmes. Many single-issue **pressure group**s have developed in recent years. Some, like that which launched the **Snowdrop campaign,** have disappeared once their goal is attained. Preoccupation with individual issues is appealing to campaigners, who can often create or articulate moral concern and attract media interest for their cause.

**single-member system** Also known as simple plurality system or **first past the post** (FPTP). An electoral system in which the candidate who gets the most votes in a **single-member constituency** is declared the winner, regardless of whether he or she had an absolute majority. The system is used in Westminster elections and also in Canada, India and the United States. Supporters associate FPTP with effective **single-party government** and like the link it provides between a **Member of Parliament** (MP) and their constituents. Critics point out that under FPTP the outcome is distorted, the winning party enjoying an exaggerated victory at the expense of third and small parties who are under-represented. No British Government since 1945 has ever won a majority of the votes and many MPs are minority members, who were wanted by fewer people than did not want them. The debate over **electoral reform** was highlighted by the

2005 election in which Labour gained a comfortable major-ity on the basis of only 35.2 per cent of the popular vote.

Further reading: D. Farrell, *Electoral Systems: A Comparative Introduction*, Palgrave, 2001

**single-member constituency** Or single-member electoral dis-trict. Constituencies that have one representative each in **Parliament**. For their use in practice, see also **single-member system**.

**single-party government** **Government** based on a single **polit-ical party** which has a secure majority in the **legislature**. Supporters of the simple plurality electoral system (**first past the post**) admire the way in which it consistently delivers effective government based on one party that can be held responsible for what is done and left undone.

See also: **coalition, first past the post, minority gov-ernment**.

**single transferable vote** A form of **proportional representation** based on **multi-member constituencies**, used for European and local elections in Northern Ireland, local government elections in Scotland and for all elections in the Irish Republic and Malta. To get elected, the candidate needs to obtain a quota. The voter marks the candidates in order of preference on the ballot paper. The first preferences are then counted. Those with the quota are declared elected, their surplus votes being redistributed on the basis of the second preferences on their ballot papers to the remaining candidates. When no further candidate can be elected via these means, then candidates are eliminated from the bottom, one at a time. Their second preferences are then redistributed, until the remaining vacancies are filled.

Supporters claim that it enables voters to discriminate between candidates of the same party, thereby enhancing voter choice. It delivers a reasonably proportional result, depending on the size of constituency employed. As with other systems of proportional representation, it makes it easier for third parties to gain representation and **coalition government** more likely.

Further reading: D. Farrell, *Electoral Systems: A Comparative Introduction*, Palgrave, 2001

**Sinn Féin Party (SF)** An Irish nationalist, **republican** party formed in 1902 by Arthur Griffith, the words meaning 'we ourselves'. It was reorganised and re-invented at different times in the twentieth century, appearing in its present form in the 1970s as a party committed to the creation of a socialist united republic for the whole of Ireland. Having at one time justified the use of 'the armalite and the ballot paper', it now claims to reject political violence and under the leadership of Gerry **Adams** has participated in the peace process. In the past, Unionist leaders such as Ian **Paisley** were unimpressed by the claim, arguing that senior Sinn Féin members have continuing links with the **Irish Republican Army**.

Sinn Féin has fared well in recent elections in the province, winning five seats in the 2005 election. Its members do not take their seats at Westminster, for they do not accept the partition of Ireland or the **authority** of the British **Government** to rule in the six counties of the North. However, since May 2007 the party has been in a **power-sharing** agreement with the Democratic Unionist Party and is a partner in the devolved administration. Martin **McGuinness** is Deputy **First Minister** and three other members belong to Sinn Féin.

**sleaze** A popular term much used in the 1990s referring to dark, corrupt or improper behaviour of **ministers** and **Members of Parliament** (MPs), initially on the Conservative side of the House. Several episodes involved financial wrongdoing, others sexual behaviour. The revelations led to the establishment of the **Committee on Standards in Public Life**, in 1994. Labour campaigned strongly against sleaze in 1997 and promised to conduct a 'cleaner' style of government, but on various occasions – often involving the business interests of paymasters of the party – there has been public disquiet about the allegedly discreditable behaviour of MPs and party supporters. In 2006, the making of **life peers** was a cause of difficulty for ministers, when it became apparent that the nearly £14 million worth of loans Labour received in order to fight the election campaign often appeared to result in nomination for a place in the upper chamber.

See also: **Ecclestone affair, loans for peerages**

**Snowdrop campaign** Following the shootings in Dunblane primary school, a group of bereaved parents and their friends mounted the Snowdrop petition, followed by a whole series of other initiatives designed to attract publicity for their cause, the abolition of handguns. As an example of campaigning on **single-issue politics**, the activists were highly successful. Their efforts convinced Labour of the need to promise a ban in the 1997 election, a pledge honoured shortly after the party came to power. Snowdrop was then dissolved.

**SNP** see **Scottish National Party**

**Social Chapter** The Social Chapter was a protocol of the **Maastricht Treaty** committing 11 member states to 'the promotion of employment, improved living and working conditions, proper social protection, dialogue between management and labour, the development of human resources with a view to lasting high employment and the combating of exclusion'. On behalf of the British

Government, John **Major** opted out of the Social Chapter for – along with many Conservatives – he saw it as **socialism** by the back door.

Labour was committed to 'sign up' to the Chapter on coming to **power** and soon after the election of May 1997 announced that it would do so. At Amsterdam, the substance of the protocol was written into the **Treaty of Rome** (Articles 117–20). Since then, various initiatives have been introduced in Britain under its auspices, notably those dealing with works councils, parental leave and regulations for part-time workers. However, a number of rightwing business leaders and politicians remain uneasy about the **European Union**'s social agenda, which is seen as a threat to enterprise.

**social class**  The broad division of society into strata based on income and related socio-economic criteria. A class is a group of people who share a common social position and economic interests.

Class is often defined by the occupational category a person occupies – the categorisation used by the Registrar General in assessing census returns – but background, education, income, lifestyle, property ownership and speech are among other determinants. Today, there is much more mobility between social classes as people born into a working-class background may, because of their educational opportunities, end up with a degree and qualify for entry into one of the middle-class professions.

Voting in Britain was traditionally much influenced by social class. It still is, but the relationship is much weaker and less clear cut than a few decades ago.

**social democracy**  A moderate, reformist strand of **socialism** that favours a balance between the market and the **state**, rather than the wholesale abolition of **capitalism**.

Originally deriving from Marxian socialism, social democracy has become associated with revisionism that allows for the possibility of peaceful change as a means of attaining the end goal, rather than revolution. In Britain, most members of the political **Left** argue that capitalism can be transformed and fundamental social and political change achieved by a gradualist approach to reform. Some still describe themselves as socialists, but in the postwar era 'social democracy' was increasingly the term commonly applied to those on the centre-right of the party who were uninterested in public ownership but favoured movement towards a more equal society.

According to its **constitution**, Labour has always been a social democratic party.

**Social Democratic Party** In Britain, the social democratic wing of the **Labour Party** often criticised public owner-ship. In 1981, several **Members of Parliament** on the **right** of the party were uneasy at its drift to the **left** in opposition and its anti-European Community stance. The split led to the creation of a separate Social Democratic Party, which fought the 1983 and 1987 elections alongside the **Liberals** as members of the Alliance. The two parties merged in 1988 to form the **Liberal Democrat Party**, although a rump remained and kept the Social Democratic Party alive until it was finally dissolved in 1990.

**social exclusion** Refers to the experience of people who suffer from a combination of connected problems – bad health, family breakdown, inadequate education and skills, low incomes, poor housing and unemployment among them – which deter them from assuming a full role in society. A broader concept than poverty, it is nonetheless closely identified with it.

The **Blair Government** has established a Social Exclusion Unit in the Policy Department of **Ten Downing Street** to tackle the issues relating to those who fall through the safety net of welfare protection. In 2006, responsibility for social exclusion was given to a **minister** of **Cabinet** rank.

**socialism**  One of the major Western ideologies, socialism is a product of modern industrial **capitalism**. Under a socialist system, the means of production, distribution and exchange would be **state** owned and controlled on behalf of all of the people, so that the wealth could be distributed more fairly.

Socialist theory argues for the collective ownership or control of key parts of the economy, state economic planning and state provision of basic services, but it opposes complete state control of the economy (the command economy) as is associated with communist regimes and favours the retention of large areas of economic, social and political and economic life beyond state interference.

For socialists, the most important goal is to provide a high quality and relatively equal standard of living for all **citizens**. Each individual is encouraged to increase the collective good of all, in an environment that encourages cooperation and sharing. **Government** plays a crucial role as it attempts to use its allocation of values and control of resources to increase the material, social and political **equality** of all citizens.

In Britain, a number of socialist parties were formed in the late nineteenth century, some of which combined with the **trades unions** in 1900 to form the Labour Representation Committee, later renamed as the **Labour Party**. Labour has always adopted a gradualist approach to socialism, those on the **left** associating the idea with public ownership, those on the **right** preferring to emphasise the commitment to a more equal and just society. **New Labour** describes itself as a democratic socialist party in the revised version of **Clause IV** of its **constitution,** although most writers would be wary of calling it socialist in any meaningful sense.

**social movement** Movements comprise a large body of people who organise themselves in support of some broad area of policy such as **environmentalism, feminism** or single-sex relationships. Those who involve themselves in such causes often provide a radical critique of mainstream societies and institutions and are interested in finding different ways of organising political activity. They tend to exhibit a high level of commitment and political activism. Such social movements existed in the nineteenth century but those of the present time are often referred to as **new social movement**s. The 'old' social movements of the nineteenth century included a myriad of small groups and combinations that were protesting against harsh industrial conditions, with workers struggling to achieve a new social order in which they could enjoy better living and working conditions. They were challenging the dominant ideas and **power** structure of their day.

**soundbite** A short saying, full of concentrated meaning, which consists of a few easily remembered words and yet conveys a particular message. The Reverend Jesse Jackson is a master of 'soundbitese'. Recognising that he will get perhaps 15 seconds on a news bulletin, he can summarise his argument in an exciting epigram. His rhyming soundbite 'we're going to have demonstrations without hesitation and jail without bail' was a more memorable and catchy way of saying 'we are not going to spend a long time deciding whether to have a demonstration. We are willing to go to jail for our cause and will not accept bail'.

In Britain, an oft-quoted soundbite is that of Tony **Blair** when he was an Opposition spokesman on home affairs: 'Tough on crime and tough on the causes of crime'. Another is his 'Education, education, education', summarising the priorities of his new administration in 1997.

**sovereignty** Complete or supreme **power**. The idea is that a country or institution is sovereign if it is free to act as it wishes, independently of the way other bodies or countries choose to behave. National sovereignty implies that British **governments** can in theory determine British policy, acting freely and unilaterally. In reality, this **freedom** has inevitably been eroded in recent decades. Membership of **NATO** and the **European Union** (EU), and the ratification of the **European Convention on Human Rights**, all impair freedom of manoeuvre. In the modern world, governments seek to preserve real influence and – as with the relationship with the EU – might conclude that Britain has more influence in the world as a member than we would if we were outside and retained our national sovereignty. National sovereignty is today only a theoretical or nominal independence.

Membership of the EU has had a significant effect not only on national sovereignty, but also on **parliamentary sovereignty**.

**Speaker** The impartial officer who presides over legislative bodies such as the **House of Commons**. In Britain, the Speaker is an experienced **Member of Parliament** (MP) who is elected to chair the proceedings of the House. Among the functions of the office, Speakers: call those who wish to participate in House debates, generally giving precedence to Privy Councillors but also acknowledging the interests of particular MPs and the period that has elapsed since they last addressed the House; try to ensure that parties receive a fair share of debate time and that opinions within parties are fairly represented; discipline MPs where necessary, making them apologise for unparliamentary language and even on occasion suspending them; and rule on points of parliamentary procedure. They do not themselves speak in debate.

To carry out such functions, incumbents need to be firm but fair, possess the confidence of the House, be able to follow the course of debates, have a knowledge and understanding of how **Parliament** works, and – ideally – a ready wit to defuse potentially difficult situations, when the atmosphere of the House is highly charged.

**Speaker's Conference** An all-party conference called to discuss matters which it is thought should be handled in a non-partisan way. Such conferences have been used to deal with issues of **electoral reform**, for example by the **Wilson Government**.

**special adviser** Special advisers have been used by all British **government**s of the last generation, their number nearly doubling after Labour's victory in the 1997 election. They are usually active members of the governing party, political appointees whose function is to add a political dimension to the advice **minister**s receive from civil servants. They provide support and political focus, assist and fortify ministers in exercising influence over the direction of policy, and ensure that it is presented in a favourable light from the party's point of view.

Their numbers and presence can cause tensions with officials in the relevant departments. In 2000, the **Neill Committee** recommended that the number of special advisers appointed by the government should be limited, perhaps to around 100 – more than 20 more than are presently on the payroll. He pointed to the danger that their authority might outweigh that of objective advisers (civil servants) and urged that their activities be subject to a code of conduct to spell out the relationship between special advisers, the media and ministers. The code should make it clear that all advisers have a duty to uphold the impartiality of the **Civil Service**.

**special relationship**  A term used to describe the warm political and diplomatic relations between the United States (US) and some Western nations, particularly **Great Britain**. The relationship has been the centrepiece of British foreign policy in the post-1945 era. It is based on bonds of culture, history and language, as well as a perceived similarity of political interest and outlook. Its strength has varied according to the leadership on both sides of the Atlantic, but the ties between **Churchill** and President Roosevelt, **Macmillan** and Kennedy, **Thatcher** and Reagan, **Blair** and Clinton/George W. Bush have been particularly close and strong.

The personal understanding and political cooperation of the British and US leadership in 1939–45 was based on a common desire to defeat Fascist aggression. After the war, the countries were even more closely bonded by the growing threat posed by the Soviet Union, as the **Cold War** developed. Once the Cold War was over, the need for such close military cooperation initially no longer seemed as great a priority, but the Iraqi invasion of Kuwait brought the two countries into battle on the same side once more. The aftermath of the **September 11th attacks on the World Trade Center**, including the **war on terror** and the decision to go to war with Iraq in 2003, showed how supportive Britain was of the American position.

Europeans, perhaps especially the British, have always been tempted to overrate their importance in American eyes to whom the term 'special relationship' might cause confusion, especially for those living on the West coast. But members of several American administrations continue to regard Britain as not only a loyal ally, but also a useful bridge between the US and the **European Union**, as Britain has important links with both.

See also: **first Gulf war, Iraq war**

**spin**  Spin is a term which originated in the United States and derives from the spin applied by baseball pitchers to make the ball go in a particular direction. First applied to politics in the late 1970s, it refers to the attempt to give a favourable slant to an item of news or potentially unpopular policy on behalf of a particular personality or policy. Although the phrase is relatively new, putting a gloss on the way information is presented and seeking to manage expectations are traditional political practices.

Spin can be counter-productive when its use becomes a more important story than the one that politicians are trying to present in the best possible light, a problem which came to afflict the **Blair Government** whose spokespersons regularly employed the art of spinning.

Spin doctors are public-relations experts whose task it is to change the way the public perceives an **issue** or event. They try to manipulate the news and encourage favourable media coverage for the party and its leader.

**spin doctor**  see **spin**

**SSP**  see **Scottish Socialist Party**

**stakeholding**  A concept deriving from management theory, by which it was suggested that a firm's obligations are not just to the shareholders to maximise company profits, but also to others with a stake in the enterprise, notably employees, customers, suppliers and the community it serves.

In the stakeholder society, everyone has a stake and nobody is excluded. In politics, the term was made fashionable by economist Will Hutton and taken up by Tony **Blair** and **New Labour**, spokespersons for whom inclusion became a key buzz word. Hutton was influenced by the perception that the heavy emphasis upon the free market during the Conservative years had created a society in which there was a widening gap between rich and poor, with consequent social division and a growing sense of exclusion among those who were deprived or insecure.

Further reading: W. Hutton, *The State We're In*, Vintage, 1996

**standing committee** Committees of the British **Parliament** used for a variety of legislative business, including the detailed consideration of **Bills** and the handling of **secondary legislation**; a number are appointed for each parliamentary session.

Standing committees examine Bills after their second reading to make them more acceptable for their third reading. They comprise party members in proportion to numbers in the House and are known as standing committee A, B, C and so on, each having 30 or so members. A Bill awaiting its committee state is sent to the next available committee, meaning that the hearings are conducted by non-specialists. See also **select committees**, whose membership is more expert, for **Members of Parliament** sitting on them handle issues within the same policy area all of the time.

**state** The legal notion of the state is that is a political association that establishes sovereign jurisdiction within defined territorial borders. The term 'country' usually refers to a state's territory and population, rather than its **government**. We normally use 'a' state when we refer to a country and 'the' state when we refer to its institutions.

States are distinguished from other forms of association in that: they have a territory over which they claim absolute legal **authority** or **sovereignty** and will recognise no higher or competing authority – in effect, sovereignty here means independence; states have a monopoly on the legitimate use of violence to enforce the **law**s and decisions of the society; and membership of the state is compulsory, something we are born into – we are as members of a state subject to one government that has authority over us.

**statute law** The **law** which is contained within acts of **Parliament** and **secondary legislation**, in contrast to European law or **common law**, the law which is contained in judicial opinions.

**statutory instrument** The most important form of **secondary** (or delegated) **legislation**. It enables the **minister** to exercise their right deriving from a particular statute to make **law** for certain purposes.

**Stormont** The seat of the devolved Northern Ireland **parliament** and administrative offices of the Northern Ireland **government**.

There was a parliament in existence prior to direct rule, often known as 'the Stormont Parliament'. The operation of the new evolved machinery following the **Good Friday Agreement** has been suspended on four occasions and remains so at the time of writing.

**sub-national government** All of the tiers of **government** below the national level. This includes any **state** or regional government, **local government** and any neigh-bourhood or community government.

In the **United Kingdom,** the elected tiers include the devolved governments that operate in Scotland and Wales, the **Greater London Assembly** and the local-government units of various types, ranging from the large metropolitan districts to smaller town councils.

**subsidiarity** A description of a political system in which the functions of **government** are carried out at the lowest appropriate level for efficient administration – at the closest level possible to the people affected by the decision; the idea that each level of government has its suit-able geographical level.

Subsidiarity is believed to enhance **democracy.** Germans would portray it as the very essence of **federalism** but – post-Maastricht – Majorite Conservatives saw its adoption as a means of fending off a more deeply integrated and federal **European Union.**

**Suez crisis** (1956) A conflict over control of the Suez Canal in which an alliance of France, Israel and the **United Kingdom** was pitted against Egypt. In 1956, Egyptian President Colonel Nasser nationalised the Suez Canal Company which operated the canal. The British and French **government**s feared that he might close the canal and cut off petroleum shipments which were vital to its economic and trading interests in the region. In concert with Israel, they secretly prepared military action to regain control of the canal and if possible depose Nasser as well.

British forces were sent to Port Said but the armed action quickly ended when it became apparent that the United States (US) would not back the **Eden** Government. There was in addition considerable anxiety among **Commonwealth** countries.

The enforced withdrawal of forces marks an important stage in postwar British history, for the failure of the action to achieve its goals exposed the limitations of Britain as a **Great Power**. It encouraged some politicians to turn away from reliance on the **special relationship** with the US and – over a period of time – to contemplate joining with those European countries who were actively engaged in a drive towards economic and political cooperation.

Suez was a bitterly divisive issue in Britain, some people strongly opposing the initial intervention, others lamenting the humiliating withdrawal. It seriously damaged the reputation of **Prime Minister** Eden who resigned soon afterwards.

**suffrage** The legal right to vote in public elections. Hence suffragists and suffragettes were women who campaigned for the vote, the former by using quiet, constitutional means involving pamphleteering and addressing meetings, the latter being also willing to engage in methods of **direct action** and law-breaking, such as disrupting parliamentary proceedings, smashing shop windows, cutting telephone wires, planting bombs, setting fire to the contents of letterboxes and damaging pictures and statues in art galleries.

**Sunningdale Agreement** (1973) The agreement reached by the **Heath** Conservative **Government** to establish a **power-sharing executive** in Northern Ireland possessing many domestic functions in which Unionist and Social Democratic and Labour Party (SDLP) representatives worked together. The agreement on power-sharing split the Unionist party, more hard-line loyalists preferring a return to old-style **Stormont** politics in which Unionism was a dominant force.

The executive, led by Brian Faulkner, survived for four months, before being brought down in 1974 by a workers general strike which brought the province to a standstill.

**supply days** Now usually referred to as Opposition days, these are the 20 days set aside in each parliamentary session on which the opposition selects the topics for parliamentary debate.

**supplementary vote** Used in Sri Lanka for presidential elections and for elections to the mayoralty of Greater London, the supplementary vote represents a cross between the French double ballot and the **alternative vote** (AV). In Britain, it would allow the existing 646 constituencies to express a second preference on their ballot paper. If no candidate obtains an overall majority, then the second preferences of all but the top two candidates would be counted and redistributed to those who remain. Effectively, it is a speeded-up version of the French presidential method, for it spares the voter the necessity of making a second excursion to the polling booth. It shares many of the advantages and disadvantages of the AV system.

Further reading: D. Farrell, *Electoral Systems: A Comparative Introduction*, Palgrave, 2001

**supranationalism** A system of **government** under which some form of transnational organisation such as the **European Union** (EU) is able to impose its will on member nation states which agree to pool their **sovereignty** in specified areas. Supranational institutions within the EU such as the European Commission and the European Parliament examine issues from a European rather than a national point of view.

By joining the Union, Britain agreed to the transfer of powers to the EU in which there is joint decision-making in several policy sectors.

**sustainable development** Development capable of being maintained at a steady level without exhausting natural resources or causing severe ecological damage. The term was first developed by the **United Nations** Commission on the Environment and Development 1987, in its report 'Our Common Future', in which a sustainable society was defined as one that 'meets the needs of the present, without compromising the ability of future generations to meet their own needs'.

**swing voter**  see **floating voter**

# T

**tabloid**  Tabloids are small newspapers such as the *Sun* that convey information in a sensational style, with bold or even lurid headlines. Stories are often about figures in sport and entertainment. They are presented in a salacious manner and may be shamelessly biased, the style being designed to have popular appeal to readers whose attention span and/or available time may be limited. Lively presentation is intended to help the paper in the 'ratings war' with other papers of the genre.

Whereas the *Daily Express* and *Daily Mail* have black nameplates, tabloids such as the *Sun*, the *Daily Mirror* and *Daily Star* have red nameplates, hence their popular label as 'redtops'. These papers are usually written in simpler language, are more sensationalist and have more pictures than 'blacktops'.

**tactical voting** The practice of voting for a candidate other than the voter's first preference, in order to keep out another candidate of whom the voter particularly disapproves. A Labour supporter in a seat where the Liberal Democrats are the most effective challenger to the Conservatives might vote tactically for the Liberal Democrats. Having assessed the candidates' relative strength, the voter would be voting for a second-choice party with a better chance of winning than their first choice, thereby increasing the chance of defeating the Conservatives, the party most disliked. Tactical voting worked to the advantage of the centre-left parties and the disadvantage of the Conservatives in 1997 and to a lesser extent again in 2001.

**targeted benefit**    see **selective benefit**

**taxonomy** Most political analysis begins with a taxonomy, a set of categories that classifies phenomena or data (for example, the different varieties of **pressure group**s) into different types. Categories should ideally be exhaustive, mutually exclusive and differentiated by consistent criteria. The categories of any taxonomy establish the crucial concepts that structure the analysis.

**tendency** Tendencies are groupings within a **political party** that are less cohesive than **faction**s. They are looser organisations of people who adopt a broadly similar approach on some issue and campaign to persuade the party to move towards its viewpoint. Within the **Conservative Party**, an example would be the **Bruges Group** that stresses the need for a Europe of independent nations.

**Ten Downing Street** The residence and office of the **Prime Minister** of the **United Kingdom**, situated in the City of

Westminster. It is actually the official residence of the First Lord of the Treasury but in modern times this post has always been held simultaneously with the office of Prime Minister. Number Ten is the centre of the British **government**, physically and politically. As well as being the Prime Minister's home, it is also his place of work. It has offices for himself, his secretaries, assistants and advisors, and numerous conference rooms and dining rooms where he meets with and entertains other British leaders and foreign dignitaries.

**Ten Minute Rule** Also known as Standing Order No. 23. A procedure in Parliament for the introduction of **private members' Bills**.

**terrorism** The use of premeditated violence. It employs methods such as bombing, hijacking, kidnapping, murder and torture to spread fear and horror in the service of political ends. Those who practise it tend to see themselves as freedom fighters for a particular cause. The victims may be carefully targeted by organised cells or they may innocents who were present in the area at the time.

In Britain, terrorism has been used in the past by groups such as the **Irish Republican Army**. Whereas Irish **republicans** used it in their bid to achieve a political or strategic goal, today's Islamic terrorism is of a different order. Those who perpetrated the attacks in London on 7 July 2005 and a fortnight later, arguably the worst in British history, made no demands concerning grievances that could be addressed. As with previous attacks in Madrid, Bali and New York, this seemed to be – from a Western perspective – arbitrary and nihilistic brutality. Moreover, it was the first example of suicide bombing on British soil. The suicide bomber represents a unique kind of threat: an enemy that does not fear being captured or killed is always bound to be potent.

See also: **al-Qaeda, London bombings, Prevention of Terrorism Act**

**Thatcher, Margaret** (1925– ) Margaret Thatcher became a Conservative **Member of Parliament** in 1959. She served as Secretary of State for Education and Science under Edward **Heath** whom she successfully challenged for the leadership following the party's second electoral defeat in 1974. In opposition, she became associated with **New Right** policies and in her victorious **general election** campaign in 1979 urged a radical change of direction after years of drift and **consensus politics**. A strong conviction politician, she had a number of distinctive policies which later were collectively labelled **Thatcherism**. As **Prime Minister,** she was a domineering figure whose performance did much to fuel the debate about **prime ministerial government**. Her personal style and performance did and still do arouse sharply contrasting views, some seeing her as divisive and harsh, others as someone who was not afraid to lead. It is evident in such observations as: 'Standing in the middle of the road is very dangerous; you get knocked down by the traffic from both sides'; 'To me, consensus seems to be the process of abandoning all beliefs, principles, values and policies'; and 'U-turn if you want to. The lady's not for turning'.

For several years she was an electoral asset to the **Conservative Party**. She won three successive general elections, until then the only British politician to do this in the twentieth century. However, although she had strong support from the largest minority of voters for most of her tenure she was eventually elected out of leadership by her own party and replaced by John **Major** in 1990. Her popularity had finally declined when she replaced the unpopular **local government** rates (a tax on property) with the even less popular **community charge,** more commonly known as the poll tax. At the same time the Conservative Party had also begun to split over her sceptical approach towards the **European Union** (then Community). A **life peer** since 1992, Baroness Thatcher has given her name to an era, an indication of the impact she had on both Conservative and British politics. She was the longest-serving British Prime Minister since Gladstone, and had the longest single period in office since Lord Liverpool (1812–27). She is also the only woman to be **United Kingdom** prime minister or leader of a major British **political party**.

Further reading: P. Hennessy, *The Prime Minister*, Allen Lane, 2000

**Thatcherism** Margaret **Thatcher** gave her name to a set of political attitudes and a style of leadership that became known as Thatcherism. Even before coming to **power** she was nicknamed the 'Iron Lady' in Soviet media (because of her vocal opposition to communism), an appellation that stuck. The profound changes Thatcher set in motion as **Prime Minister** altered much of the economic and cultural landscape of the **United Kingdom** (UK). She curtailed the power of the **trades unions**, cut back the role of the **state** in business, dramatically expanded home ownership, and helped to create a more entrepreneurial culture. She also aimed to cut back the **welfare state** and foster a more flexible labour market that would create jobs and could adapt to market conditions. Exacerbated by the global recession of the early 1980s, such policies initially caused large-scale unemployment, especially in the industrial heartlands of northern England and the coalfields of South Wales, and increased wealth inequalities. However, from the mid-1980s, a period of sustained economic growth occurred that led to an improvement in the UK's economic performance for which supporters of

Margaret Thatcher claim she was responsible. They also laud her policy of **privatisation** as part of a drive to introduce popular **capitalism**.

In foreign relations, she supported the 'special relationship' with the United States and formed a close bond with Ronald Reagan. In 1982 her **Government** dispatched a Royal Navy task force to retake the Falkland Islands from Argentina in the Falklands War. Her role as war-leader enabled her to adopt the Churchillian mantle and hone her developing image as a strong, formidable leader. She became increasingly antagonistic towards the **European Union** (then Community) as her premiership developed, her views being set out in her **Bruges** speech.

There has always been debate as to whether Thatcherism was more a matter of style or substance. The strength of her personality and the rhetoric she employed made it sound as though she were an agent of fundamental transformation. For all of her single-mindedness and clear vision of what she wanted to achieve, she was not totally inflexible and did not always go as far in shifting the direction of policy as she might have wished. She had a shrewd sense of what the public would accept, a quality that only failed her over the introduction of the **community charge**.

Further reading: A. Gamble, *The Free Economy and the Strong State: The Politics of Thatcherism*, Palgrave, 1994; P. Hennessy, *The Prime Minister*, Allen Lane, 2000

**think-tank** A group formed to research and develop policy proposals and campaign for their acceptance among opinion formers and policy makers. Think-tanks are often ideologically based, their ideas sometimes being influential with the parties with which they share a broad affinity. They become especially important after 1970, when organisations such as the Institute of Economic

Affairs and the Centre for Policy Studies pushed for radical changes in social and economic policy and exerted intellectual influence on Conservative thinking. Think-tanks associated with progressive politics include Demos and the Institute for Public Policy Research.

**third way** The doctrine advanced by Anthony Giddens which seeks to transcend the old ideological cleavage of **capitalism** and **socialism** and create a middle way that blends economic efficiency and social **justice**. The idea of a 'third way' is not entirely new. Harold **Macmillan** adopted a middle way for the **Conservative Party** in the 1930s. Essentially, the third way is an attempt to find a middle route between **left** and **right**, between the unrestrained free market and **state** planning. It appeals to centre-left progressives and moderate social democrats.

The third way is the theoretical basis of the **Blair Government**'s thinking and vision for the reshaping of British politics and society. It is also a strategy about creating a new left-of-centre progressive consensus in Britain and elsewhere. Its exponents share a commitment to practical **social democracy**. Shunning an excess of **ideology**, they proclaim that 'what matters is what works'.

Further reading: A. Giddens, *The Third Way: The Renewal of Social Democracy*, Polity, 1998

**Third World** A phrase first used in the early 1950s to distinguish nations that were not aligned to the West or the Soviet Union in the **Cold War**. However, it became increasingly applied to countries that lagged behind in their economic development, being less industrialised or technologically advanced than more prosperous nations.

Today, 'Third World' is much less used, commentators opting for 'developing', 'less developed' or 'undeveloped' world instead. The term is inappropriate because some of the countries once described as belonging to that category became the 'Asian tigers' of the late twentieth century. Some development workers now refer to the 'two-thirds world', as that is the proportion of the world which is underdeveloped.

**three-day week** (January–February 1974) As a result of industrial action by the National Union of Mineworkers (NUM) in pursuit of wage demands, coal supplies were dwindling in late 1973. The **Heath Government** was unable to reach agreement with NUM leaders and – fearing a total shutdown if power supplies ran out – introduced a three-day week for manufacturing industry as part of its attempt to curb usage of electricity. Politically, the conflict with the miners and anxiety over the impact on industrial production damaged the administration, contributing to the Conservative defeat when Heath called a snap election in February 1974.

See also: **miners' strike**

*Today* **programme** The **BBC**'s long-running early-morning flagship news and current affairs programme, broadcast on Radio 4 every day from Monday to Saturday. It comprises regular news bulletins, serious political interviews and in-depth reports. Its discussions are often thought to set the political agenda for the day, leading as they do to follow-up analysis on later radio and television programmes.

**Ministers**, their shadows and other politicians are often listeners and are keen to go on the programme and air their views. However, some male interviewers have attracted criticism for excessively tough interrogation, even bias. In the past, Brian Redhead and more recently John Humphrys have been viewed as unduly confrontational and hostile to the government of the day. In 2003, controversy arose after a report by correspondent Andrew **Gilligan** included the allegation that – with the active connivance of Alastair **Campbell** – ministers had deliberately exaggerated the case for war with Iraq, including in a dossier information they knew to be untrue.

See also: **Iraq war**

**Tory** In the late 1670s there was a proposal to exclude Charles II's younger brother James from the throne because of his avowed Catholicism. Those who supported his succession were accused of being sympathetic to the Catholic Church. Tory was an originally abusive name used to describe Irish Catholic outlaws who lived in the middle, 'bog' counties of Ireland, hence the literal meaning 'bog trotters'. The term has tended to be employed to describe a Conservative of a more reactionary kind, the literary Dr Johnson characterising a Tory as someone 'with an instinctive reverence for what was established, a respect for **government** and the **Crown**, a loyalty towards the Church of England and a prejudice in favour of the landed interest'.

Today, Tory remains a popular name for a member of the **Conservative Party**, being often used to describe a person who espouses traditional rather than modern Conservative values. The term is often used by the party's opponents, to remind people of allegedly unsympathetic, harsh and uncaring rightwing governments.

**trade union** An organisation created with the intention of obtaining the best possible living standards and working conditions for its members. Trades unions were legalised by an Act of **Parliament** in 1824 but for many years struggle to achieve full legal recognition and protection. Today, individual unions such as Amicus and UNISON are involved in collective bargaining over wage levels and in discussions about hours, manning levels, redundancies, the introduction of new technology, security of employment and other **issues** relating to their members' interests.

Trades unions have in most countries suffered from a shrinking membership, partly as a result of the decline of manufacturing, with new, less-unionised service industries becoming ever more significant in many economies. As a general trend, unions have failed to cater for the growing number of office workers and those in services (often small-scale and harder to motivate) but membership has suffered from other factors such as unemployment, public attitudes, the increase in the amount of part-time working, and the increased diversity of workforces in terms of qualifications and working conditions.

Trade union membership fell in Britain every year between 1979 and 1997, before rising each year until 2000 and remaining more or less static ever since. Union density – the proportion of a workforce that belongs to a union – actually rose in 2003 and 2005 for the first time since the 1970s. This is happening because organised labour is finally beginning to penetrate parts of the workforce that used to be off-limits, particularly professional workers and the voluntary sector.

**Trades Union Congress (TUC)** The central organisation representing British **trades unions**, an umbrella **interest group**.

The TUC held its first meeting in Manchester in 1868. Today, it has 66 affiliated trades unions and nearly 7 million members, approximately 19 per cent of the workforce. It is not an **executive** body, so that it can wield influence but not bind other unions to any of its resolutions. It is nominally politically independent, for it recognises that it must be ready to deal with whichever party is in **power**. But many of its member unions are affiliated to the **Labour Party** and the bulk of the membership is likely to incline to the **left** in their political attitudes.

The TUC's principal officer is the general secretary.

**transparency** Opening up decision-making, documents and institutions to the public gaze, with more openness in decision-making and improving access to information and documents.

**Treasury** see **HM Treasury**

**Treaty of Rome** see **Rome Treaty**

**tribunal** A quasi-judicial institution established to resolve conflict between public or private individuals or bodies. Tribunals are a means of avoiding the expensive and time-consuming needs of the courts and of settling a large number of relatively small, straightforward, routine cases.

Tribunals developed as a pattern of administrative **justice** in the twentieth century in response to the growth of **state** involvement in the social and economic life of the country. This created the possibility of the individual **citizen** coming into conflict with **minister**s and their departments, and local authorities, on questions of an administrative kind. Tribunals exist to arbitrate in such conflicts, whether it concerns the payment of benefits, disputes between a landlord and their tenant or the alleged malpractice of a doctor brought before the Disciplinary Committee of the General Medical Council.

**Trimble, David** (1944– ) Formerly a barrister, Trimble was the legal adviser to the Ulster Workers' Council during the strike which broke the **Sunningdale Agreement**. He was associated with hard-line unionism as a member of the Vanguard Progressive Unionist Party until its collapse. He then joined the **Ulster Unionist Party** (UUP) in 1978 which he led from 1995 until just after his **general election** defeat in May 2005; he had been a **Member of Parliament** at Westminster since 1990.

As leader of the UUP, Trimble showed flexibility and appeared to modify some previous attitudes. He was instrumental in persuading his party to accept the **Good Friday Agreement** and for his efforts shared the Nobel Peace prize in 1998. However, within his party, his stance was frequently questioned and his tenure as **First Minister** of the **Northern Ireland Assembly** was interrupted by its four suspensions. His party has lost much of its former influence, the principal beneficiaries of its decline being the Democratic Unionists.

**tripartism** An approach to economic policy in the 1970s which emphasises the need for consensual agreements between the Government, employers and the unions.

A loose, less centralised form of **corporatism** (and sometimes known as neo-corporatism) that involves close Government consultation with business organisations and the **trades unions** over the conduct of economic policy and in particular over wage and price restraint. It was operated under Governments of both British parties in the 1960s and 70s. It is a rather weaker variety of corporatism than that practised in parts of the continent where corporatist decision-making has often been institutionalised.

**Troubles** The label 'the Troubles' is sometimes applied to the events in southern Ireland at the time of the Irish struggle for independence after the end of World War One (1919–23). Here, it refers to the period of communal violence that lasted from the late 1960s until the late 1990s, culminating in the signing of the **Good Friday Agreement**

in 1998. The period has been variously described as one of low-intensity conflict to one of civil war. In these years, there was a continuation of sporadic incidents of armed conflict which sometimes took on a more dramatic and extremely violent character. Massive destruction was created by bombing and other activities, resulting in heavy casualties in Northern Irish towns and cities, both of innocent by-standers as well as those more personally committed. The conflict involved **paramilitary group**s representing elements on the **loyalist** and **republican** sides, the Royal Ulster Constabulary and the British Army, which was sent in to 'hold the ring' in the sectarian strife but soon found itself caught up in conflict with the **Irish Republican Army** and other paramilitary forces.

**TUC**  see **Trades Union Congress**

**turnout**  The proportion of people who turn out to vote in any election. Figures between countries vary, some showing the proportion of the registered electorate who vote, some the proportion of people over the lower voting age limit who do so. In some countries registration and voting is made easier than in others. In a few cases, it is compulsory.

Electoral turnout is variable, its level varying from country to country and – within Britain – from one type of election to another. It varies from one election to the next, across constituencies and **local government** wards and from person to person. Some people always vote, some occasionally do and some never vote.

In recent years, levels of turnout have been falling in much of the democratic world, Denmark and Sweden resisting the general trend which has been marked in **United Kingdom** (UK) **general election**s. UK turnout fell to a postwar low of 59.4 per cent in 2001, only slightly improving in 2005 (61.3 per cent). Turnout in Britain has tended for many years to be lower than on the continent.

**two-party system**  A type of **party system** in which two large parties dominate all others, so that only they have a chance of obtaining a majority of seats in the **legislature** and forming a **single-party government**. There will be other parties – some sizeable – but they have not in the past meaningfully competed for office. Such systems are encouraged by use of the **first past the post** electoral system.

Supporters claim that two-party systems promote effective, stable and strong government, simplify voter choice and make government clearly accountable to the electorate, for the voters know who to praise or blame for the policies in operation. Critics suggest that they restrict voter choice, make politics unduly adversarial and deny **justice** to third and other parties.

# U

**UDHR**  see **Universal Declaration of Human Rights**

**UK**  see **United Kingdom**

**UKIP**  see **United Kingdom Independence Party**

**Ulster Unionist Party (UUP)**  The UUP was for many years the largest party in Northern Ireland. It formed the governing party in the **Stormont** administration from 1921 to 1972. Members were united in their desire to maintain the **Parliament** and remain under British rule. After the fall of Stormont, the UUP suffered from a series of schisms that led to secession by breakaway groups, the issue of **power-sharing** often proving a thorny one. From the early 1980s, the UUP faced stiff electoral competition from the Democratic Unionist Party (DUP).

Led by David **Trimble**, the UUP continued to experience divisions over the party's constitutional policy and his willingness to engage in talks in which the **Sinn Féin Party** were represented, sign the **Good Friday Agreement** and lead the power-sharing **Executive** which has subsequently been suspended. Trimble resigned the leadership in 2005.

UUP fortunes have been on the wane in recent local, devolved, European and **general elections**, its paramountcy among unionists having been ceded to the DUP which – in the eyes of many inhabitants – adopted a tougher view in its approach to Sinn Féin, particularly over decommissioning.

**ultra vires** Literally, beyond the scope or in excess of the legal **power** or **authority** of an agency, corporation or tier of **government**. The legal doctrine which states that any public authority must act within the powers accorded it.

In British constitutional **law**, an act may be judicially reviewable if the administrator did not have the power to make a decision or the process of decision-making was conducted with procedural defects, or if there was an abuse of power (for example, through unreasonableness or bad faith). In municipal law, attempts at local **legislation** that go beyond the powers granted to local authorities are said to be ultra vires. In running and operating a school, the relevant local authority must comply with the procedural standards of administrative law. If it fails to do so – in other words, if the authority is acting beyond its powers – then the actions taken have no legal standing and will be actionable.

**UN** see **United Nations**

**unicameralism**  A political system in which there is only one chamber in the **legislature**. Unicameralism is the norm today, with around two-thirds of the world's **parliament**s falling into this category.

**unitary state**  A **state** in which there is no constitutional division of **sovereignty**, so that all **powers** derive from central **authority**. **Sub-national government**s, regional or local, may exist, but they do so only at the behest of the centre. National **government** can in theory abolish lower levels. Unitary systems normally exist in relatively homogeneous countries which lack significant ethnic, geographical, linguistic or religious distinctions. Most countries are unitary, examples being France, Israel and the **United Kingdom** (UK).

Countries such as France and the UK are sometimes classified as 'devolving unitary' states. There is some elected regional machinery with a degree of – but not necessarily uniform – autonomy. In the UK, power has been devolved to Scotland, Wales and – when the system is up and running – Northern Ireland; a system of **local government** exists too. But devolved and local power can be revoked. They operate at the behest of Westminster, to which they are entirely subordinate.

See also: **devolution**

**United Kingdom (UK)**  The official title of the sovereign **state**, the full version being the United Kingdom of Great Britain and Northern Ireland. '**Great Britain**' technically refers to the mainland only, although the term is sometimes used synonymously with United Kingdom. Apart from England, Scotland and Wales, other component parts of the UK are the province of Northern Ireland (the

British part of the partitioned island of Ireland), the Isle of Man and other small islands.

**United Kingdom Independence Party (UKIP)** The United Kingdom Independence Party (commonly known as UKIP, pronounced 'you kip') is a eurosceptic **political party** that aims at British withdrawal from the **European Union**. In the 2004 European Parliamentary elections, the party's profile was raised substantially in April and May 2004 by the surprise candidacy of former **Labour Party Member of Parliament** and chat show host Robert Kilroy-Silk. However, in January 2005, Kilroy-Silk headed a now-defunct breakaway movement which formed a new party, Veritas, with a broadly similar political outlook. UKIP has a few dozen local **councillors**, many of whom are defectors from other parties. In the 2004 elections it picked up two seats in the London Assembly and an impressive twelve in the **European Parliament**. It made no headway in the 2005 **general election**, fought under an electoral system that does not help small parties (**first past the post**).

See also: **europhobe, eurosceptic**

**United Nations (UN)** The international organisation established in October 1945, with the aims of avoiding war, preserving the fundamental rights of human beings and promoting the economic and social advancement of all peoples. Its headquarters is in New York, its chief official being the Secretary General, currently Kofi Annan. Membership is open to all 'peace-loving nations', there being 191 in 2006. Every member country has a seat in the General Assembly which meets once every year. Key decisions are taken by the Security Council which has five permanent members and a number of smaller powers elected for two years.

Britain retains the seat on the Security Council which it has held since the beginnings of the UN. Working alongside the United States, the **Blair Government** was unable to find sufficient support in the Council for a second resolution in favour of military action against Iraq in early 2003.

See also: **Iraq war**

**universal benefit** A benefit given to whole categories of a population, like children or old people, without any form of **means testing**. Universal benefits are administratively convenient. Proponents argue that they are simple, and also fair, because everyone has paid National Insurance contributions and should therefore receive benefits such as old age pensions, sickness and unemployment payments as a right. Opponents argue that such wide, blanket coverage makes them expensive and means that there is insufficient money available to help adequately those who are genuinely in need and who merit some special targeting.

**Universal Declaration of Human Rights (UDHR)** A declaration comprising 30 articles that was adopted by the United Nations General Assembly in December 1948. It set out the view of the **United Nations** on the **human rights** guaranteed to all people.

**universal suffrage** Also known as franchise. Refers to the extension of the right to vote, to all adults, without distinction as to **race**, sex, belief or social status. In most old established democracies, only a limited number of people at first had a say in the running of the **government** but the number of people who could vote increased gradually with time. The nineteenth century featured movements advocating universal male **suffrage** – the extension to all males regardless of **social class** or race. This right later spread to women in the twentieth century.

See also: **women and the right to vote**

**usual channels** The informal system by which the **whip**s of the major parties in the **House of Commons** arrange parliamentary business and communicate over matters of common interest to them.

**UUP** see **Ulster Unionist Party**

# V

**voting behaviour** The study of voting behaviour developed in the mid-twentieth century and was based on the new developments in survey research. Much has been written about the relationships between voting behaviour and **social class**, education, religion and social attitudes. Political scientists have developed various models to explain changes that have taken place in voting over recent decades, none of which explains voting patterns entirely.

Long-term influences include party identification and loyalty, social class and other factors relating to the social structure, such as age, gender, occupation, **race** and religion. Short-term influences include the economy, the personal qualities and appeal of the party leaders, the style and effectiveness of party campaigning, the impact of the **mass media**, and the events leading up to the election. Broadly, the long-term factors have declined in their importance in British politics and the short-term ones have assumed an increased significance.

The breakdown of the traditional associations has been of considerable importance for the parties that can no longer count on the support they once took for granted. The academic literature of the postwar era pointed to a positive relationship between membership of a social class and the way people cast their vote. However, from the 1970s onwards, the process of **class dealignment** was reflected in a reduction in Conservative support from the professional and managerial classes and a reduction in Labour support from the working classes. In 1997, Labour increased its support across all social classes and for some years it continued to broaden its appeal in Middle England. In 2005, it suffered a sharp decline in the number and percentage of votes it polled. Over the country as a whole: women rallied to Labour and the Liberal Democrats; younger voters (especially the under-35s, if they voted) overwhelmingly backed Labour or, in university constituencies, the Liberal Democrats; the over-65s inclined to the Conservatives; and in all classes other than AB and the C1s, Labour was ahead of its main rival.

Further reading: D. Denver, *Elections and Voters in Britain*, Palgrave, 2002

# W

**Wales Act** (1998) Following the **referendum** of September 1997 which narrowly approved the **Blair Government**'s **devolution** proposals, the Wales Act established the **Welsh National Assembly** in 1999. It transferred most of the rights, **powers** and duties of the Welsh Secretary to the new 60-member body which has delegated many of its **executive** Powers to nine **cabinet ministers** – headed by a **First Minister** – who together form the Welsh Assembly government.

**war on terror**  The global war on terror, or terrorism, has the stated objective of ending international **terrorism** by preventing groups said to be terrorist in nature from posing a threat and putting an end to **state** sponsorship of terrorism. The invasion of Afghanistan by United States and **NATO** forces was the first action of this war

The war had its origin in the attacks on the Twin Towers of 9/11 which **NATO** members saw as an attack upon them all. From the beginning, it was active in response to the terrorist threat and quickly supported the 'coalition of the willing' which sent troops into Afghanistan to root out **al-Qaeda** activists and topple the Taliban regime said to have harboured them. The war has subsequently been waged in other theatres such as Africa, Southeast Asia and the Middle East. However, the decision to invade Iraq as a further step in the war was controversial even among some countries that had been part of the 'coalition of the willing'. So too have other policies, such as the attitude to the events in Lebanon, in 2006.

Critics argue that the attempt to carry on waging the war until every terrorist group has been defeated means that the world will be in a perpetual state of conflict and war. Indeed, sometimes the methods used to wage the fighting may have the effect of creating resentment and so antagonising moderate groups that they become more sympathetic to terrorism. Some point out that the very name 'war on terrorism' is misleading, for terrorism is a method rather than a country and you cannot wage war against a tactic. Others make the point that one man's terrorist is another man's **freedom** fighter.

See also: **Iraq war, September 11th attacks on the World Trade Center**

**weapon of mass destruction (WMD)**  The term used to describe a massive weapon with the capacity to kill indiscriminately large numbers of people. The phrase broadly includes nuclear, biological and chemical weapons. It entered widespread popular usage in relation to the invasion of Iraq in 2003. The threat of potential WMD in Iraq was used by George W. Bush and Tony **Blair** to generate public support for the 2003 invasion but to date coalition forces have only found remnants of chemical weapons from degraded artillery shells. Most observers are deeply cynical of the claim that Saddam Hussein was stockpiling WMD. Others say that they did exist but were transported to Syria before the war.

The United States military defines WMD as: 'Weapons that are capable of a high order of destruction and/or of being used in such a manner as to destroy large numbers of people. Weapons of mass destruction can be high explosives or nuclear, biological, chemical, and radiological weapons, but exclude the means of transporting or propelling the weapon where such means is a separable and divisible part of the weapon'.

**welfare state** The system of social welfare the origins of which can be traced back to the **Liberal** reforms of 1906–11 but which was really created by Labour after World War Two, as its response to the Beveridge Report of 1942. Via the welfare state, the **Government** accepts responsibility for the welfare of its **citizen**s with regard to education, health, housing and social security, much of the money for such provision coming from taxation. Key Labour measures included the creation of the **National Health Service** and the introduction of the National Insurance scheme, which came into effect on what was designated welfare state day (5 July 1948).

For several years, most politicians of all parties came to accept the desirability and popularity of the welfare state and especially of the **National Health Service**, including even some Conservative doubters who felt that it undermined personal initiative and responsibility. In the 1970s, the **New Right** became increasingly and vocally critical of a system that was said to encourage a 'dependency culture', as well as being wasteful and excessively costly because of the universality of the benefits paid out. Since the 1980s, **ministers** of both parties have sought to curb spending and have used the language of remodelling welfare provision to make it more attuned to the needs of a more affluent and healthy society. Similar systems of welfare have been under attack in other European countries once noted for the generosity of their provision.

**Welsh National Assembly** The **Wales Act** established a National Assembly based in Cardiff, comprising 60 members. Members of the Welsh Assembly (AMs) are elected in the same way as MSPs (see **Scottish Parliament**), there being 40 constituency and 20 additional members. The Assembly does not currently have the **power** to introduce **primary legislation**, nor does it have fund-raising powers. It is responsible for **secondary legislation,** having scope to flesh out **Bills** already passed at Westminster by filling in details making them appropriate for Welsh conditions – for example, it can define the content of the national curriculum in Wales. The National Assembly can also act as a kind of **pressure group** on the London **Government**, pressing for greater consideration of Welsh interests.

An **executive** is formed from the membership of the Assembly, known as the Welsh Assembly Government. Initially, a Labour minority administration assumed office, but this gave way to a Labour–Liberal Democrat **coalition**. Following the 2003 elections, Labour ruled in Wales under the leadership of the **First Minister**, Rhodri

Morgan. After 2007, he is again head of a coalition, this time with **Plaid Cymru**.

Further reading: R. Deacon and A. Sandry, *Devolution in the United Kingdom*, Edinburgh University Press, 2007

**Welsh nationalism** Welsh **nationalism** has always been concerned more with preserving the Welsh culture and language than with the pursuit of self-government. It has tended to thrive in times of economic difficulty and a general sense of dissatisfaction with Westminster rule. It ends to be stronger in the Welsh-speaking areas of rural North and central Wales, rather than in the traditionally Labour valleys of the South. It often expresses itself in support for **Plaid Cymru**, the Welsh nationalist party.

Wales is often seen as less of a nation than Scotland, not least because of its smaller size and different history as a conquered territory; it has never retained its own distinctive identity to the same extent as Scotland. The overwhelming rejection of **devolution** in 1979 and the very narrow vote in favour in 1997 suggested that there was less demand for devolution in the principality than there was in Scotland. Hence the decision of **ministers** to offer a weaker form of devolution as a means of meeting the demands of Welsh nationalists.

**Welsh Office** A Labour **Government** established the Welsh Office in Cardiff in 1964. It was headed by a Secretary of State for Wales and had limited **powers** over areas such as primary and secondary education, health, housing, social services and the environment.

Following **devolution**, the Welsh Office remains (though it is now under the aegis of the **Department for Constitutional Affairs**), as does a more truncated version of the position of Secretary of State for Wales.

**Westland affair** (1986)  The Westland helicopter company ran into serious financial difficulties between late 1985 and early 1986 and was unable to continue operations. Because of its importance to the defence industry, **ministers** had an interest in any rescue package concerning its future ownership. Most of them (including the Secretary of State for Trade and Industry, Leon Brittan) favoured an American buy-out by the Sikorski company (as eventually happened), whereas Michael Heseltine (the Secretary of State for Defence) preferred to see a European consortium in charge.

The significance of the episode was twofold. There was firstly dispute over whether Britain should generally commit itself to a more European future, befitting a member of the **European Union**. Secondly, the handling of the controversy ignited a major discussion concerning the downgrading of the **Cabinet** in modern **government**. Heseltine claimed that Cabinet discussion was being discouraged by **Prime Minister** Margaret **Thatcher** and he was unwilling to accept **collective ministerial responsibility** for a policy he could not support. He dramatically walked out of a Cabinet meeting and resigned. Brittan found himself under intense media scrutiny for his attempts to discredit Heseltine's position and resigned in response to adverse comment about his handling of the issue.

For a short time, Thatcher felt her own position to be in jeopardy, but in a later Commons vote of confidence she secured the unanimous backing of Conservative **Members of Parliament** – including that of Michael Heseltine.

**West Lothian question**  The name given to the anomaly detected by the then **Member of Parliament** (MP) for West Lothian Tam Dalyell in Labour's **devolution** proposals of the late 1970s. Subsequently taken up by

Conservative and other critics of devolution, the question posed is why Scottish MPs cannot vote on, say, Scottish education decided north of the border but can vote on English education. Dalyell actually asked: 'Why should Scottish MPs at Westminster continue to vote on purely English matters whereas English MPs will not be able to vote on purely Scottish matters?' William Hague, former leader of the **Conservative Party**, has urged that there should be only 'English votes on English laws'.

There is a difficulty that cannot be easily answered. It derives from piecemeal devolution in the **United Kingdom** (UK), by which different countries are treated distinctly. If all four component elements of the UK had an assembly with similar **powers** as part of a federal devolution, the question would not arise. The issue was not seen as important in the days when Northern Ireland sent MPs to Westminster at the same time that there was an administration running the province in **Stormont**, prior to **direct rule**. If devolved **government** is re-established in the province, it will be the case that Northern Irish MPs can influence discussion of and **legislation** on purely English issues, whereas English MPs will be unable to so influence policy in the province. However, it is the Scottish issue that gains more attention, perhaps because Scotland sends 59 (72 prior to the 2005 election) MPs to the **House of Commons**, a significant addition to Labour's majority.

**Westminster Hall** The oldest surviving part of the Palace of Westminster that has long been used mainly for ceremonial occasions. However, since 1999 it has been used to stage debates on Tuesday, Wednesday and Thursday afternoons on **issues** that cannot be fitted into the timetable for the main chamber. The occasions are good opportunities for members to raise matters of constituency or regional importance, as well as those that fall outside the normal scope of party discourse. Thursday sittings are reserved for debating reports from **select committees**. Overall, though attendances are often limited to a dozen or so interested **Members** of **Parliament,** the sittings are being viewed as a useful complement to the work of the main chamber, not least because it makes some 400 hours or so available in an average parliamentary session.

**Westminster model**  The system of **parliamentary government** found in the **United Kingdom** and subsequently exported to **Commonwealth** countries such as Australia, Canada and India which has features that distinguish it from continental practice. In particular, a **single-party government** is invariably formed out of the majority party in the **House of Commons** and an official Opposition party exposes the deficiencies of its performance and prepares itself to take over should it win the next election. Supporters associate single-party administrations with effective and stable **government,** whereas opponents argue that the **first past the post** electoral system that underpins British arrangements is unfair to minority parties and makes politics adversarial rather than consensual.

**wets**  The derogatory label applied by **Prime Minister Thatcher** to her **One Nation** critics such as Sir Ian Gilmour and Norman St John Stevas within the **Conservative Party** in the early 1980s. They disliked her divisive economic and social policies and wished to emphasise the Disraelian traditions of ensuring that the **Conservative Party** retained a broad appeal to all **social classes** and in all parts of the **United Kingdom.**
See also: **One Nation Conservatism**

**whip**  The name given to officials who manage the supporters of their party in a **legislature**. The term derives from the 'whipper in' of English hunting parlance, whose role it is to keep the pack together in chasing its quarry. The whips are key figures in party organisation, with responsibility for maintaining discipline and unity. In British politics, the **Chief Whip** is assisted by between 8 and 10 assistant whips, all **Members of Parliament** (MPs).

Whipped votes are votes in which the party whips instruct members on the line they are expected to adopt, the term 'whip' also being applied to the notice of business that requires attendance to vote with the party in forthcoming divisions. Items are underlined once, twice or three times, according to their importance. For a 'three-line whip', MPs are expected to attend, absence only being countenanced if a member is out of the country on parliamentary business or seriously ill, or has other exceptional reasons. On occasion, MPs may be allowed to miss votes, if they can make an approved **pairing** arrangement.

**whipping**  see **whip**

**White Paper**  A document that sets out Governmental thinking in a policy area and is indicative of the **Government**'s legislative intentions. Consultation on a White Paper is still possible, hence occasional references to 'White papers with green edges'. However, this stage is a much clearer indication of current thinking that a **Green Paper**.

**Wilson, James Harold** (1916–95)  Harold Wilson served as a postwar Labour **minister** in the **Attlee Government** and later became **Prime Minister** from 1964 to 1970 and 1974 to 1976. His Governments were undermined by long-standing economic problems that limited the scope for achievement in the social field. His Governments' creation of the Open University and the office of **Parliamentary Commissioner for Administration** and passage of the first

**legislation** on **race** relations are among the most memorable innovations.

Wilson possessed finely tuned leadership skills that enabled him to keep the wings of the party united as a 'broad church'. While in opposition between 1970 and 1974, divisions over attitudes to the **European Economic Community** caused schism. To plaster over his difficulties, he committed Labour to a **referendum** on British membership should the party be returned in the next election. This vote was held in 1975.

Possessed of a sharp brain, he was a formidable debater and opponent, but some colleagues found him too short-termist ('a week is a long time in politics'), concerned with tactics and opportunistic. The verdict of his colleague Nye Bevan (the leftwinger credited with the creation of the **National Health Service**), was 'all facts and no bloody vision'.

**Winter of Discontent**  The label applied to the series of industrial stoppages that occurred between late 1978 and early 1979 as the **Callaghan Government** endeavoured to impose a strict pay policy. The scenes of rubbish piled in the streets, the stories of hospitals having to operate a very basic service and of the dead being left unburied seriously harmed the image of the Government, damaging Labour's claim that it could manage the **trade union**s more effectively than the Conservatives. During the **Thatcher** years, film of those scenes was frequently used to illustrate the alleged perils of electing another Labour administration.

**WMD**  see **Weapon of Mass Destruction**

**women and the right to vote**  The female right to vote was recognised in many countries in the early twentieth century, often following a long, sustained struggle by pioneering women and through the support of some sympathetic men. In Britain, the vote was denied to women in national – but not local – elections until 1918. The Suffragists and Suffragettes had been keen advocates of women's **suffrage**. The former employed peaceful means, attempting to persuade men through education, information and reason. The latter revealed a flair for publicity and attracted enormous public attention, primarily due to the militant tactics adopted by Mrs Emmeline Pankhurst, members of her family and many other women. They were enthusiasts for **direct action**, being willing to create disorder to gain publicity for their cause. However, it was arguably service to the country in World War One that earned women the vote in the eyes of many men. In 1918, women over the age of 30 and university graduates were given the vote. In 1928, it was granted to all remaining women over 21. In 1969, the voting age for men and women was lowered to 18.

**women in political office**  Women are still underrepresented in most of the world's **legislature**s, partly because of lack of educational opportunities in some parts of the world, but also because of their traditional responsibilities in childbearing and homemaking. Males often see themselves as especially suited to the conduct of political discussion and fitted for the role of political leadership. This tends to be a self-perpetuating situation, for women are liable to be deterred by the perception that politics is a man's world, a macho experience which they will find daunting and intimidating.

Women fare better where a form of **proportional representation** is employed, rather than the **first past the post** electoral system. Scandinavia has the highest percentage of women among European legislative bodies, Protestant countries generally faring better than Catholic or Orthodox ones such as France, Greece and Italy.

Representation of women in the **House of Commons** has significantly increased in recent years, averaging around 3 per cent in the 1950s and fractionally under 20 per cent in the 2005 Parliament. Much of the increase of recent years has been due to Labour's determination to boost women's representation, through the use of **all-women shortlist**s.

The use of the **additional member system** in Scotland and Wales has helped the female cause, with 51 and 30 women members respectively in the Scottish and Welsh devolved bodies. The **Welsh National Assembly** is the only elected legislature in the world with an equal number of male and female members.

Of course, there are other ways in which women participate in the political system, for example by service in **local government** and on the Bench, and by membership of **pressure group**s and involvement in political protest.

**women's movement** The name given to those women who campaign for more rights for women, in areas such as childcare, pay levels, the workplace and parliamentary representation. The movement is not formally organised with a known national leadership. Much of its activity is conducted through local groups, sometimes highly factionalised. Some is carried out via **pressure groups** (particularly the **trade**s **union**s) and **political parties**.

Among campaigning individuals and groups, there are differences over goals and tactics, some women being primarily concerned with a single **issue** such as abortion rights, childcare or equal pay, others with the denial of fair treatment over a range of social issues. Some adopt a 'moderate', reformist approach, working by education and persuasion to achieve helpful **legislation** such as the

Equal Pay (1970) and Sex Discrimination (1975) Acts. Others are 'radicals' who note the continuing differences in pay rates and point to a range of present inequalities such as under-representation in high positions in commerce, politics and the **judiciary**, as well as exploitation – including male violence – in the home. A few are prepared to be more militant, such as the Greenham Common anti-Cruise weapons protesters of the 1980s and 90s.

Abortion is a controversial and divisive issue within the women's movement. Whereas many feminists strongly argue for the 'woman's right to choose', other women – especially Roman Catholics and evangelicals – place great emphasis on the 'right to life'.

See also: **feminism, women in political office**